本书同时获得海南师范大学科研出版基金和教育部人文社科基金项目：
"认知语境等值的界面研究"（项目号：14YJC740064）资助

翻译过程中认知语境等值的界面研究

An Integrated Study of the Cognitive Contextual Equivalence in Translating Process

马海燕 著

MaHaiyan

中国社会科学出版社

图书在版编目（CIP）数据

翻译过程中认知语境等值的界面研究／马海燕著 . —北京：
中国社会科学出版社，2016.1
ISBN 978 - 7 - 5161 - 7509 - 5

Ⅰ . ①翻… Ⅱ . ①马… Ⅲ . ①翻译—研究 Ⅳ . ①H059

中国版本图书馆 CIP 数据核字（2016）第 018026 号

出 版 人	赵剑英	
责任编辑	任 明	
特约编辑	付 钢	
责任校对	李 姐	
责任印制	何 艳	

出 版	中国社会科学出版社	
社 址	北京鼓楼西大街甲 158 号	
邮 编	100720	
网 址	http://www.csspw.cn	
发 行 部	010 - 84083685	
门 市 部	010 - 84029450	
经 销	新华书店及其他书店	

印刷装订	北京市兴怀印刷厂	
版 次	2016 年 1 月第 1 版	
印 次	2016 年 1 月第 1 次印刷	

开 本	710 × 1000 1/16	
印 张	17.5	
插 页	2	
字 数	301 千字	
定 价	66.00 元	

序　言

　　近日，马海燕博士寄来她的书稿《翻译过程中认知语境等值的界面研究》，请我为书稿写序。她博士毕业两三年内喜事不断，获得教育部人文社科青年课题立项，晋升为副教授，今又见到她出书，为她的勤奋与努力感到十分高兴。该书稿即将付梓出版，翻译理论园地很快又要绽放一株幼苗，这是值得祝贺的事情，也是对译学园地新作者的一种鞭策和激励。马海燕曾以高级访问学者的身份在广东外语外贸大学访学，我是她的指导老师，她经过一番努力备考顺利考上高级翻译学院的翻译学博士生，我又成了她的博士生导师。她在读博期间的表现给我留下了深刻印象，体现在她的博士论文选题的新意性及其在理论研究方法方面所面临的挑战性，她在解决难题和迎接挑战所做的努力方面尤其难能可贵。可贵之处在于该选题能从一个特定视角切入研究一个重要的译学理论概念，小题大做，以点及面，对传统译论给予另辟蹊径的阐释，既具有一定的理论认识价值，又具有一定的翻译实践指导意义，能在一定程度上深化和拓展翻译理论研究范畴。该书是在她的博士论文修改润色后成型的，书名中研究视角的概念表述有所变化，以"界面研究"整合了"心理空间与概念整合研究视角"，文字比博士论文的题目更精简，却也涵盖了原先的理论方法。心理空间与概念整合属于认知语言学研究范畴，从不同的学科理论范畴切入研究翻译学理论问题，无疑涉及两个不同界面的桥接。潘文国先生（2012）认为，界面研究是将本来是独立的、"不搭界"的两个"界"人为地放在一起进行研究，对两个"界"相接的"面"进行研究。"面"是研究时的切入点或角度，角度不同，落脚点和结果必然不同。如"语篇-句法界面研究"、"文学-语言学界面研究"、"文化-语言学界面研究"，等等。界面研究属于语言研究的方法论，语言研究要做到三个"打通"：古今打通，中外打通，语言文学打通，否则语言研究就无法深入。他还提倡界面研究一定要把眼光放得远一点，要在继续现有领域的基础上，不断探索新的领域，寻找新的切入点，这是界面研究作为方法论的真正价值所在。翻译理论研究的深化与拓展必然要求探索新的研究领域，寻找新的研究增长点。翻译研究涉及语言理解与表达转换的问题，而语言研究最基础的问题涉及语义，语义问题又涉及概念，概念又涉及概念内涵与外延，内涵与外延问题又涉及语境（因为翻译是以文本为主的语际转换活动）。美国哲学家奎恩曾认为概念的外延是不变的，内涵是可变的；在他看来，语言意义的本体论是外延本体论，应将内涵从意义本体论中驱除出去。概念内涵的变化是由于概念使用的语境发生了变化，语境的变化赋予了概念内涵某种语境化关系语义特征，而语境又必然涉及认知语境和文化语境的互动性关系问题。故翻译理论研究的认知视角构成了"翻译学-认知语言学界面研究"的增长点，马海燕博士所做的研究因此也可以说是具有方法论特点的界面研究的一种尝试，其理论价值和实践意义如何，值得译学界同仁给予检验。

　　"理论"在本质上就是一种解释或阐释视角的运用。英语语词 theory 起源于希腊语 thea，由"view"与"-horan"（看+视野）构成，与 theater 同词源。一种翻译理论就是从一个特定的角度或视域为翻译实践过程中有关意义与形式的选择与操作提供理据，也就是说，翻译的选择是一种有理据的选择，只不过理据的合理性程度还需要主体间性的批评和交流。我在 2012 年出版的《翻译学理论多维视角探索》（上海外语教育出版社）一书中提出，只有从不同的理论视域或视角去认识和揭示翻译的本质特征，才能全面深入系统地认识翻译的多重本质属性及其运作的内在规律性。故理论是用来说明翻译现象和事实的，具有认识论功能，同时还具有方法论特点。从这个角度看，马海燕博士的著作《翻译过程中认知语境等值的界面研究》的新意体现在该题目结构中的四个关键概念方面，下面对这四个方面作一说明。

　　其一，"翻译过程"研究是译学界面临的一个挑战，一个较为普遍的观点认为，翻译过程是人脑思维的反映，人脑是个黑匣子，难以观察，故要真正反映翻译思维过程是非常困难的。国内外也有人在做实验口语报告法，即让受试者将自己在翻译过程中对文本概念或命题语义的感知、知觉、辨析、判断、析取、综合、加工等一系列思维活动大声说出来，并进行录音，然后再根据录音来研究"译者"大脑中呈现的"翻译过程"。这种翻译过程研究方法的局限性在于"受试者"和受试所采用的翻译材料的典型性和篇幅导致"研究结果"的效度和信度大打折扣。这种受试者往往是学生，将口语报告法研究集中于对翻译理论认识十分有限的学生群体难以揭示翻译的本质特点，对其翻译思维过程的简单"记录"和"整理"难以发现真正有价值的东西；而材料的典型与否、篇幅长短、难点的分布、重点内容等实验设计的科学性程度也大大影响研究的有效性，因为翻译研究的目的在于发现具有普遍意义的原理性或规律性认识，这种有限报告研究的结果难以达到此目的。这就是为什么口语报告法这几年已归于沉寂，难有有价值的理论提炼和新的增长点。从理论的效度看，要研究翻译过程，必然涉及认知思维，若没有认知语言学理论作为可行的分析工具，缺乏一系列相应的、具体可感的理论概念，则无从描述思维过程，无从揭示翻译思维中主观与客观之间互动的各种联系。

　　另一种可行的研究路向是基于实践问题导向的翻译过程研究，这种研究是从某些值得研究的实践现象或某类翻译事实出发的带有认识论和方法论意义的理论探讨，如文本翻译中所遇到的一系列复杂多样的典型文本特征：抽象性、隐喻性、隐晦性、模糊性、不定性、多义性、间接性、经济性、缺省性、空白性、语境性、关系性、连贯性、衔接性、互文性、新异性、美感性、暂构性、变体性、嬗变性、陌生化等（曾利沙，2013）。这些反映文本典型特征的现象或事实是客观存在的，对这些问题的解决如何从翻译思维过程去研究，给予可描述、可阐释、可推论、可印证、可操作性的研究，值得从一定的理论方法上给予深入系统的探讨。在跨语言文化交际的条件下，译者对这些翻译实践现象的操作处理不可能是进行简单地移译，而是有意识地对其作出一定的"改造"，译者主体这种变革实践客体的行为必然烙上主体的审美价值观和操作理据。由于理论研究的旨归在于力求揭示实践活动的"区间性规律"（列宁语），对这些问题的研究应上升为一定的普遍原理性层面作出理论阐释，否则仍落入传统翻译散论和印象式评说的窠臼。理论研究的特点之一在于其理论认识具有一定的主观性，有待于进一步在译学界同仁之间获得共识，这不仅是学术共同体之间形成合力研究的原动力，也是学科理论发展的重要支撑点：对于某个或某类特定的研究问题，研究者本人进行的是证实性研究，学术群体的其他成员则可能对其进行证伪性研究，以此来推动研究问题的发展。当然，对于证伪者来说，不可能简单而武断地否定了事，也需要提供一定可信或可行的理论视角和论证方法，大多情况下则是提供修正方案或视角的完善。对于以翻译实践问题为导向的过程研究，若能在学界引起一定范围内的研究兴趣，能反映现有的译学理论问题，甚至成为若干研究者共同努力的方向，那么这个研究选题就可能发展成为创新性的研究课题，从一定的层次、一定的视角推动翻译学理论研究范畴的发展。我认为，马海燕博士的研究问题具有上述这些特点，即对翻译的认知思维过程的描述性和阐释性并举，可证性与可操作性并重，而且具有一定的研究深度和理论价值，能激发一些翻译理论研究者的思考。

其二，"认知语境"是个令人感兴趣的研究对象，内容十分丰富，有着广阔的研究前景。翻译过程所论的"认知"涉及一系列感知、知觉、辨析、判断、推论、论证、抽象、概括、综合、加工、优化、析取、建构、定形、语境适切、检验等思维形式和思维特征，这些思维活动又是在一定的语境中进行的。但由于语境自己不会直接明确地呈现出来，多数情况下需要译者或研究者自己通过认知思维识别一系列或显性或隐性的语境参数去建构，这就构成了建构性的"认知语境"。又由于研究者的差异性和局限性，不同研究者建构的语境可能不一样，得出的结论也可能不一样，对相应的翻译实践过程问题的认识也会出现异同性，这就使得研究问题具有了商讨的空间，而这正是翻译理论研究特点的反映和研究价值所在，因为只有具有争议的理论与实践问题才具有典型意义，只有集中学术群体的集体智慧才能逐渐将复杂的认识问题推向深入。众所周知，翻译活动是一个非常复杂的思维过程，有关意义的问题是一个永恒探究的研究课题。长期以来译学界对"忠实（信）"原则理论问题的辩论，对"意义不定性"和"忠实（信）"原则规约理论与实践矛盾冲突的关系问题的质疑等，无不体现在对意义的理解认识与表达再现的"度"的探讨。马海燕博士从心理空间和概念整合角度研究翻译过程，必然涉及特定问题引起双语心理空间活动的认知语境。为此，她引入"语境参数理论"作为辅助性的分析和论证工具，对所研究的实践问题进行可描述性、可阐述性、可推论性的剖析。例如，针对下列翻译实践问题，就必然涉及认知语境建构的过程，否则方框内的概念就无法得到正确的理解，翻译表达也就无从着手。

（1）It's the latest R&D trend: penciling in tinkering time on the company clock. …

（2）Now the international finance system has come to depend on what looks more like a global Rube Goldberg machine running on hot money.

（3）One of the key features … has thus been *a transfer* of the *less sophisticated* end of the manufacturing market, *such as toys, textiles* and *footwear*, and the like，from the more to the less developed nations. （*EUROMONEY*）

传统翻译理论中的信、达、雅、准确、通顺等原则概念，或异化和归化等翻译策略，或直译和意译等一些抽象方法概念不能解决上述实例中框形内概念的理解与表达问题。只有将类似的实践问题纳入认知语境内予以分析和阐释，找出这些概念的语境化语义嬗变的原理性认识及其运作的规律性，才能为有效的翻译表达提供译文语境中概念语义生成或整合的主客观理据。如例（1）的字面意思是："最近的研发趋势：在公司的钟上在修补时间内用铅笔写画"，这种字面意思是源语读者和译文读者都无法理解的。字面翻译造成语句之间的语义不连贯，不符合人们有关公司研发的经验常规认识，故使读者对整个句子不理解。对于此类实践问题，我们要质疑的翻译理论问题是：忠实于"原文意义"的"意义"究竟是什么意义？"原文意义"是否就是原文概念的词典释义（经验结构意义），或其命题结构意义？若否，那么忠实原则所要规约的或要取"信"的意义本质上应是什么意义？若原文的意义是不定的，那么，从翻译的角度看，不同的译者译出的意义是否都是合理而可接受的？针对文本这种典型的语言现象的翻译构成，如何从"等值"理论进行重新认识，应是译学界所期待的。在大多情况下，原作者所要表达的意思并非停留在字面上或一般约定俗成的经验结构意义之上，而是需要读者或译者对相关概念从认知语境中进行概念语义的重构或整合，需要读者或译者经过语境关系分析参与意义建构的过程才能确定。对于原文不定的概念意义形态，任何译者都必须确定一种意义形态，必须通过重构概念的方式将其在译语中固定下来，以便读者或受众获得一种连贯性的理解。译者这种在译文中的概念化重构,其正确性与否或程度与翻译的忠实原则理论无关,而是与译者自身的认知思维能力和翻译经验知识的积累有关。但要为缺乏翻译理论或实践经验的翻译爱好者提供理论依据,就必须对此类翻译作出过程性的原理认识。若现有的理论不能提供过程分析的解决方法,只能另辟蹊径,寻找可行的理论工具。对于上述列举的实践难点问题,必须从认知语境的理论视角才能解决。从这个意义上说,马海燕博士从认知语境切入翻译问题的研究具有客观基础,而且对理论研究具有典型意义,可以小题大做,特征为一系列相辅相成的翻译学理论研究范畴:基于认识论和方法论的语境化概念整合性研究范畴。

其三,对"等值"理论概念的重新认识。马海燕博士著作题目中的另一关键词"等值"是翻译学基础理论中的一个重要概念。这个概念在美国翻译理论家奈达(Nida)那里得到理论研究范畴的拓展,如"dynamic equivalence"和"functional equivalence",后来又和金隄一起拓展为"equivalence of effect",并且是作为翻译原则来定性的。严格地说,英语概念"equivalence"的语义特征并不等于汉语的"等值",前者宽泛,缺乏指向性;后者具体和明确,具有指向性。从概念的关系特征考察"dynamic equivalence"和"functional equivalence"两组概念:"dynamic"与"equivalence"是一种相对于静态的关系表述,是从事物的发展变化状态来认识事物 A 和 B 之间的相等或相同性,表达的仅是一种状态关系特征,并没有揭示事物相同或相等的是什么样的属性。而"functional"与"equivalence"之间的关系则不同,"functional"是用来指向事物本身的某种属性特征的。例如,我们可以说 A 和 B 都是具有某种功能属性的事物,它们之间只是在功能上具有"equivalent"的关系,揭示的是事物的一个侧面或一种性质。从概念的理论价值看,"dynamic equivalence"理论价值最小,"functional equivalence"的理论价值较大,因为后者可以作为一个可描述的、可阐释的理论范畴来研究翻译过程中有关源语转换成译语的概念语义或命题语义的重构问题,如那些具有美学或修辞或交际功能的双关语、习语、惯用语、隐喻、公示语、文化缺省的概念置换等语际翻译现象。问题是,"functional equivalence"不能作为翻译的普遍原则来规约翻译实践,只能作为一种系统理论中的理论范畴来表征,其理论职能只能限定于从"功能"属性去描述的翻译现象。一旦超出这些翻译现象，"functional equivalence"就不能统摄这些现象，也就不具有可阐释性和可证性，其理论价值也就受到制约和弱化。

汉语的"等值"译自于英语的"equivalence"。考察英语词典对"equivalence"的释义：

（1） equal in value, amount, meaning, importance, etc.（指在价值、数量、意义、重要性等方面的相等。）

（2） （of）a thing, amount, word, etc. that is equivalent to something else（旨在事物、数量、语词等方面的相等，参见《牛津高阶英语词典》。）

（3） something that has the same value, purpose, job, etc. as something else（指某物与另一物具有相同价值、目的、工作等，参见《朗文当代英语词典》。）

（4） （of） the same size, value, importance, or meaning as something else（指某物与他物之间具有相同或相等的尺寸、价值、重要性或意义，参见《麦克米兰英语词典》。）

（5） equal in value, measure, force, effect, significance, etc.（指在价值、估量、力量、效果，意义或重要性等方面相当或相等，如：*His silence is equivalent to an admission of guilt.*//corresponding in position, function, etc.(e.g. *In some ways their prime minister is equivalent to our president.*)《兰登书屋韦伯完整词典》

可见，英语的"equivalence"作为一个日常概念，其内涵是多样性的、多层面的。作为翻译理论而言，"equivalence"只是一个空泛概念，必须结合具体语境才能明确相等或相当的是什么。如当我们抽象地说源语语言单位 A 与目的语语言单位 B 相等或相同，可以是指在 A 所具有的某个或某些潜在特征（potential features）方面的相等或相同，可表征为：

$$A (Fx, Fy, Fz, ...F\text{-}n) = B（Fx）/ \quad B(Fy) / B(Fz) / B（x+y） ....B(F\text{-}n)$$

其中 x, y, z 等可以被事物某种不同的属性特征替代，如 x=价值，y=效果，z=意义。也就是说，当我们说 "A is equivalent to B" 可能指向 B 与 A 的某个属性特征相等或相同，并非指 B 与 A 具有的所有属性特征相等或相同或一致。明确这一点对从翻译理论角度研究 "equivalence" 这个译学概念非常重要。

"Equivalence" 在英语中是个中性的日常概念，而汉语译文概念 "等值" 的内涵已不同于英语概念 "equivalence"。我认为 "等值" 相对于 "equivalence" 而言更像一个翻译理论化了的概念，更具有指向性、涵盖性、描述性，更能反映客体的属性特征在语际转换中的主观认识。因为，"等值" 之 "值" 既不同于 "功能"，又不同于原文的 "意义"，而是一种具有价值判断特征的观念化了的概念，指向的是客体的价值属性。"等值" 之 "值" 可以涵盖语义特征、语意（语用含意）特征、形式特征、美学特征、功能特征等一切被认知主体价值化了的客体属性特征，即只要是符合认知主体所需的客体之 "值"，都可以纳入 "值" 的范畴，从而使 "等值" 这一理论概念具有更广泛的阐释空间。"等值" 概念更能在源语和目的语之间架起桥接的纽带，使得源语的语言单位各种属性特征在向目的语转换的过程中趋于价值化、析取化、突显化、可弱化、可虚化。"等值" 还具有价值哲学的理论基础，因为，价值是连接主体与客体之间的中介，没有翻译实践的客体就没有译者主体，没有对客体（如文本）价值属性的认识，就没有译者主体的观念化认识（如原则或策略的概念化表征）。只有将翻译客体某种（些）潜在的价值属性加以突显，在源语和目的语之间考察它们这种（些）被突显的相等或相同的属性特征的转化形式与意义，才能有效地、科学地揭示 "等值" 的本质内容及其实践结构的规律性。从理论职能看，无论是英语的 "equivalence" 或是汉语的 "等值"，都不是目的论原则或策略论原则。这是因为，翻译活动并非是为了追求等值而等值，等值不是目的；等值也不是策略，所谓策略原则是指为了实现某种目的而采用的某种或某些规约性的手段、计划、方案等，等值本身并不说明如何实现目的。而从理论性质看，"等值" 更具有描述性和阐释性特征。这就是马海燕博士在她的研究中突出的一个不同于传统认识的新颖观点。请看她的有关论述：

此前的等值研究多局限于形式对等、功能对等或等效几个层面，主要是从原则要求上对双语转换过程中源语与目的语之间的关系进行说明，研究多停留在抽象的理论规约以及简单的主观经验性阐释，并没有对其从理论建构上进行深化与扩展，更未能提出相应的辅助性理论概念，或借助相邻相关学科理论作为方法论对其进行比较系统的研究，致使等值研究陷入争端并跌入低谷。而借助认知语言学最新研究成果——概念整合理论，从认知语境入手研究等值的实现过程，能在一定程度上揭示翻译的本质特征。

本研究主要在基于认知和语境的框架分析中拓展了等值研究的新维度，不是将"等值"（equivalence）作为一个原则概念，而是作为一个描写性概念，即等值研究不是去探求或要求语言形式的对应或字面意义的对等，而是从认知层面入手探究和描写如何实现认知语境中的意义等值的本质特征。（参见本书"前言"）

其四，马海燕博士在研究中采用的理论方法分析视角突出了"界面研究"，将认知语言学相关理论与翻译学理论研究融合起来，根据翻译过程中英汉两种语言概念在不同语言文化背景中的解码心理、感知方式、解析视角、突显方式、审美习惯等异同，从翻译理论方法上进行了研究范畴化的建构。

所谓界面研究的本质就是一种交叉或相邻相关学科理论视角的综合运用，本书所涉的理论视角源自于认知语言学的心理空间理论及其拓展的理论次范畴——概念整合理论。心理空间理论为美国加州大学认知语言学家福柯尼耶（Fauconnier）所创，后来又和他的同事一道创立、发展了概念整合理论。心理空间理论（Mental Space Theory）是两个或多个心理空间合成而产生的层创（novel）推理。映射（mapping）被用来建立和开发概念整合的处理过程，对背景知识的激活。概念整合过程可以把真实的东西、虚构的东西、意象中的东西概念化；概念整合理论或叫概念融合理论（Conceptual Blending / Integration Theory），旨在探讨概念的形式与意义的关系，将语言表征形式幕后运作的、对于概念整合隐匿的复杂性揭示出来。概念整合理论建立在动态的概念、时间、空间的基础上，概念整合是心智的加工，不同功能信息、概念特点在不同时间维度和心理维度经过心智加工形成新的概念包，概念的分裂、整合、变化、传输是意义产品产生的认知路线。（参见王正元所著《概念整合及其应用研究》《前言》，高等教育出版社，2010）。心理空间理论及其相关联的概念整合理论的理论效度在于能用于分析和揭示翻译过程中的概念语义变化、概念重构、概念语义生成与语境的制约关系等一系列涉及认知思维加工的过程。

　　翻译过程中的概念整合是翻译心理过程中的一种重要形式，是对英汉语语言文化和民族思维差异制约语言概念使用的一种协调手段，值得从方法论层面进行深入探讨。如她将翻译过程中的概念整合分为两个次范畴：偶合型概念整合和偏离型概念整合。在她看来，偶合型概念整合的本质是再词汇化，如动词化、动作词的再词汇化和冗余词的再词汇化。再词汇化通过隐喻投射、转喻投射、映射和义素的析取等认知机制实现。通过再词汇化，译者旨在整合原语的原型意象特征和目的语的各种典型特征，从而使译文更加简洁和新颖。这就将我们平时在做翻译实践研究过程中一些被忽略的语言文化翻译现象纳入了体系化的理论表征中。如：

（1）　她打了他一巴掌。（She slapped him.）
（2）　他从人群中奋力挤过去。（He shouldered his way through the crowd.）
（3）　她点头/招手示意他过去。（She beckoned him to come over.）
（4）　Essex held the end of the desk *with strong white knuckles*.

　　　＊？艾瑟克斯用他那又壮又白的指关节握着桌沿。

　　　艾瑟克斯用力抬起桌沿，指关节涨得粗大泛白。

　　上述实例中，例（1-3）可以归纳为偶合型概念整合，例（4）则为偏离型概念整合次范畴。对于例（1-3）而言，从汉英翻译过程看，译文中的概念整合在语言形式上体现为动作的再词汇化，源语和译入语在认知语境中是等值的。她在论述这种概念整合的原理性认识时指出，"出于译语表达简洁美感策略的运用,源语中某些冗余概念在认知语境中被整合过滤掉,目的语译文会出现概念数量和形式上的变化,然而源语中的整体交际意义或信息可通过受众的认知语境建构或经验知识推论而保持不变,可以说是等值的"。对于偏离型概念整合,她认为,"其实质上是意象、信息或意义的重新建构。通过重构,译者旨在增加译文的可读性和美学效果。在重构过程中,虽然译文的意象、信息甚至是字面意义都发生了变化,然而译文在目的语受众中所引起的认知联想和原文基本上是一致的,因为重构是建立在译者的认知体验基础之上且受语境参数的制约"。

此外,马海燕博士在研究中还揭示了译者在进行概念整合过程中的各种影响因素,详述了语境参数如何影响各个心理空间并进入整合空间。她得出的结论是,在翻译的概念整合过程中,语境参数或以上下文语境参数的形式或以认知语境参数的形式参与整合,且随着语篇的展开,上下文语境随时可以转化为认知语境,所以语境可以随时进入各个心理空间。从翻译理论方法的建构与拓展看,她的研究也有自己的从下而上的研究路向,如她发现并概括推导出十几种经验性操作法则,这些经验法对于指导翻译实践具有一定的实用价值。

马海燕博士研究内容的一个显著特点是:理论研究的问题导向化,实践研究的理论方法化,形成了理论与实践的紧密结合,既有经验感性认识,也有理论感性认识,这是值得肯定的。当然,作为一本形成于博士论文基础上的翻译研究著作,还存在一些值得完善的薄弱环节:一是对整个翻译学系统理论的宏观理论把握与本研究的关系问题的论述显得不足,如未能充分剖析"忠实"、"取信"原则理论和翻译过程中"等值"之"意义形态"的价值取向的关系问题,未能从理论范畴化建构与拓展角度明确该研究在译学系统中的理论价值。因为,从意义的语境化建构性本质特征看,"等值"无疑具有动态性,故"忠实"原则的规约性理论职能也应具有动态性,而非传统翻译观所认为的静态性。二是对客体"意义形态"的价值特征和译者主观认识之间的辩证关系问题的论述缺乏详实的论述。三是对一些典型实例的分析过程未能程序性地充分展开和详实地论证。也就是说,作者还需要提高科学研究的方法论意识和理论表述的综合能力,如微观研究的论证过程需要从概念自身的语义义素结构特征出发,再结合语境关系的判断，综合认知语境的各种要素，逐步论证概念语义在心理空间中整合的思维路径，作出可证性的程序化描写，再上升为规律性或原理性理论认识，形成开放性经验模块的建构（曾利沙，2013, 2014），这样才能使翻译学习者有效地做到举一反三、触类旁通。总之，作为翻译研究领域的一名新人，本书的出版是一个良好的起点，我期待她在今后的研究中，瞄准一个有价值的研究方向，持之以恒地努力探索，将其做深做透，为丰富翻译学系统理论范畴的发展做出贡献。

曾利沙

2015 年 6 月 8 日

于广州白云山寓所

CONTENTS

LIST OF ABBREVIATIONS

Adj.	adjective
Adv.	adverb
N.	noun
Prep.	preposition
V.	verb
C	Chinese
E	English
AHD	*American Heritage Dictionary*
CIT	conceptual integration theory
CMT	conceptual metaphor theory
CPT	contextual parameter theory
MS	mental space
MST	mental space theory
LF	linguistic form
SL	source language
ST	source text
TL	target language
TT	target text
CC	cognitive context
CCE	cognitive contextual equivalence
CNKI	*China National Knowledge Infrastructure*
OAED	*Oxford Advanced English Dictionary*

OAECD	*Oxford Advanced English Chinese Dictionary*
TAPs	Thinking-Aloud Protocols
TCM	Traditional Chinese Medicine

LIST OF FIGURES

Preface

Equivalence as the final pursuit of translation has always been the kernel of translation studies. Former studies of equivalence, however, have been mostly confined to surface phenomena, such as formal equivalence, functional equivalence and equivalent effect, which are mainly interpretations of relations between ST and TT in translating process from perspective of principle. Such studies remain at the level of abstract theoretical prescription and empirical interpretation, without promotion or expansion in theory, to say nothing of developing auxiliary theoretical concepts or borrowing relevant theories from adjacent disciplines for further systematic study. Considerable controversy and consequent slump in equivalence studies have been only too natural. Borrowing the latest developed cognitive linguistic theory of conceptual integration to explore the realizing process of equivalence from cognitive context can reveal the essence of translation to some extent, which is of theoretical and practical significance. Similar studies have been rarely found both at home and abroad. This study holds that one of the important features of translation is integration----the integration of the ST and the TL in terms of content and under the restriction of culture, co-text, aesthetics and cognitive thinking mode, etc. Based on the above view, and by means of appealing to reconstruction of the ST content, intention and aesthetic features in the TL cognitive context, this study aims to reveal how conceptual integration functions as an important mechanism in realizing cognitive contextual equivalence. Therefore, one important task of this research is to provide a methodological perspective and operating rationale for the purpose of analyzing the process of fulfilling cognitive contextual equivalence.

Efforts have been made to construct a theoretical framework to describe, analyze and interpret the translating process, in which conceptual integration theory serves as its basis and contextual parameters theory as a reference. Typical cases in E-C and C-E translations are analyzed procedurally from the micro, meso and macro dimensions concerning levels of sentence, paragraph and text, with the emphasis on its descriptiveness. All these aim to deduce empirical rules to be used in future translation practice.

The research shows that conceptual integration is an important cognitive mechanism in realizing cognitive contextual equivalence. Conceptual integration in translation can be divided into two types: coincidental and deviant. Coincidental conceptual integration is in fact the re-lexicalization, such as verbalization, re-lexicalization of motion words, and re-lexicalization of the redundancy. Re-lexicalization is realized via metaphorical mappings, metonymical mappings, projection, and sememes extraction, etc. Through re-lexicalization, the translator aims to integrate the prototypical features of the source word with those of the target word so as to make the version more concise and succinct. With such aims, some redundant concepts of the ST are integrated in the cognitive context, so the number or form of concept is changed in the TT; however, the general communicative meaning or information is kept through recipients' cognitive contextual reconstruction or empirical knowledge reasoning. Deviant conceptual integration is in fact the reconstruction of image, information or meaning in the TT, aiming at its readability and aesthetic effect. Even though the image, information and surface meanings are deviant from those of the

ST through reconstruction, the cognitive imagination of the TT in recipient is basically the same with that of the ST because the reconstruction is based on the translator's cognitive embodiment and restricted by the relevant contextual parameters.

The present research also reveals various interfering factors that are involved in the process of conceptual integration and amplifies the ways in which contextual parameters influence mental spaces and get involved in blending space. The research finds that in the process of conceptual integration, contextual parameters get involved via co-textual parameters or cognitive contextual parameters; what is more, with the development of the text the co-textual parameters can be converted to cognitive contextual parameters, so contextual parameters can go into the mental spaces at any time. Through comparative analyses, the research finds and deduces more than ten local empirical rules of translation which are believed to be valuable in guiding future translation practice.

The main contribution of this research is that the framework analysis based on cognition and context expands the study of equivalence from a new dimension, in which equivalence is not regarded as a principle but a descriptive concept; that is, studies of equivalence should not focus on equivalence of linguistic form or surface meaning but to explore and describe such essential feature as how to realize meaning equivalence in cognitive context. Data analysis proves the properness and effectiveness of the analytic framework. Via logical deduction, the realization of cognitive contextual equivalence is clearly demonstrated, which provides a cognitive perspective and study method for the study of equivalence. Moreover, the analytic framework combines CIT and CPT, and is comprehensive and open for translation study. This framework is significant for the extension of translation studies, as well as the development of CIT and CPT. Besides, the research emphasizes the descriptiveness, operability and verifiability of the analyzing process, so it is of some theoretical and practical significance for the extensive translation studies. Last but not least, the study also provides abundant materials for translation teaching and sheds light on those inexperienced translators.

Chapter 1

Introduction

Viewing translating as a process of conceptual integration can help disclose the potential cognitive mechanism of the translator as well as the dynamic operating process. With the assumption that translations in general are aimed at realizing cognitive contextual equivalence (CCE) at certain levels, this research mainly explores the translator's cognitive process for finding out how the translator realizes CCE with the operating motivations also explored. Concept (conceptual meaning) and meaning belong to different layers in that concept is the basic unit of thinking or reasoning in cognition, while meaning refers to linguistic meaning in written forms (Wang, 2007: 92). This research attempts to explore one important aspect of translating process by dividing the translating process into two procedures: conceptualization and meaning reconstruction or generation which are also regarded as the processes of understanding and expressing. The research is an interface study between cognitive linguistics and translation, which integrates the mental space theory (MST), conceptual integration theory (CIT) and contextual parameters theory (CPT), aiming at constructing a theoretical framework for interpreting the translator's cognitive process in realizing CCE.

This introductory chapter defines the key working terms, justifies the research rationale, states the general research objective, raises some research questions, and outlines the organization of this research.

1.1 Key Concepts

The two key concepts *cognitive contextual equivalence* and *conceptual integration* need to be defined since they are used as the working terms.

1.1.1 Cognitive Contextual Equivalence (CCE)

"Cognitive context" refers to the context in cognition in which a set of parameters can trigger or guide the readers' or recipients' cognitive thinking processes of making semantic perception, discrimination, judgment, inference, processing, and synthesization, etc. "Cognitive context" reflects all kinds of real or imaginary situational context of social or historical culture, which is composed of a variety of knowledge schemata or experience schemata. Such schemata share common features and can be relied on by readers or recipients to do cognitive thinking. "Cognitive contextual equivalence" refers to the interrelationship between different conceptual forms and equal semantic content in cognitive processing and choosing conceptual meaning under the common experience of translation activity.

1.1.2 Conceptual Integration

Conceptual integration, conceptual blending and blending are terms invented and explained by Fauconnier referring to the same thing. He regards conceptual blending as a general cognitive operation on a par with analogy, recursion, mental modeling, conceptual categorization and framing. Blending is dynamic, supple, and active in the midst of thinking. It yields products that frequently become entrenched in conceptual structure and grammar, and it often performs new work on its previously entrenched products as inputs. Blending is easy to detect in spectacular cases but it is for the most part a routine, workaday process that escapes detection except on technical analysis. (Fauconnier,1998: 133)

In this research, the translating process is regarded as two processes of conceptual integration, with the former integration referring to the period of understanding of the source text and the second integration referring to the period of expressing of the target version. The two processes are also considered as the processes of conceptualization and meaning generation. Since emergent structure will be produced during the processes of mapping, projecting and integrating, novel meaning will also be produced in the process of translating.

1.2 Research Rationale

Nowadays, studies of translator's cognitive mechanism in translating and the process of meaning generation in certain context are still limited. Translation studies at home are confined to discussions of cultural thinking, principle summarizing, words operating and methods applying, etc. (Zeng, 2008), so the lack of a set of theoretical category and conceptual system featuring in descriptiveness, maneuverability and verification has restricted the development of translation studies as a discipline.(Zeng,2000) Translation studies abroad, although very prosperous in providing different theories, are still limited in combining the macro theory with the micro practice, or limited in systematic description of the micro operating process under guidance of the macro theory, which can be seen through review of the previous translation studies.

Although the practice of translating has been long established, the study of the field developed into an academic discipline only happened in the second half of the twentieth century(Munday,2001:7). However, if the comprehension or thinking of translation were regarded as a kind of primary translation theory, translation theory could be said to have a history of more than two thousand years (Wang,2008: 4). Various translation theories have appeared, among which studies regarding equivalence between two texts can be found in different paradigms. Structuralists, such as Wilhelm Von Humboldt, Edward Sapir, Benjamin Whorf and Ferdinand de Saussure, hold that different languages express different views of the world, and the relation and structure make language meaningful. According to their viewpoints, since different languages cut the world up in different ways, no words should be completely equivalent out of their language system. So they think translation impossible. Such proposition is strongly criticized by many theorists. As Georges Mounin argues, "...yet translators exist, they produce, and their products are found to be useful. (Pym, 2010: 10)" Under such a background, the main theories of equivalence developed. The scholars tried to explain something that the linguistics of the day could not explain or somehow did not want to explain.

Pym (ibid.: 6-42) classifies equivalence studies into two paradigms: natural and directional. Researchers of natural equivalence, led by Vinay & Darbelnet (1958/1972), Kade (1968), Catford (1965), aim to find the natural equivalence between the target and the source texts at different linguistic levels by listing different procedures, yet the fact is that natural equivalence can only solve limited translation problems but cannot explain those asymmetry phenomena between languages, such as the subjective creativity of the translator. The paradigm of directional equivalence extends the dimension of natural equivalence by classifying different kinds of equivalence chosen by the translator in achieving different translations. However, most directional equivalence theories are based on the dichotomy made by Cicero: translating like a literalist interpreter or like a public speaker. The following is a list of the dichotomies found throughout the history of the western translation theories: foreignizing or domesticating by Schleiermacher (1813/1963), formal equivalence or functional equivalence by Nida (1964/2004), semantic and communicative translation by Newmark (1981/2001), illusory and anti-illusory translations by Levy (1967/2000), overt and covert translations by House (1997), documentary and instrumental translations by Nord (1997), adequate or acceptable translation by Toury (1995/2001), fluent or resistant translation by Venuti (1995). Directional equivalence solves the apparent "impossibility of translation" posited by structuralist linguistics, and equivalence becomes so possible that there are many ways to achieve it (Pym, 2010: 38). However, since equivalence presupposes symmetry between languages and wants to realize equivalence to the source text, the translator is definitely confined to the frame of the source text which is generally considered as superior to the target text, as a result the translator's subjective creativity is still confined. Furthermore, the equivalence paradigm only prescribes different ways for translator to choose rather than explains why translator chooses in this way.

The skopos paradigm centers around the purpose and states that translation is decided by certain purpose rather than the simple relation of equivalence. Supportive institutions, clients and readers are all influential factors. Such a paradigm only regards equivalence as part of the features of translation. Although the skopos paradigm realizes the importance of the objective factors in the whole process of translation, it fails to clarify the client's purpose or rneglects the fact that the client could not break the norms of the source text casually in actual translation.

Descriptive paradigm puts translation study into a polysystem of literature and regards equivalence as "a feature of all translations" (Pym, 2010: 64). Theorists of this paradigm such as Toury (1995/2001), Chesterman (1997) use methods of systematic description by means of a set of terms, whose studies lay a foundation for the scientific translation studies. The descriptive research method is better than the traditional prescriptive method in revealing the nature of translation, and the research scope may extend to all kinds of translation phenomena, yet it cannot explain the translator's mental mechanism during translating or meaning generation in certain context. So there still exists research space in western translation theories.

Translation in China also experiences a long history, which is generalized into four periods by Luo (1984:19): "Word-for-word (*Anben*) — Faithfulness (*Qiuxin*) — Similarity in spirit (*Shensi*) — Sublimation (*Huajing*)". When talking about the weaknesses of traditional translation theories in methodology, Liu Miqing gives the following points:

> Classical and modern translation theorists in China are confined to traditional literary criticism such as using the methodology of traditional literary aesthetics, as a result, they put more emphasis on macro description by means of subjective inspiration and sentiment rather than using scientific and systematic formal argumentation to analyze the translation at the micro level. The lack of systematic and scientific categorization or logical analysis to value concepts makes traditional translation theories faint, impressive and intangible in their categorization and analysis, which causes debates between different viewpoints.Such translation theories cannot be of practical significance. (Liu,1999: preface XIII, tran. by the author)

Since translation studies have limitations in themselves and should be patched by theories from other fields, Snell-Hornby (1988/1995) proposes an integrated approach to translation studies based on the cognitive linguistic theories of Prototype and Gestalt, which offers enlightenment to this research with a new perspective to integrate the latest developed cognitive linguistic theories of Mental Space and Conceptual Integration into the translation studies.

Anyway, cognitive linguistics, with its advantage of helping describe the translator's cognitive mechanism, has been applied to translation studies by some scholars (Gutt,1991/2000; Jiang,2002). Their studies provide new perspectives of translation studies to this research. Conceptual integration theory (CIT), integrating achievements of other cognitive linguistic theories, is considered very powerful in explaining the cognitive process of human thinking and talking. Introducing CIT into the translation studies can therefore help explain the cognitive mechanism of the translator in translating (see Mandelblit，1997, Wang，2004). However, although CIT can provide a reasonable explanation to the translator's conceptualization in his/her cognition, it cannot explain the reason of concrete meaning generation in certain context. On account of various factors restricting the process of the translator's conceptualization in cognition and meaning generation in certain context, the author also borrows the contextual parameter theory (CPT).

CPT breaks through the limitations of traditional context theories. Based on the purpose of descriptiveness and interpretation, CPT regards context as a collection of concrete contextual parameters which may be better defined and characterized than those abstract concepts of intra-textual context or outer-textual context. As to CPT, the relation between contextual parameters can be cross reference (including reference between the macro and the micro propositions, reference between the superordinate and the subordinate concepts, reference between the whole and the part, etc.), mutual mapping (including mappings between conceptual meaning components, between relational characters, etc.), or mutual restriction (such as restriction of conventional experiences, etc) (Zeng 2002, 2004, 2010). CPT provides an available analytic tool to the translating process at both macro and micro levels. Thus it offers a reasonable means to this research for integrating CIT and CPT to explore the translator's operating mechanism in realizing equivalence in translating.

1.3 Research Objective and Questions

This research proposes that the purpose of general translation, taking into consideration the linguistic and cultural disparities between English and Chinese, is to realize CCE at certain levels, and conceptual integration plays an important role in achieving contextual equivalence. In order to explore its essence theoretically, the research focuses on the manifestation of contextual equivalence from the cognitive perspective. To achieve such a research objective, this study attempts to answer the following research questions:

（1）**What is the mental mechanism that reveals the essence of translating processes in which the cognitive contextual equivalence is realized?**

This research views translating as a process of conceptual integration to realize CCE, in which process the concepts of the ST are mapped onto those of the TL and finally integrated into the TT expressions. The translator's mental mechanism in realizing CCE and the operating processes of achieving CIT are also illustrated.

（2）**Why can the conceptual-integration-theory-based mental mechanism be theoretically valid in exploring CCE and how can it be verifiably demonstrated in translating practice?**

As a theoretical analytic tool, CIT is systematic and descriptive, so it is believed to demonstrate and interpret the translating process more descriptively and verifiablely. This research, by integrating MST, CIT and CPT, aims to construct a theoretical framework to interpret the translating process in a more descriptive and verifiable way.

（**3**）**How can systematical cognitive patterns be constructed to methodologically interpret and describe the translating mechanism that reveals the essence of CCE? And what contribution will this research offer to enrich the theory of Equivalence in translation studies?**

By analyzing different kinds of examples under the theoretical framework, the research tries to find and deduce some empirical rules of translation so as to guide translation practice.

1.4 Research Methodology

This research is mainly a qualitative study featuring analysis and synthesis. Apart from giving an insight into the essence of CCE with general theoretic discussion, the research makes efforts to provide demonstrative descriptions of the mental mechanism that reveals the essential features of rendering processes in achieving CCE by integrating top-down and bottom-up approaches so as to build relevant empirical rules. In descriptive translation studies, Toury describes the top-down thinking mode, which is elaborated by Delabastita (2008: 234) as follows: 1) Level of system: theoretical possibilities (can be); 2) Level of norms: culture-bound constraints (should be); 3) Level of performance: empirical discursive practice (is) (Pym 2010: 71). This research emphasizes the bottom-up mode, which goes on the opposite way: a) describing what the actual translation is; b) explaining why the translation is in this way or what factors influence the translation; c) summarizing the possible empirical rule to guide translation. It has been widely accepted that no single research method or approach is adequately effective in translation studies and the complicated phenomenon of translation requires a multi-dimensional perspective. As Bell (1991: 29) states, "A multiple approach, involving both induction and deduction in a cyclic investigation, is more likely to be revealing than the strict adherence to either induction or deduction alone." This research actually integrates methods such as qualitative study, demonstrative analysis, induction and deduction through construction of the empirical rules.

1.4.1 Qualitative Study

This research assumes that translation in general is aimed at realizing cognitive contextual equivalence at certain levels, so the essential features of CCE realized in different situations are classified and analyzed. As translating is regarded as the process of conceptual integration in this research, qualitative analyses are also made in discussing different kinds of conceptual integration.

1.4.2 Demonstrative Analysis

In translation studies, it is a weak point in explaining the translator's mental mechanism of conceptualization and meaning reconstruction or generation. This study tries to give demonstrative analyses of the translator's mental mechanism in realizing CCE. Contrastive and comparative analyses are also made to identify the results of different conceptual integrations by different translators.

1.4.3 Induction and Deduction

Methodologically, this research takes an integration of deductive (top-down) and inductive (bottom-up) approaches.

Deduction refers to theoretical construction from other subjects or fields, such as applying concepts, theories and methods of other subjects to translation studies, so as to get new viewpoint of translation and make new conclusions (Wang 2008). This research introduces the existed concepts and terms of CIT and CPT to the study of translating process for describing the translator's mental mechanism and meaning generation in certain context. The research is also inductive in that we start from the bottom by focusing on the data: classifying examples, describing the process, exploring local rules, and inducing empirical rules. The study provides some empirical rules to guide translation practice.

1.4.4 Data Collection

Examples are collected first-hand and second-hand from different kinds of materials with their translated versions, including literary works, poems, theoretical books, as well as scientific and technological reading materials, aiming at explaining the various kinds of conceptual integration in translation.

1.5 Organization of the Book

This book mainly consists of six chapters. The first chapter talks about the reason for choosing the topic, in which the origin, the rationale, the objective and questions, as well as the methodology of the research are proposed. In order to make the study more understandable, two key concepts are explained in the first place and the outline of the research is put at the end of this chapter.

Chapter two is literature review regarding the relevant studies. Three different aspects are reviewed including studies concerning translating process, studies on context, and studies on equivalence theory. Of course, a detailed discussion of the review and objective evaluation are unavoidable in introducing the three aspects.

In chapter three, an integrated theoretical framework is constructed to guide the analyses of examples in the following chapters. The framework is based on those background theories such as MST, CIT, Mappings and CPT, which are also introduced in detail.

Chapter four and five are two core chapters, in which different conceptual integrations in translation are discussed to reveal the translator's mental operating process in achieving CCE. Chapter four mainly concerns translations of coincidental conceptual integration, and chapter five is about the translations of deviant conceptual integration.

Chapter six is the closing part of this book. It is a summarization of the whole research, including the major findings and significances. Meanwhile, the limitations of the study and suggestions for future research are also discussed.

Chapter 2

Literature Review

This book is an interface study of cognitive contextual equivalence, which concerns the cognitive mechanism of translator, context and equivalence, as well as the translating process, so the previous and present studies of these aspects are reviewed respectively.

2.1 Review of Studies Concerning Translating Process

As translating activity is very complex in nature and the development of cognitive science and psychology is actually confined, the study of translating process is definitely very difficult. Nevertheless scholars are still working hard to do such a research. According to Li (2005), articles and monographs abroad concerning studies of translating process surpassed 100 from 1982 to 2002. Studies at home are also in a growing trend. By using "Fanyi Guocheng" (translating process) as the key word to search the relative articles in *China National Knowledge Infrastructure(CNKI)* within the duration from 1980 to 2014, the author found several thousand articles including PHD dissertations and MA thesis. Those studies abroad and at home can be reviewed from three paradigms: linguistic, psychological and cognitive.

2.1.1 Linguistic Studies of Translating Process

Traditional studies of translating process belong to Linguistic ones in which translation is either divided into two general procedures: understanding and expressing (Fan,1994; Lao,1996), or the process is summarized into a series of concrete operating procedures (Nida,1969/1982; Liu,1999: 135-161). Among them, Nida can be a representative.

Nida states that there are basically two different systems for translating studies. The first consists in setting up a series of rules which are intended to be applied strictly in order and are designed to specify exactly what should be done with each item or combination of items in the source language so as to select the appropriate corresponding form in the receptor language. Some theoreticians have contended that this automatic selection process is best accomplished by working through an intermediate, neutral, universal linguistic structure. This go-between language into which the source is translated and from which the finished translation is derived may be either another natural language or a completely artificial language. But whether or not such an intermediate stage being used is based on the application of rules to what linguists call the "surface structure" of language, or in other words, the level of the structure is overtly spoken and heard, or written and read. This approach may be diagrammed as in figure 2-1:

$$A \text{ ———— } [X] \longrightarrow B$$

Figure 2-1 System one of translating (cf Nida & Taber 1969/1982: 32)

A represents the source language and B represents the receptor or target language. The letter X in parentheses stands for any intermediate structure which may have been set up as a kind of universal structure to which any and all languages might be related for more economic transfer (ibid: 32) .

The second system of translation consists of a more elaborate procedure of three stages: (1) analysis, in which the surface structure (i.e., the message as given in language A) is analyzed in terms of (a) the grammatical relationships and (b) the meanings of the words and combinations of words, (2) transfer, in which the analyzed material is transferred in the mind of the translator from language A to language B, and (3) restructuring, in which the transferred material is restructured in order to make the final message fully acceptable in the receptor language. This approach may be diagrammed as in figure 2-2 (ibid: 32).

By means of figure illustration, Nida makes a clear description of the transferring process. However, his description of the translating process is a static one and cannot disclose the dynamic cognitive mechanism of the translator. So the studies from psychological and cognitive paradigms are called out.

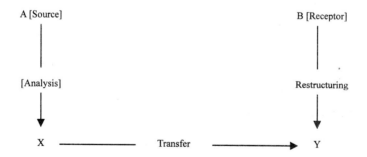

Figure 2-2 System two of translating (cf Nida & Taber 1969/1982: 32)

2.1.2 Psychological Studies of Translating Process

The psychological paradigm of translating studies consists of the theoretical study and experimental study. Bell (1991) is the representative of the former and TAPs belongs to the latter.

Theoretical studies of the psychological paradigm

One important theoretical study of the psychological paradigm is that of Bell. Bell (1991: 43-60) proposes his own model of translating on the basis of psycholinguistics and artificial intelligence. His model is based on a number of assumptions about the nature of the process and the characteristics it has in satisfactorily explaining the phenomenon of translation. His assumptions of translating process can be simplified as follows: First, it is a special case for the more general phenomenon of human information processing. Second, it should be modeled in a way that reflects its position within the psychological domain of information processing. Third, it takes place in both short-time and long-time memories through devices for decoding text in the SL and encoding text into the TL. Fourth, it operates at the linguistic level of clause. Fifth, it proceeds in both a bottom-up and a top-down manner in processing the text and integrates both approaches by means of a style of operation which is both cascaded and interactive. Sixth, both languages should have a visual word-recognition system and a writing system. He also divides the process into analysis and synthesis, both consisting of three distinguishable areas of operation: syntactic, semantic and pragmatic. As for each area, he makes a detailed description respectively. Bell's translating process model can be clearly shown in figure 2-3.

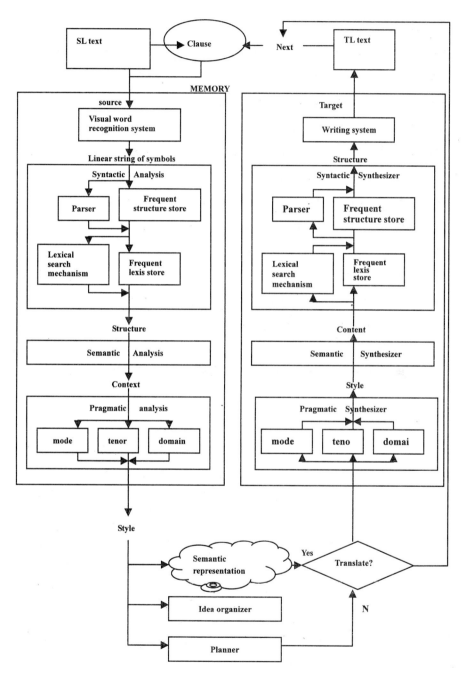

Figure 2-3 Bell's figure of translating process

Bell's model describes the translating process in a comparatively overall way from the psychological aspect, which is of great significance in helping disclose the nature of translating. However, his description of the process is a static one in that he does not consider the role of the specific context. Since meaning is decided by context and the translator is guided by context in the translating process, the ignorance of context is inappropriate. What is more, this model is also a static linguistic description of the translating process, which can not disclose the translator's dynamic mental mechanism. Sun (2003: 61) criticizes it in this way: "Although the second step of Bell's model is to integrate the source text into the target text, he could not explain the concrete steps of the integration." Last but not least, Bell's model is too complicated to use. In a word, the complicatedness and absence of contextual consideration restrict the spread and application of Bell's model.

Experimental studies of the psychological paradigm

The experimental methods are mainly used in the interpreting studies. Such methods include measuring the translator's Eye Movements (McDonald & Carpenter,1981), investigating correlations between Pupil Dilation and the Mental Load experienced by simultaneous interpreters (Tommola & Hyona ,1990), as well as Thinking-Aloud Protocols (TAPs), among which the last method is the most influential. (see Toury,1995/2001: 234)

In the experiment of TAPs, subjects who are faced with the task of producing a translation are asked to say aloud whatever comes into their minds while they are working on it. The verbalization is recorded—ideally, video-recorded, in order to catch non-verbal features as well, the recorded protocols transcribed, and the running transcripts submitted to meticulous analysis. (Toury,1995/2001: 234)

TAPs is in fact data collection of the mental process, which belongs to the introspective method or verbal report procedure of psychology. It originates from the studies of Buhler Edo & Claparede in the early 1930s (see Li,2005).In the 1980s, some researchers made detailed studies in their PHD dissertations, which makes this method well known and extensively used till in the 1990s (Krings,1986; Youssef,1986; Tirkkonen-Condit & Laukkanen, 1996; Jaaskelainen,1999; Fraser,2000; references see Li,2005).

There are two different opinions on whether TAPs is suitable to the study of translating process. The first opinion states that if the thinking process is regarded as a kind of information operating rather than a single activity of the nervous system, then TAPs can totally reflect the thinking process, and what's more it should be the most natural and suitable one to be used in the study of thinking process in translating (Krings,1987;Fraser,2000, Jaaskelainen,1999; Loscher,1991; references cf Toury,1995/2001:235). The second opinion is doubtful about TAPs' being used in translating studies with the following reasons: first, TAPs can only reflect the thinking process indirectly; second, the interpretation of data is mingled with the researchers' subjectivity; third, the influence between the spoken translation of the subjects and their final written version is still a mystery (ibid: 235). Apart from these, there are big differences between spoken and written languages, so as to the translation. This research also holds the idea that TAPs has defects in that it neglects the contextual parameters which influence the final written translation from the former spoken translation.

2.1.3 Cognitive Studies of Translating Process

There are many cognitive approaches in the study of translating process, such as Relevance, Relevance and Adjustability (Li, 2007), Gestalt (Jiang, 2002),

Prototype (Li & Zhang,2003), Schema (Wang,2001:19-25), Re- verbalization (Liu & Li,2009), Mental Space and Conceptual Integration (Mandelblit,1997; Wang,2004). Among those approaches the relevance theory used to be the most influential, and MST and CIT show great power and are used in translation studies with a rising trend, so they are reviewed as representatives in the following.

2.1.3.1 Relevance Theory

Since the publication of Gutt (1991), relevance theory has become one of the hot topics in translation studies. Relevance theory regards relevance as an existing principle in human mind, which must be obeyed in communication. Translation is regarded as a cognitive and inferential process. The whole process of translation consists of two rounds of ostensive-inferential process, involving three communicators: ST author, translator and TT reader. During the first round of ostensive-inferential process, the translator makes relevant inference through the ST context and understands the intention and meaning of the ST. During the second round of ostensive-inferential process, the translator shares the ST intention and content with the TT reader by means of translation. The optimal relevance is what the translator seeks to reach.

Gutt's relevance-translation theory provides a powerful explanation to the translator's cognitive process of translation and it has gained a place in the field of western translation studies. However, this theory also has its shortcomings and is criticized by scholars. Tirkkonen-Condit (1996) questions Gutt's dependence on a general principle of relevance and asks "by what criteria, other than hierarchization of purposes, can a translator decide what must be retained and what can be legitimately sacrificed?" Wang (2000) maintains that the relevance approach to translation fails to explain translation as cross-cultural communication on account of its incompetence in showing how to transmit the cultural defaults. Li (2007: 24) lists three weak points:

first, Gutt does not point out whether communicative clash between the translator and his target readers has anything to do with the maximal relevance and the optimal relevance in secondary communication situations; second, the principles are too abstract; third, he does not mention cultural defaults in the translating process. In my view, this theory cannot explain why the translator infers in this way instead of in that way, nor does it consider the concrete contextual factors.

2.1.3.2 Conceptual Integration Theory

Mandelblit (1997) is the first abroad using the theory to explore translation. He studies the Creative and Schematic Aspects in Sentence Processing and English-Hebrew Translation from the perspective of Grammatical Blending. What Mandelblit does is to apply the theory to translation studies and the cases he uses are mostly caused-motion patterns. Later when MST and CIT are introduced to China, they are applied in a greater scope.

The first article introducing CIT at home is that of Wang & Zheng (2000: 7-11). Later, more and more articles and monographs on CIT appear. Those articles can be classified into five main types: 1) introduction or review of the theories (such as Meng,2004; Wang,2004: 6-12; Wang,2006 X: 65-70); 2) Using the theories to reinterpret language phenomena, including figures of speech, grammar, syntactic, and word-formation, etc. (such as Jiang,2003; Liang & Sun,2002; Miu,2007; Shen,2006b; Li,2013; Peng,2013; Chen & Bai ,2014); 3) Exploring the explanatory power of the theories to text (such as Song,2000; Su,2007; Wang & Sun,2008; Wang,2005: 5-8); 4) discussing the inspiration of the theories to foreign language teaching (such as Zhang,2008: 115-118; Wang,2014); 5) On the theories' explanatory power to translation and translation studies (see the following part). Among the five types, the second type takes the largest proportion; the third type mainly concerns MST; the fifth type is comparatively limited.

Apart from the articles and dissertations, there are also some monographs concerning the theories, such as Zhang (2003), Wang (2009), Wang (2004) and Yang (2008), etc. What is more some compilations of cognitive linguistics also involve the introduction and application of MST or CIT, such as Sun (2008), Wang (2007), Li (2008), Liu (2006), and Zhang (2009), etc.

Among those studies regarding translation, Wang Bin is a representative in that his study is a comprehensive one of CIT combining with translation studies (Wang 2001a, b, c, 2002, 2004). Translating process is described by Wang in this way:

> *"If a source text is treated as the blend of source language structures and schemata of communicated events, in translating, when we digest the source text, we are actually disintegrating the text and discovering the schemata of communicated events carried by the text, and when we do actual translation, we integrate the digested schemata from the source text with the target language structures. Translating is, as a matter of fact, a mental process of embodied mind, a way to illustrate how the same communicated event is mapped onto different language structures in different cultures through our mind."* (Wang,2004: 6)

Wang's study is a pilot one in combining CIT with translation study at home, which sheds light on the later studies. However, his study can be seen as the usage of CIT to explain translation, and his explanation of translation is in a limited way. He does not show concern for the way of meaning generation in concrete context, so his study is of little help in solving translation problems.

Apart from Wang, there are other scholars using the theory to explain translation phenomena from different aspects, to name a list: Chen (2002), Chen & Yin (2007), Yin (2007), Wang & Ma (2006), Sun (2001), Dong & Feng

(2005), Zhou & Liu (2007), Wang (2008: 72-75), Zhang (2006), Miao & Wang (2014), Li (2014), etc. All these studies only concern translator's conceptualization process, without a reasonable explanation of meaning generation in certain context. Nevertheless the study of Zhang (2009) can be regarded as the expansion of CIT because he makes an integrated study of the theory.

Zhang's multi-meaning-driven pattern

Based on the cognitive theories of prototypical categorization, Gestalt, Mental space and Conceptual integration, Zhang(2009) proposes his comprehensive translation pattern: multi-meaning-driven translation pattern.

According to his pattern, linguistic expression is the representation of meaning. Since linguistic form and textual configuration are subject to the need of meaning representation, to grasp meaning is the first thing in dealing with information. As the object of translation, text is a reflection of language's communicative function, so linguistic communication is driven by meaning (Zhang,2009: 289). In inter-translation, translator should begin with the understanding and expressing of meaning. Through understanding the communicative mode of the source language, he may judge the role of certain words in the communicative mode and then decide the linguistic schema and conceptual schema of the words and sentences. After that, he can decide the corresponding schema in the target language by means of mappings between the source communicative mode and the target communicative mode, and finally choose the corresponding expression. Accordingly, translation in certain aspect is the process of mapping (or matching) and transformation of the communicative mode between languages and cultures. (ibid: 292)

Zhang's multi-meaning-driven communicative pattern is shown in figure

2-4. According to this pattern, the ST consists of linguistic schema and knowledge schema, which are transferred into conceptual schema through conceptual integration and acquire certain meaning representation. Under control of TT features, it is transferred to the target schema by means of conceptual integration, and then the target schema is re-conceptualized into suitable representations. Finally, meaning is formed under control of the target linguistic roles. In this pattern, Zhang regards the ST knowledge and TT features as background, and factors such as discourse phenomena, discourse intention and discourse receptor as controlling factors.

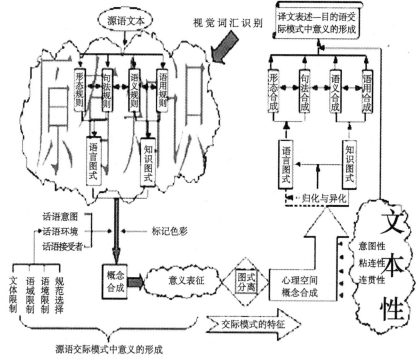

Figure 2-4 Multi-meaning-driven communicative pattern (cf Zhang 2009: 292)

Zhang's pattern is very clear in describing the translating process. His regarding the transferring process as a conceptual integration is of great significance in reflecting the dynamic feature of translating process. However, he uses too much of the communicative model transference instead of the way of conceptual integration, which, I think, is a weak point in revealing the real mental mechanism of translator. As to the different types of conceptual integration, he (ibid: 300-307) classifies five types of translation according to the four kinds of networks made by Fauconnier & Turner (2002: 120-137). I think his classification is too general to explain the complex translation phenomena. He does not mention the ways of mapping in the conceptual integrating process and their roles in producing different kinds of translation. Based on his pattern, this research aims at constructing a theoretical framework to describe and interpret the translating process.

2.2 Review of Context Studies

Studies of context in this section are reviewed from four aspects: non-cognitive studies of context, cognitive studies of context, context studies in translation, and contextual parameters theory, aiming at introducing the combination of cognitive context in translating studies.

2.2.1 Non-Cognitive Studies of Context

The notion of context is initiated by Malinowski (1923) in the complementary of *The Sense of Sense* by Ogden and Richards. He distinguishes three types of context: first, situations in which speech interrelates with bodily activity; second, narrative situation; third, situations in which speech is used to fill a speech vacuum— "PHATIC COMMUNION". Sparkled by Malinowski, Firth (1957) is interested in how language functions in the context of situation. He develops Malinowski's view and gives a more detailed description of context. Firth points out that not only the previous sentence, the following sentence, and passage of a discourse are context, but the relation between language and social environment is also context. He views the context of situation as a suitable schematic construct to apply to language events, and he suggests the categories involved in situation of context as follows: a) the relevant features of participants, persons and personalities, including the verbal and non-verbal actions of the participants; b) the relevant objects, including objects, events and non-linguistic and non-human events; c) the effect of verbal action. Firth is the first person who analyzes language from the angle of context, so he sketches a framework for the study of context thereafter.

Halliday, one of Firth's students, further develops the theory of context. As to what determines variation in language use, Halliday (1978) recommends a framework of two dimensions: user-related and use-related. The former is called dialect and the latter register. Context is reflected by register in three aspects: field, mode and tenor of discourse. Field refers to the environment where the speech event takes place, which includes topic, participants and the whole process of interaction. It reflects the social function of the text. Tenor is the relation between participants when social status and roles are taking into consideration. Tenor in effect directly determines the formality of the language used. Mode determines the medium of language activity. It is a manifestation of the nature of language code. In other words, mode is the channel through which a language is used.

Halliday is the founder of the Systemic Functional Linguistics (SFL). After him the SF approach has been succeeded and extended to context studies by many of his followers, to name a list: Dik (1981), Ventola (1995), Butler (1985), Martin (1985, 1992, 1999), Givon (1989, 1995, 2005), Fetzer (2004), etc. However, any theory or approach will be old-dated if not changed or made anew, so is the SF approach to context. Van Dijk (2008: 28-54) uses a whole chapter to talk about SF approach to context and summarizes its defects from five aspects: a) theoretically closed conceptualization; b) vague, heterogeneous, terminologically idiosyncratic and theoretically confused; c) too much linguistic sentence and grammar; d) the rather arbitrary nature of the three "variables" making the three functions of language and language structures arbitrary, incomplete and confused; e) no social research into the nature of contexts; f) anti-mentalist or lack of interest in cognition.

Although van Dijk criticizes SF in bitter words, he admits its contributions in some way:

> "But, the main point of the account of context, namely how properties of a social situation of interaction or communication are systematically related to grammar or other discourse properties, is a fertile and productive area of SFL. Thus, more than most other approaches to language, SFL has thought about genre, register and other ways contexts leave their traces in (or are expressed in) the structures of language use...much of this systematic work on language and discourse structure, and on the relations between text and context, remains relevant today." (van Dijk 2008: 55)

Van Dijk is correct in criticizing SF's lack of self criticism and updating, but he is too fault-finding in talking about their anti-cognition. In my opinion, at the time when Halliday proposed his SF approach to context, cognitive linguistics was not so developed or studied as it is today. What Halliday concerned is discourse analysis from the linguistic aspect instead of from pragmatic or cognitive aspects. So we can still borrow the idea of SFL even nowadays but need to make a more detailed description of the contextual parameters including both the co-text ones and cognitive ones.

Studies of context at home mainly follow the way of studies abroad and the main characteristic is to classify the context into different types (Hu,2002;

Si,2007; Wang,2006). The classification of context into different types by different scholars makes the study of context in a scattered way. What is more, the abstract and general classification of context is of little help in discussing translation problems unless they provide a systematic classification to concrete contextual parameters.

2.2.2 Cognitive Studies of Context

With the deepening study of context, researchers begin to apply the cognitive approach to text translating studies and cognition becomes a powerful tool in exploring context. For instance, van Dijk emphasizes the importance of cognition in studying context. He argues that "contexts as such are not social situations but mental constructs" (van Dijk,2001a: 582), that they "are not 'out there', but 'in there': they are mental constructs of participants" (van Dijk,2001b:18). Later, he clearly defines context as "a socially based but subjective construct of participants about the for-them-relevant properties of such a situation, that is, a mental modal" (van Dijk,2008:56) or "a special kind of mental model of everyday experience" (ibid: 71). He even thinks that context models "do claim to represent a plausible mental interface between discourse and social situations" (ibid: 57) and he lists several properties (ibid: 71).

One thing to point out here is that van Dijk (ibid: 98) also proposes the concept of "contextual parameters", and he sets concrete contextual parameters in the context models of the discourse participants. He also regards contextual parameters as a dynamic and open system, and which parameters are chosen is decided by the participants (ibid: 104-106). Van Dijk's definition and construction of context models is very significant in describing the mental mechanism of the translating process, while his study is about the realization of the communicative and pragmatic function of the discourse in mono-language communication rather than the meaning decision in co-text concerning bi-lingual translation. So his context model is a significant reference to this study, but as to the concrete contextual parameters concerned and how these parameters act in bilingual meaning generalization, contextual parameters theory (CPT) by Zeng Lisha is available.

In China, studies of the cognitive approach mainly follow the viewpoints of the studies abroad by regarding context as mental representation of social situation (Xiong, 1999; Wang, 2001c, 2002).

Studies from other perspectives should also be mentioned here in a general way, such as social/interactive approach (Hymes,1964), philosophical approach of Wittgenstein & Austin, social semiotic approach of Bakhtin & Vygotsky, language and cultural communication theory of Gumperz, and Relevance theory of Sperber & Wilson (1995/2001), etc., which approaches and theories extend the researches of context from different aspects. (see Liu, 2008: 127-128)

2.2.3 Studies of Context in Translation

In text comprehension, it has been widely recognized that meaning is to be determined in context and both internal and external contexts play an important role in interpretation of meaning. It is true with translation studies and scholars used to talk about context generally from different aspects of culture (Katan,1999/2004), ideology (Calzada Perez, 2003) or power (Tymoczko & Gentzler, 2002) respectively (see Baker, 2006: 322). Later when Gutt (1990, 1991, 1996, 1998) applies the concept of context in his writing of translation, what he ultimately takes as a point of departure in his analysis is not some readily identifiable and stable social reality but the assumptions of target readers. These assumptions are not 'out there' for translators to recover;

they are products of our own cognitive processes, but they do guide us in making decisions about how to render a text from one language and social context into another (Baker,2006: 323). Apparently, Gutt's context is fuzzy and cannot act as a systemic rule to guide translation. Nida (2001: 31-41) classifies nine types of contexts in translating: 1) Syntagmatic contexts; 2) Paradigmatic contexts; 3) Contexts involving cultural values; 4) Contexts that favor radical shifts in meaning so as to attract attention; 5) The context of a source text; 6) The audience of a discourse as context; 7) Different characters and circumstances in a discourse as contexts for different language registers; 8) The imprecise content of a text as the context for symbolic language; 9) The content of a text as a context for phonetic symbolism. According to his view, "the preceding types of contexts are not exhaustive, but they may serve as some of the more important ways in which a context may lead to certain types of content and reinforce the meaning and form of a text."(ibid: 41) However, his classification is still unsystematic and static, which is not verifiable or descriptive. Baker (2006: 325) also disagrees on the static classification of contexts. As she states, "However, defining context as a list of components of the type outlined by Hymes in his SPEAKING model or Scollon & Scollon (1995: 22-23) in their 'grammar of context' suffers from serious limitations. The weakest point is that the components and entities are often treated as static phenomena that exist in a fairly stable environment which the analyst can simply document and use to generate an analysis of events and behavior." Viewing from the above studies of context on translation, the author finds that a systematic theory of context is urgently needed to guide translation, and contextual parameters theory just meets the need.

2.2.4 Contextual Parameters Theory (CPT)

As context is a rather general concept, it is far from adequate in qualifying its significance in textual translation and requires improvement in the aspects such as descriptiveness and interpretation. So it is very significant to set various parameters for describing how context works and revealing the essence of those contextual meaning variations in mental mechanism. Zeng Lisha, after summarizing the inadequate aspects of other context studies, proposes CPT (2002, 2004). In order to make a persuasive description of the faithfulness in translation, Zeng classifies and qualifies different contextual parameters which act as references for meaning decision in translation. Zeng (2005, 2007a, 2010) also makes descriptive studies of contextual parameters with the illustration of concrete examples. His classification of contextual parameters is in a systematic and clarified way; moreover the descriptions of parameters are very persuasive. His study provides an available descriptive and interpretive method to translation studies.

Since its proposition, CPT has shown great power in deciding concrete meaning of polysemy, ambiguity, fuzziness, meaning shift in certain context (Zeng, 2002, 2004, 2007b, 2010; Ma, 2009; Wu, 2010; Yang, 2010). Nevertheless, as a primary theory, CPT also has some limitations in that its description of the translator's mental mechanism is not in a systematic way and the classification of parameters is not complicated, which needs to be further developed. This research also aims to deepen the study of contextual parameters theory by compensating it with MST and CIT.

2.3 Review of Equivalence Studies

In this section, equivalence studies abroad and at home are both reviewed, together with the discussion of their inadequacy, and then CCE is proposed and introduced with the purpose of making a complementary contribution to the theory of Equivalence.

2.3.1 Equivalence Studies Abroad

The Infancy Period of Equivalence

According to *Oxford Advanced English Dictionary*, the adjective "equivalent" goes back to 1460, while the noun "equivalence" is first recorded in 1541. In other words, the lexemes of equivalent/equivalence are used in English both as sharply defined scientific terms and in the notoriously fuzzy area of general vocabulary to mean 'of similar significance', "virtually the same thing' (*OAED*). (Snell-Hornby,1995/2001: 17)

Generally, Tytler is regarded as the predecessor of translation equivalence. Tytler (1791) proposes the standard of a good translation as follows:

> "*I would therefore describe a good translation to be, that, in which the merit of the original work is so completely transfused into another language, as to be as distinctly apprehended, and as strongly felt, by a native of the country to which that language belongs, as it is by those who speak the language of the original work …*
>
> *It will follow: 1) That the Translation should give a complete transcript of the ideas of the original work; 2) That the style and manner of writing should be of the same character with that of the original; 3) That the Translation should have all the ease of original composition.* " (cf. Snell-Hornby, 1995/2001: 190)

Although Holmes doubts that Tytler's principles "possibly borrowed—or plagiarized—from his contemporary and fellow townsman George Campbell", he still regards Tytler as a great influence in that "Tytler's thinking about translating takes on the shape of a system, a normative model that the translator can actually make use of, to a greater extent than any earlier text." (ibid: 189) Although not using the term 'equivalence' or 'fidelity', his words completely implies the idea.

Mathesius, one of the founders of the Plague School, expresses his idea in 1913 that the basic aim of literal translation is to get the same artistic effect as the original text, and the equivalent artistic effect is more important than the corresponding expressions. (see Liao,2000: 51, tran. by the author) Mathesius may be the first person using the term "equivalence" in translation.

The Development of Equivalence Theory

Later, Fedorov (1955) proposes two principles of translation. According to his principles, the target text and the source text can be totally equivalent to each other, and the translator must "transfuse the original thought clearly and exactly to the target reader, which is the primary condition for the reader's easy understanding and reception" (ibid: 11, tran. by the author).

Fedorov strengthens total and exact equivalence in thought and language, which is a hard work even for languages in the same family, to say nothing of the equivalence between English and Chinese, so it can be hardly reached. Just like what Barkhudarov comments, "complete equivalent translation is an ideal rather than a reality" (Barkhudarov,1985: 160, tran. by the author).

Barkhudarov defines translation as "the process of shifting one language's production to another with the content or meaning unchanged" (ibid: 4) The content or meaning he used in the definition needs to be understood in a broader sense and referred to the different relations between language units. And "keeping the content or meaning unchanged" is also an ideal target as meaning will definitely get loss during the shift. Therefore, the translation cannot be exactly equivalent to the source text (ibid: 5). According to the dividing standard of modern linguistics, Barkhudarov divides translation units into six levels (phoneme, morpheme, word, phrase, sentence and discourse) and he discusses the different translations respectively, which is helpful in setting evaluative standards to translation.

He argues that those necessary and sufficient translations are equivalent translations, those low-leveled are word-for-word ones, and those high-leveled are meaning translations. In order to reach equivalent translation, he suggests four methods: displacement, replacement, adding words, and omitting words (ibid: 145-204).

Barkhudarov's equivalent translation theory is more practical than that of Fedorov in that he does not prescribe the terms in a dead way but provides some details in a practical way. Nevertheless, Barkhudarov's translation theory can be regarded as the development and extension of Fedorov's viewpoint.

The term 'equivalence' is also discussed by Jakobson in his essay *On Linguistic Aspects of Translation*. He states that "Equivalence in difference is the cardinal problem of language and the pivotal concern of linguistics. Like any receiver of verbal messages, the linguist acts as their interpreter". The phrase "equivalence in difference" was—ironically—taken over as a focal concept in German Ubersetzungswissenschaft (cf Snell-Hornby, 1995/2001: 19).

During the boom of the scientific linguistic theories in the 1960s, English-speaking linguists also develop theoretical approaches to translation. In England, Catford develops his translation theory on the basis of Halliday's systemic grammar. Catford (1965: 20) defines translation as "the replacement of textual material in one language (SL) by equivalent textural material in another language (TL)". He even maintains that "the central problem of translation practice is that of finding TL translation equivalents and a central task of translation theory is that of defining the nature and conditions on translation equivalence" (ibid: 21). He makes a distinction between "formal correspondence" and "textual equivalence" in this way:

"*A textual equivalent is any TL text or portion of text which is observed on a particular occasion, by methods described below, to be*

the equivalent of a given SL text or portion of text." (ibid: 27)

According to Catford, the discovery of textual equivalents is "based on the authority of a competent bilingual informant or translator". If the key factors are contributed to the competent of the translator, then translation cannot be guided by any law, which means translation theory will be trapped in vain. Snell-Hornby (1995/2001:19) also views Catford's concept of equivalence as more general and abstract.

In the United States, the representative of equivalence study is Eugene A. Nida, who, on the basis of his own rich experience in Bible translating, develops a theory of translation which includes concepts from transformational grammar. Nida (1964) makes a dichotomy concept of "formal vs. dynamic equivalence". His examples are chosen from Bible translation. As to those cultural images which in reaching formal equivalence may cause confusion or conflict in another culture, he advocates being changed into the familiar images in the target culture to fulfill dynamic equivalence. The ideal translation for Nida & Taber (1969:12) is to "reproduce in the receptor language the closest natural equivalent of the source language message, first in terms of meaning and secondly in terms of style".

Nida's viewpoint of closest natural equivalence is influenced by his religious belief that Bible should be accepted by the target readers via natural target linguistic expression. Later Nida (1986) revises dynamic equivalence into functional equivalence which is thought more accurate in that meaning equivalence is impossible to be totally fulfilled between languages. Apart from content and meaning, he also realizes the importance of linguistic form and rhetorical features in language communication. He even proposes new principles of translation: understandable, readable, and acceptable. Although he makes some revision and development in his later book, Nida does not give deeper clarification to those problems (Tan, 1989: 28-49). Nida's limitation is caused by his translation of religious text and particularly his missionary demands, so his theory may cause confusion in dealing with other types of translation.

Nevertheless, equivalence studies have become a hot issue at that time. Snell-Hornby (1995/2001: 15) states the phenomena of translation studies during the 1960-70s in this way: "All the linguistic-oriented schools of translation theory were interested in the concept of translation equivalence (German Aquivalenz), which shifted the focus of translation theory away from the traditional dichotomy of 'faithful' or 'free' to a presupposed interlingual tertium comparasions." As Svejcer states, "equivalence is one of the central issues in the theory of translation and yet one on which linguists seem to have agreed to disagree" (Wilss, 1982/2001:134).

Theorists in Germany also discuss the term "equivalence" in translation in the 1970s. Koller (1979: 187-91, 1989: 100-104) bases his equivalence on some conditions. For instance, the ST and TT words supposedly refer to the same thing in the real world, such as on the basis of the referential or denotative equivalence; the ST and TT words trigger the same or similar associations in the minds of native speakers of the two languages, such as their connotative equivalence; the ST and TT words are used in the same or similar contexts in their respective languages, such as what he calls text-normative equivalence (Baker & Saldanha 2009: 96).

According to Wilss (1982/2001:135), other German scholars also introduce the term "equivalence" in one way or another. To name a list, Kade put forward "retention of translation invariance on the content level" in 1968; Levy proposed the concept of "illusionist vs. anti-illusionist translation" in 1969; Roganova was in favor of "functional invariance" in 1971; Ablbrecht advocated "total equivalence" in 1973; Jager brought forward "functional equivalence" in 1973; Popovic used the concept of "stylistic equivalence" in 1976; Reiss raised the issue of "communicative equivalence" in 1976; Kopczynski put forward the concept of "pragmatic appropriateness of translation" in 1980; Wilss introduced the issue of "text-pragmatic equivalence" in 1980 (cf Baker & Saldanha, 2009: 96). Equivalence studies boomed in that period.

Challenges to Equivalence Theory

Even in its flourishing period, "equivalence" is doubted by different scholars. Dagut remarks on its problems in translating metaphor in this way, "...any 'equivalence' in this case cannot be 'found' but will have to be 'created'. The crucial question that arises is thus whether a metaphor can, strictly speaking, be translated as such, or whether it can only be 'reproduced' in some way" (cf Bassnett,2005:33). Raymond van den Broeck challenges the excessive use of "equivalence" in translation studies and claims that the precise definition of equivalence in mathematics is a serious obstacle to its use in translation theory (ibid: 34). Nida's classification of *formal* and *dynamic* equivalence is challenged by the action of E.V. Rieu in that Rieu deliberately translates Homer into English prose because the significance of the epic form in Ancient Greece could be considered equivalent to the significance of prose in modern Europe, which is a case of dynamic equivalence applied to the formal properties of a text (ibid: 35). His aim is to show that Nida's categories could actually be in conflict with each other.

The works of the Russian Formalists and the Prague Linguists, together with the more recent developments in discourse analysis, have broadened the problem of equivalence in its application to the translation of literary texts.

James Holmes feels that the use of the term equivalence is "perverse", since to ask for sameness is to ask too much. Durisin argues that the translator of a literary text is not concerned with establishing equivalence of natural language but of artistic procedures. And those procedures cannot be considered in isolation, but must be located within the specific cultural–temporal context within which they are utilized (ibid: 35) .

 Ross (1981) goes even further by suggesting that the term *equivalence* should be replaced by the even vaguer term *similarity* (cf Snell-Hornby, 1995/2001:21). In the same year, Newmark (1981/2001: x) declares with refreshing candor that "Other subjects, such as the unit of translation, translation equivalence, translation invariance, I regard as dead ducks—either too theoretical or too arbitrary". Snell-Hornby (1995/2001:21) summarizes the two terms in this way: "while Aquivalenz—as a narrow, purpose-specific and rigorously scientific constant—has become increasingly static and one-dimensional, equivalence (leaving aside the TG-influenced concepts of the 1960s) has become increasingly approximate and vague to the point of complete insignificance." She even doubts the suitability of equivalence as a basic concept in translation theory. She states that "the term equivalence, apart from being imprecise and ill-defined (even after a heated debate of over twenty years) presents an illusion of symmetry between languages which hardly exist beyond the level of vague approximations and which distorts the basic problems of translation."(ibid: 22)

In responding to these criticism of equivalence, Nida (2001: 112) states that "in fact they went so far as to insist that true translating can only apply to nonliterary or nonfigurative texts, since they considered literary texts as structurally marginal uses of language." Originally, Nida's purpose of using dynamic equivalence is to show the similar effect of translation to the target readers with that of the original text to the original readers, which can be seen through his examples. He also expresses his viewpoint in this way: "Absolute equivalence in translating is never possible. But effective translating can be accomplished, and for three reasons: the existence of language universals, the extent of cultural similarities, and certain intellectual capacities of all peoples." (Nida,1984: 14) But the critics neglect that fact and are cornered with the expression of equivalence. Thus the problem can hardly be solved in this way. Just as Bassnett (2005) states, "equivalence in translation should not be approached as a search for sameness, since sameness cannot even exist between two TL versions of the same text, let alone between the SL and the TL version." It seems that to evaluate equivalence between two texts from the linguistic form is impossible.

Defects of Former Equivalence Studies

Former studies of equivalence have been mostly confined to surface phenomena, such as formal equivalence, stylistic equivalence, pragmatic equivalence or functional equivalence, which are mainly interpretations of relations between ST and TT in translating process from perspective of principle. Such studies remain at the level of abstract theoretical prescription and empirical interpretation, without promotion or expansion in theory, to say nothing of developing auxiliary theoretical concepts or borrowing relevant theories from adjacent disciplines for further systematic study. Considerable controversy and consequent slump in equivalence studies have been only too natural.

2.3.2 Equivalence Studies in China

Although equivalence is not used as a term by traditional translation theorists in China, similar viewpoints are proposed by them throughout the translation history. Dao An in eastern Jin Dynasty proposes "five lost and three difficulties (*wushiben, sanbuyi*)" which means that translation should be faithful to the source text in content, linguistic expression and style. Dao An's viewpoint can be seen as strict equivalence to the source text. Later Kumarajiva proposes that in keeping the content of the source text, the syntactic inversions should be smoothed out according to the target language usage (*qu cong fangyan, er qu bu guaiben*). Kumarajiva's viewpoint is similar to content equivalence to the source text. Xuan Zang pays attention to both content and style in translation and proposes that translation should express the content of the source text in fluent target language (*jixu qiuzhen, youxu yusu*). Later, Ma Jianzhong proposes that "good translation should bring target readers the same effect as that of the source text to the source text readers." Ma's viewpoint is a little similar to Nida's "closest natural equivalence". Other theorists in Chinese modern history also propose their translation viewpoints: Yan Fu proposes "faithfulness, expressiveness and elegance" (*Xin, Da, Ya*); Lu Xun argues for keeping the style and spirit (*Fengzi*) of the source text; Qu Qiubai states that translation should make the concepts acquired by the Chinese readers similar to those acquired by the source text readers; Fu Lei proposes that translation should be "more similar in spirit than in linguistic form"; Qian Zhongshu proposes the theory of "sublimation" (*Huajing*); Liu Zhongde proposes "faithfulness, expressiveness and properness" (*Xin, Da, Qie*); Xu Yuanzhong argues for "being similar in meaning rather than in linguistic form", etc. All of their viewpoints are about equivalence to the source text to some extent.

The only Chinese who directly uses the term "equivalence" is Jin Di. Based on Nida's equivalent principle, Jin proposes "equivalent effect" in translating *Ulysses*. Jin regards "equivalent effect" as both a theory to explore translating law and an ideal principle to pursue. As he states, his aim is "to reappear in the Chinese text the source text's artistic effect as loyal and complete as possible so that the Chinese readers can get the closest effect as what the source text readers get." (Jin,1998: 179) For example, he thinks that "cough it up" should be translated into "咳出来吧" in stead of "干脆说吧" in that the former can give the Chinese readers a similar effect considering Malligan's social position as a medical student and his habit of showing off knowledge (ibid: 184). But the problem is how to check the readers' reaction in reading such a translation and what kind of readers should be checked. If the common readers can not really understand the translation, equivalent effect can hardly be reached. So Jin's reader seems to be acted by the translator.

Compared to western theories, traditional Chinese translation theories of equivalence are more general and abstract. It seems that those theorists want to make principles to fit for all situations. But the fact is that those general and abstract prescriptive principles are not available in guiding specific translation practice. What is more, a similar defect between Chinese and western translation theories is that both regard source text as a steady and static system to be corresponding to and both neglect the subjectivity of the reader and translator in understanding the source and target texts.

2.3.3 Proposition of Cognitive Contextual Equivalence

Although Jin Di does not use the term of cognition, his equivalence effect is closely connected with cognition. According to his nine translating procedures, we see that he is unconsciously following the cognitive process of integrating the source text content with the target language and the equivalent effect he wants to reach is also checked from the cognitive aspect (see Jin, 1998: 184). Based on the former equivalence studies, this research proposes "cognitive contextual equivalence" (CCE). By combining mental space theory and conceptual integration theory, this research aims to explore the realizion of equivalence from cognitive context so as to reveal an essential feature of translating from a new perspective.

The principle of CCE goes like this: In translating, the translator first transmits the source text into suitable mental phenomena according to the contexts, and then he or she expresses the mental phenomena in the proper target language. Due to the different thinking modes and linguistic expressions between English and Chinese, an expression in one language may not have a corresponding one in another language. In such a situation, the translator has to choose some other expressions to adapt to the context. Sometimes one word in language A may correspond to more than one meaning items or concepts in language B, so choosing a new concept to replace one of the meaning items is quite acceptable and suitable. In principle, if the translator is restricted or guided by the concrete contextual parameters in his cognition and produces an appropriate translated version, we may regard the translation as cognitive contextual equivalent to the ST. Cognitive contextual equivalence is open, dynamic and context-guided in nature, which should be evaluated in cognitive context rather than in linguistic form as a meaning container or vehicle carrying its so-called "original meaning".

2.4 Summary

In this chapter, literature concerning relevant studies is reviewed. First of all, through reviewing studies of translating process from different paradigms, this research finds that former studies are either prescriptive in process interpreting or static in process describing, none considering the concrete roles that contextual parameters play in the process. Besides, conceptual integration theory is also reviewed, including its studies abroad and at home, as well as its usage in translation studies. Through the overview, the research finds that former studies concerning translation are mainly using the theory, which does little help to the theoretical development. What is more, CIT can only show us the cognitive mechanism of translating process. As for how to deal with the translating problems of vagueness, polysemy, meaning default, etc., it is helpless.

Since translation is influenced by context, studies on context are also reviewed. Traditional studies on context either center on social context or center on co-text, which are classified in a general way. Van Dijk studies context in a cognitive way and he induces all the former contexts into cognitive schemata which guide people's understanding of the latter discourse. His viewpoint is helpful in discussing text but is too general to qualify the relations between different contextual factors. Zeng's contextual parameters in textual translation compensates for van Dijk's defect in that Zeng's contextual parameters are open, systematic, qualitative and descriptive. By combining Zeng's classification of contextual parameters with van Dijk's cognitive viewpoint on context, this research can give a qualitative analysis of contextual parameters involved in the translating process.

At last, through reviewing traditional studies on equivalence, the research finds that to achieve equivalence from linguistic form is impossible in most cases and is easy to cause debate, so the research suggests that equivalence be studied from the cognitive perspective in specific context; as a result, the author proposes "CCE". Based on the former relevant studies, this research aims to combine the advantages of different theories to construct an integrated theoretical framework to study CCE.

Chapter 3

Theoretical Framework

3.1 Introduction

On the strength of the rationale and literature review, this chapter is devoted to construction of the theoretical framework for this research. To guarantee the validity of ensuing discussions, we intend to recapitulate the background theories involved first. By integrating MST, CIT and CPT with the analysis of translating process, we will also develop a feasible and operable theoretical construct for our empirical research so as to find out the mental mechanism in realizing CCE.

3.2 Background Theories

MST, CIT, *Mappings in Thought and Language*, and CPT are all background theories acting as theoretical analytic tools, and they will be recapitulated in the first place.

3.2.1 Mental Space Theory

Mental space theory is first presented by Fauconnier in 1979 at the Accademia della Crusca, in Florence (Fauconnier,1994/2008: preface 57). Later, a series of articles are presented and discussed from 1979 to 1983 in seminars of different universities. The publishing of *Mental Spaces: Aspects of Meaning Construction in Natural Language* (1985) makes the theory well known. Gradually the theory is discussed by different scholars from different aspects (Lakoff,1987; Encreve,1988; Sweetser,1989; Takubo & Kinsui,1992), which develop the theory. After more than 20 years' development, MST has become one of the five most important orientations of Cognitive Linguistics and a new paradigm of Cognitive Linguistic Study (see Fauconnier,1994/2008: preface 67). Many monographs exploring the inner constructions and governing principles from various aspects have been published (Fauconnier, 1996, 1997; Coulson & Oakley,2000; Fauconnier & Turner,2002; Dancygier & Sweetser,2005), which supplement and amplify the research space of the theory.

According to Fauconnier & Turner (1998: 137), "Mental spaces are small conceptual packets constructed as we think and talk, for purposes of local understanding and action. Mental spaces are very partial assemblies containing elements, and structured by frames and cognitive models. They are interconnected, and can be modified as thought and discourse unfold. Mental spaces can be used generally to model dynamical mappings in thought and language." Fauconnier (1994/2008: preface) regards mental space as a significant part of what is happening backstage, behind the scenes, in the cognitive background of everyday speaking and commonsense reasoning. This hidden, backstage cognition defines our mental and social life. Language is one of its prominent external manifestations. Cognitive scientists, including cognitive linguists, all agree that visible language is only the tip of the iceberg of invisible meaning construction that goes on as we think and talk. The essence of language, in Fauconnier's view (1997:190), is the meaning construction system—mappings, frames, integrations and spaces, and the words and sentences are surface manifestation of this activity.

Fauconnier (1997:40) also defines the concept of space-builder, which is a grammatical expression that either opens a new space or shifts focus to an existing space. According to his viewpoint, linguistic expressions will typically establish new spaces with elements within them and relations between the elements. He mentions such space-builders as prepositional phrases (in Len's pictures, in John's mind, in 1929, at the factory, from the point of view), adverbs (really, probably, possibly, theoretically), connectives (if A then..., either...or...), underlying subject-verb combinations (Max believes..., Mary hopes..., Gertrude claims...), etc. Space-builders come with linguistic clauses, which typically, but not always, predicate relations between space elements.

Fauconnier & Turner (2002: 23) admit that the notion of mental space construction is distinct from linguistic structures in that it is built up in any discourse according to guidelines provided by the linguistic expressions. In the model, mental spaces will be represented as structured incremental sets—that is, sets with elements (a, b, c,...) and relations holding between them (Rab, Ra, Rcbf...) so that new elements can be added to them and new relations can be established between these elements.

MST is the basic theory of this research which focuses on the translator's mental mechanism of conceptualization and meaning generation in the process of translating, which happens in the translator's mental spaces.

3.2.2 Conceptual Integration Theory

Conceptual Integration or Blending Theory (CIT) is derived from Conceptual Metaphor Theory (CMT) and MST. Its formation is featured by a series of articles and books by Fauconnier, such as: *Blending as Central*

Process of Grammar (1996), *Mapping in Thought and Language* (1997), *Principles of Conceptual Integration* (1996), *Metaphor, Metonymy, and Binding* (2000) and his coauthored works with Mark Turner *Conceptual Integration Networks* (1998), *The Way We Think: Conceptual Blending and The Mind's Hidden Complexities* (2002), the last of which is the collective masterwork of MST and CIT, and further improvement of the inner constructs and binding principles of the two theories. Coulson & Oakley (2000) explore roles of mental spaces and conceptual integrations in language understanding. Their experimental study of Event-Related Potential (ERP) provides objective proof to Mental Space and Conceptual Integration theories. Apart from this, cognitive linguistics such as Brandt & Brandt (2002, 2005), Coulson (2001), Coulson & Oakley (2005), Hutchins (2005), Bache (2005), Harder (2005), Hougaard (2005), etc. all make deep exploration to CIT from different aspects (see Wang, 2008: 22-26; Zhang & Yang, 2008), all of which studies develop CIT. Moreover, studies on MST and CIT can also be found in these world-famous journals such as Coulson & Oakley (2000), Coulson & Oakley (2005), Dancygier & Sweetser (2005). Zhang (2003) has made an introduction to Coulson & Oakley (2000).

The following part describes how the conceptual integration networks work. In blending, the structures from input mental spaces are projected to a separate, "blended" mental space. The projection is selective. Through completion and elaboration, the blend develops structure not provided by the inputs. Fauconnier & Turner (1998: 137-144) lists the main components in conceptual integration networks:

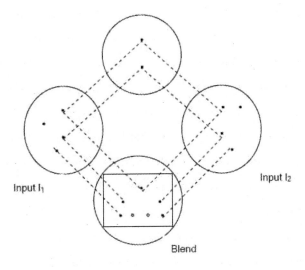

Figure 3-1 Conceptual integration

Mental spaces. The circles in figure 3-1 represent mental spaces. There are also background frames recruited to build these mental spaces, such as the background frame of two people approaching each other on a path. This is a minimal network. Networks in other cases of conceptual integration may have yet more input spaces and even multiple blended spaces.

Cross-space mapping of counterpart connections. In conceptual integration, there are partial counterpart connections between input spaces. The solid lines in figure 3-1 represent counterpart connections. Such counterpart connections are of many kinds: connections between frames and roles in frames; connections of identity or transformation or representation; metaphoric connections, etc.

Generic space. As conceptual projection unfolds, whatever structure recognized as belonging to both of the input spaces constitutes a generic space. At any moment in the construction, the generic space maps onto each of the inputs. It defines the current cross-space mapping between them. A given element in the generic space maps onto paired counterparts in the two input spaces.

Blending. In blending, structures from two input mental spaces are projected to a third space, the "blend." Generic spaces and blended spaces are related: blends not only contain generic structure captured in the generic space, but also contain more specific structure, and can contain structure that is impossible for the inputs.

Selective projection. The projection from the inputs to the blend is typically partial. In figure 3-1, not all elements from the inputs are projected to the blend.

Besides, there are three operations involved in constructing the blend: composition, completion, and elaboration.

Composition. Blending composes elements from the input spaces, providing relations that do not exist in the separate inputs. Counterparts may be brought into the blend as separate elements or as a fused element. Figure 3-1 represents one case in which counterparts are fused in the blend and one case in which counterparts are brought into the blend as distinct entities.

Completion. Blends recruit a great range of background conceptual structure and knowledge without our recognizing it consciously. In this way, composed structure is completed with other structure. The fundamental subtype of recruitment is pattern completion. A minimal composition in the blend can be extensively completed by a larger conventional pattern.

Elaboration. Elaboration develops the blend through imaginative mental simulation according to principles and logic in the blend. Some of these principles will have been brought to the blend by completion. Continued dynamic completion can recruit new principles and logic during elaboration. But new principles and logic may also arise through elaboration itself.

Emergent structure. Composition, completion, and elaboration lead to emergent structure in the blend; the blend contains structure that is not copied from the inputs. In figure 3-1, the square inside the blend represents emergent structure.

The network model is concerned with on-line, dynamic cognitive work people do to construct meaning for local purposes of thought and action. It focuses specifically on conceptual projection as an instrument of on-line work. Its central process is conceptual blending. In order to make the blending a good one, Fauconnier (1998:162-163) also proposes the optimality principles as follows:

Integration. The blend must constitute a tightly integrated scene that can be manipulated as a unit. More generally, every space in the blend structure should have integration.

Topology. For any input space and any element in that space projected into the blend, it is optimal for the relations of the element in the blend to match the relations of its counterpart.

Web. Manipulating the blend as a unit must maintain the web of appropriate connections to the input spaces easily and without additional surveillance or computation.

Unpacking. The blend alone must enable the understander to unpack the blend to reconstruct the inputs, the cross-space mapping, the generic space, and the network of connections between all these spaces.

Good reason. All things being equal, if an element appears in the blend, there will be pressure to find significance for this element. Significance will include relevant links to other spaces and relevant functions in running the blend.

Translating process is regarded as the process of conceptual integration in this research. The translator's operation is in fact a process of mapping, projecting and integrating that occur in mental spaces. During the process, those relevant concepts are foregrounded and projected to the mental spaces (short-time memory) to do on-line operation. Concepts or elements in different spaces are connected by mapping, and under the guidance of various contextual parameters, those relevant concepts or elements are projected into the blend space, and the process of conceptualization is completed. In the blending space, the blended concepts experience the process of composition, completion and elaboration with the restriction of contextual parameters, and finally form the concrete concept the translator needs, which is then put into the written form and becomes the contextual meaning. Till now, the process of conceptualization and meaning generation is completed.

From the above introduction and explanation, we are clear that CIT is only responsible for the static description of conceptualization. As to the factors restricting the process of conceptualization and meaning generation, CPT can be relied on.

3.2.3 Mappings in Thought and Language

The former part shows the general process of the translator's conceptualization occurring in the conceptual integration network. As to the concrete way of mapping and projecting, we need to go further into the theories concerning mapping.

"Mapping" is a metaphor originally used in cartography and later taken over by mathematicians and cognitive linguists (Ungerer & Schmid,2008:118). Cognitive linguists use the term to describe the corresponding relations between domains at the heart of the unique human cognitive faculty of producing, transferring, and processing meaning (Fauconnier,1997: 1). The case for metaphorical mappings has been studied by Reddy (1979), Lakoff & Johnson (1980), Turner (1986, 1991), Lakoff & Turner (1989), Sweetser (1990), Indurkhya (1992), Gibbs (1994), and many others. Fauconnier extends the scope of mapping to the whole human cognition. According to Fauconnier (1997: 1), meaning construction refers to the high-level, complex mental operations that apply within and across domains when we think, act, or communicate. The domains are also mental, and they include background cognitive and conceptual models as well as locally introduced mental spaces, which have only partial structure. Mappings are connections between different domains. Fauconnier (1997:12) classifies mappings into three main types and talks about the significance of cross-space mappings:

> *Mappings, including projection mappings, pragmatic mappings and schematic mappings, are at the heart of the unique human cognitive faculty that link mental spaces, pragmatic devices and schematic structures to produce, transfer and process on-line meaning----that is, manipulate information structures in discourses.*

Fauconnier (1997: 9-11) also gives explanation to each mapping respectively.

Projection mappings

Projection mappings will project part of the structure of one domain onto another to make the talk and thought easier. That is, in order to talk and think about some domains (target domains) we use the structure of other domains (source domains) and the corresponding vocabulary. Some of these mappings are used by all members of a culture—for instance, in English, TIME AS SPACE. We use structure from our everyday conception of space and motion to organize our everyday conception of time, as when we say: Christmas is approaching; The Weeks go by; etc. (Fauconnier 1997: 9) In this way, abstract concepts can be used as entities to express meaning, and the metaphorical expressions are formed in this way.

Pragmatic function mappings

The two relevant domains, which may be set up locally, typically correspond to two categories of objects, which are mapped onto each other by a pragmatic function. For example, authors are matched with the books they write, or hospital patients are matched with the illnesses for which they are treated. This kind of mapping plays an important role in structuring our knowledge base and provides means to identify elements of one domain via their counterparts in the other. Metonymy and synecdoche are pragmatic function mappings. In language use, pragmatic function mappings allow an entity to be identified in terms of its counterpart in the projection (Fauconnier, 1997:11).

Schema mappings

When a general schema, frame, or model is used to structure a situation in context, schema mappings operate (Fauconnier,1997: 11). Fauconnier elaborates his schema mappings from the schema in grammatical construction of Langacker (1987, 1991) and borrows the idea of Lakoff (1987) that mental spaces are structured by ICMs (idealized cognitive models), which is regarded by him as a kind of schema mapping.

As the theoretical tools for describing the translating process, these terms used by Fauconnier will be applied in my research.

Access Principle of cognitive constructions and conceptual links

Fauconnier proposes the Access Principle (also called Identification principle) and describes it as a crucial property of language, cognitive constructions, and conceptual links. The principle goes like this:

> *If two elements a and b are linked by a connector F (b=F (a)), then element b can be identified by naming, describing, or pointing to its counterpart a.* (1994/2008:1, 1997:41)

He also makes analysis of the cognitive operation of discourse configurations:

> *A language expression E does not have a meaning in itself; rather, it has a meaning potential and it is only within a complete discourse and in context that meaning will actually be produced. The unfolding of discourse brings into play complex cognitive constructions. They include the setting up of internally structured domains linked to each other by connectors; this is affected on the basis of linguistic, contextual, and situational clues. Grammatical clues, although crucial. to the building process, are in themselves insufficient to determine it.*
> (Fauconnier,1997: 37-38)

The configurations produced will undergo further pragmatic elaboration. They have the important characteristic of partitioning information, by relativizing it to different domains. The importance of partitioning for reasoning, and more general cognitive purposes, is stressed in Dinsmore (1991). The domains constructed in this fashion are partially ordered by a subordinate relation: a new space M^1 is always set up by following a focused space M. M is called the parent space of M^1, and in subsequent diagrams the subordination relation will be represented by a dashed line. (Fauconnier, 1997: 38)

The spaces set up by a discourse in this way are organized into a partially ordered lattice (figure 3-2). At any given stage of the discourse, one of the spaces is a base for the system, and one of the spaces (possibly the same one) is in focus space. Construction at the next stage will be relative either to the Base Space or to the Focus. Metaphorically speaking, the discourse participants move through the space lattice; their viewpoint and their focus shift as they go from one space to the next. But, at any point, the Base Space remains accessible as a possible starting point for another construction. (ibid: 38)

The mental spaces set up in this way are internally structured by frames and cognitive models, and externally linked by connectors, which relate elements across spaces, and more generally, structures across spaces. (ibid: 39)

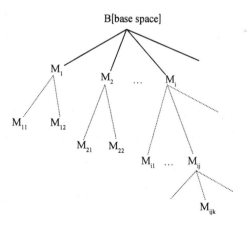

Figure 3-2 Network configuration of mental spaces

Based on the above introduction, the author proposes the idea that the network configuration of mental spaces under the guidance of the Access Principle can provide a vivid and effective description to the complicated inner relevance of textual development, and it can also provide a theoretical method to the descriptive study of textual coherence in translation. Although it has such advantages, it can not explain the cognitive mechanism in achieving coherence, nor can it explain how to operate those incoherent translated versions, so it has limitation in the study of textual translation. CPT can be borrowed for compensation.

3.2.4 Contextual Parameters Theory (CPT)

As has been introduced in the former chapter, CPT is proposed by Zeng (2002, 2004) in his study of textual translation on the basis of traditional contextual theories. Zeng breaks through the traditional approaches of classifying contexts and generalizing elements by specifying those abstract contextual concepts into a collection of referential parameters. He also discusses the descriptiveness, operability and objective demonstrability of those referential parameters (Zeng, 2000, 2001, 2005, 2007, 2010). As to CPT, the relations between referential parameters are of mutual references, including references between the macro and the micro proposition, the superordinate and the subordinate, the whole and the part, etc.; mutual mappings, including mappings between conceptual meaning components, between relational characters, etc.; or mutual restriction, such as restriction of conventional experiences, etc.

Generally, the contextual parameters system can be divided into two subsystems: intra-text and extra-text. Intra-text parameters refer to those co-text language units which act as referential factors, including linguistic form and content. Content can be sub-divided into textual theme, paragraph theme, ways of action, time, space, events, relation of genus, superior and inferior meaning relations, features, communicative intention, contrast, correspondence, decision and auxiliary parameters, etc. And these parameters can also be further classified into more detailed ones. Since linguistic form and content are connected in certain language units, those parameters different levels influence each other. Extra-text parameters are regarded by Zeng as situational parameters, including social environment, natural environment, communicative environment, communicators' features, and so on. These contextual parameters can also be further sub-categorized. For instance, communicators' features comprise communicators' thoughts, characteristics, status, cultivation, situation, mood and mutual relations, etc. Mutual relations can be further sub-categorized into social role, communicative status, emotional distance, and informational background, etc. Those contextual parameters are at different levels and function as reference, restriction or guidance, etc. in the process of contextual meaning generation.

In a word, the contextual parameter system is a dynamic and open one. On the one hand, the setting of contextual parameters reflects the inner relationship of language signs as well as the restrictions of extra-textual knowledge. On the other hand, it reflects the subject's mental representation to the objective context. Instead of generally discussing those abstract concepts of contexts, this theory makes the mental representation more visible and operable (Liu, 2008). CPT provides an available analytic and interpreting tool for interpreting meaning generation in translating process from both macro and micro levels.

3.2.5 Cognitive Contextual Equivalence Studied in an Integrated Theoretical Framework

Viewing from the above introduction, we think that none of the theories is perfect in interpreting the translating process, and the combination of them may compensate their shortcomings. So the author intends to construct an integrated theoretical framework to explore this cognitive process.

Based on MST and CIT (Fauconnier, 1994, 1997), this research regards translating as an activity happening in the translator's mental spaces. Different mental spaces such as ST space, TL space and TT space are involved in the operating process and different spaces are connected by means of cross-space mappings (Mandelblit, 1997, Wang, 2004). Different types of mappings which appear in the translator's mental spaces may cause different translations. So understanding of different kinds of translations can theoretically help us interpret the translator's cognitive process.

MST and CIT provide available theoretical method to the descriptive study of translating process. However, MST is just a static relationship description, which can only illustrate the relations between different mental spaces by means of mental space network. It can not provide a cognitive analytic framework to explain the interactions between the macro and micro operative mechanisms. Although CIT provides an active process of selective mappings and projections, it can not illustrate how concepts or statements get definite meaning in certain context, moreover, it does little help to how to translate or choose translation.

CPT can compensate the defects of MST and CIT. CPT regards the relations between parameters (concepts or statements) as mutual reference, mapping or restriction. Mutual referential relations include the macro and micro proposition, the superordinate and subordinate, the genus and species, the whole and the part, etc. The mapping relations include mappings of conceptual meaning components and relational characters, etc. The relations of restriction include restriction of conventional experiences (Zeng,2002, 2004, 2010). Meaning decision and meaning change can both find reasons in the frame of CPT. Anyway, CPT provides an available analytic and interpreting tool for meaning generation from both macro and micro levels.

By combining MST, CIT and CPT, this research tends to construct an integrated theoretical framework, which can illustrate the translator's cognitive mechanism in the translating process and analyze the reasons of meaning decision and meaning shift in certain context. That is, MST and CIT can provide theoretical basis for translating process from the cognitive layer, while CPT can compensate the shortcomings of MST and CIT on the concrete descriptive layer, so the combination of the theories can prove and compensate each other, and provide an operable theoretical framework to illustrate the translating process.

3.3 Construction and Interpretation of the Theoretical Framework

Translation in general is to achieve CCE at certain level. At the same time, the translator will adopt the receptive-aesthetics-orientation so as to make the translation more acceptable, especially in literary translation. In such cases, equivalence is fulfilled by the translator in cognitive context rather than in linguistic form. During the operating process, the translator may consider the text features and integrate the linguistic and cultural attached conceptual patterns into that of the TT. Various subjective and objective constraints come into the mental spaces and involve in the integrating process. The subjective constraints include recipients' aim and needs, and the objective constraints refer to those visible and invisible contextual parameters. (see figure 3-3)

The cognitive process of translation is also the restructuring of mental spaces, in which process concepts of ST and TL are integrated to form a new TT. Conceptual integration including coincidental and deviant ones is regarded as an important cognitive mechanism to realize cognitive contextual equivalence. And the operating mechanism of conceptual integration includes:

mapping, projecting, blending, conceptual sememes extraction, composition, completion, and elaboration, etc. The cognitive process of translation can be divided into two procedures: conceptualization and meaning generation, also known as understanding and expressing. In the first procedure, ST message comes into the translator's mind and activates his/her background knowledge in the long-time memory. Related information in the long-time memory is activated and relevant concepts are selectively projected into the short-time memory (mental spaces) to do on-line operation. Concepts of input mental spaces are mapped to each other, and then useful concepts or conceptual sememes are extracted and projected into the blending space to do integration. These concepts or conceptual sememes in the blending space experience composition, completion and elaboration and finally form the integrated ST conceptual meaning. This is the completion of the first period. Then the blended ST conceptual meaning turns into the second blending procedure. The semantic representation of the blended ST conceptual meaning goes through the period of mapping, projecting and integrating with the corresponding target language expressions and then experiences composition, completion and elaboration and finally forms the TT expressive meaning. CCE works as the guiding principle as well as the final aim of the translation. Based on analyses of the realization of CCE in various conceptual integrations in translation, some empirical rules can be constructed to guide translation practice.

This theoretical framework will guide the analyses of all examples in the following chapters. As CCE is studied from the perspective of MST and CIT in this research, it will be demonstrated and illustrated by different examples of conceptual integrations in translation.

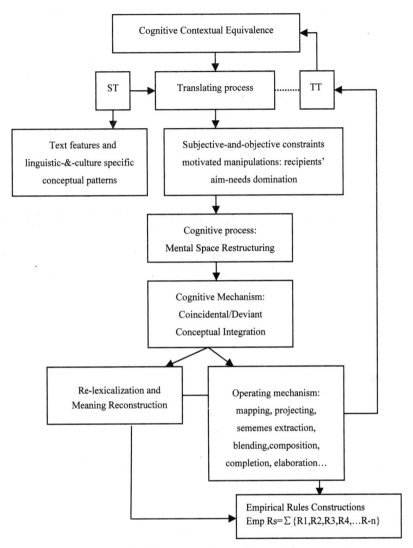

Figure 3-3 An theoretical framework of the research

(ST represents source text; TT represents target language)

Chapter 4

Cognitive Contextual Equivalence in Coincidental Conceptual Integration

4.1 Introduction

Coincidental conceptual integration can be found in two ways. The first is that a set of concepts C1+C2+C3+C4... in ST is cognitively corresponding to certain concept P in TT, and the sememes of the multi-concepts are coincidently integrated into concept P. As a result, the number of concepts is changed while sememes kept during translation. The second way is seen in the fact that an abstract concept in ST corresponds to a concrete or vivid expression in TT via re-categorization, with the target expression integrating the action and characteristic of the source concept.

Generally, the sememes of the concept P can get overall or partial correspondence with that of the multi-concepts C1+C2+C3+C4...in conceptual integration. Such a conceptual integration is undergoing in the translator's mental spaces, which is regarded as the cognitive mechanism of the translator in this research. The translator's motivation for conceptual integration is to fulfill certain aesthetic effects, such as conciseness, vividness, sarcasm or humor. With conceptual integration, the translator can better express the communicative intention of the ST or meet the needs of target language, culture or thinking mode.

Talmy (2000: 21) explores the relationship between meaning and surface expression. He believes that although the corresponding relationship between meaning and surface expression is not often clear or direct, language users can always find suitable expression. He regards the process of finding surface expression for meaning as lexicalization.

In translation, the translator will recreate the source event scenario in his cognition and then reorganize the event or scenario in the target text according to its language convention and order. Generally, the translator would not succeed the original way of lexicalization; instead, he would re-lexicalize the event and scenario according to the cognitive thinking habit of the target language users, which is called re-lexicalization (Liu,2009: 380). In this research, the author tends to regard such re-lexicalization as a kind of coincidental conceptual integration to realize CCE, which can add certain aesthetic effect to the ST. Usually different contextual parameters will come into the mental spaces to involve in the conceptual integration. CCE in coincidental conceptual integration will be discussed from three aspects: CCE in words conversion, in re-lexicalization of motion words, and in re-lexicalization of redundant words.

4.2 Cognitive Contextual Equivalence in Words Conversion

Words conversion refers to words indicating other categories converted into verbs, such as noun, adjective, adverb, etc. converted into verbs. The translator is apt to use converted words to correspond to the source expressions. Even if the surface expression is not so corresponding, the basic meaning contained in ST is maintained in TT.

Dirven (1999: 275-288) points out that re-lexicalization including N.-V. conversion is a kind of metonymy based on event schemata. According to Kovecses (2002: 145), "Metonymy is a cognitive process in which one conceptual entity, the vehicle, provides mental access to another conceptual entity, the target, within the same domain, or idealized cognitive model (ICM)." Fauconnier (1997: 11; 1994/2008: 3) regards metonymy as a kind of pragmatic function mapping.

This research holds the view that words conversion should not be regarded as a simple metonymy; sometimes they can be both metaphor and metonymy. The following part is a discussion of CCE realized in four types of words conversion: noun to verb (N.-V.) conversion, adjective to verb (Adj.-V.) conversion, adverb to verb (Adv.-V.) conversion, and numerals to verb (Numerals.-V.) conversion.

4.2.1 Cognitive Contextual Equivalence in N.–V. Conversion

Conversion from noun to verb is also called denominal verb, which has been studied by many researchers both at home and abroad. According to Wang (2008: 8-21), N.-V. conversion has been studied from five perspectives: grammatical, pragmatic, cognitive, rhetorical, and contrastive. Representatives of grammatical perspective are Jesperson (1942), Zandvoort (1961), Quirk (1972, 1985), Adams (1973), Clark & Clark (1979), Marchand (1969), Dirven (1986), Lǚ (1990), Ding (1979), Hu (1995), Lu (1983), Wang & Li (1988), Sui (2005), Lin & Liu (2005), Xu (1981), Wang (2001), etc. Some of them even classify N.-V. conversion into different kinds according to different standards. Representatives of the pragmatic perspective are

Kiparsky (1982, 1997), Kelly (1998), Xu & Gao (2000a, b), Lu (2005), Gao (2002), etc. Studies from the cognitive perspective include Xu (2001a), Liu (2000), Liu (2004), Dirven (1999), Wang (2001), and He (2006), etc., in which Liu (2004) explores the semantic relationship between the denominal verbs and the original nouns, and the others discuss the generative mechanism of denominal verbs. Researchers from the rhetorical perspective include Chen (1979), Yin (2002), Feng (2004), Wang (2006), etc. Researchers of contrastive perspective include Si (1996), Zhou (2000), Chan & Tai (1995), etc. Generally speaking, Wang's classification is not suitable in that some of the researches are overlapping. For example, even though some are classified into the grammatical perspective, they also belong to the cognitive perspective when they talk about the cognitive mechanism of the phenomena (such as Liu,2000, Dirven, Wang,2006). Nevertheless, Wang's study provides profound information of denominal verbs from the single-language aspect, which lays the foundations for further research in translation. Knowing the constructive rules and characteristics of N.-V. conversions in both languages, we can find the rule in translation and form some empirical rules to guide future translation.

The following section touches upon the features of CCE realized in four different kinds of denominal verbs: Denominal verbs concerning body parts; Denominal verbs concerning natural phenomena; Denominal verbs concerning animal names; Denominal verbs concerning object, position and other things.

4.2.1.1 CCE in Denominal Verbs Concerning Body Parts

There are many words expressing body parts in both Chinese and English, such as arm, back, head, ear, eye, nose, face, hand, finger, foot, forehead, belly, jaw, mouth, tongue, heart, etc. Zhang (2010) states that all

English words concerning body parts can be used as verbs except for "forehead" and "heart". According to my statistics of "heart" in eighteen E-E and E-C dictionaries, only three dictionaries contain the verbal explanation of "encourage" which is the ancient use without any example (*American Heritage Dictionary, Landau English Dictionary*). In fact, except for "heart" and "forehead", all the other words expressing body parts can be used as verbs. That means those widely used body parts can be converted to verbs more easily. According to cognitive linguistics, when human beings experience the world in ancient times, they interact with the environment by means of their own body parts, so they form various corresponding concepts, categories and meanings (Wang,2005). Mao Zedong (1991: 288) also talks about such a phenomenon in his works *On Practice* in 1937 that "The source of all knowledge comes from the sense of human body parts to the objective world. Whoever denies the sense or the direct experience of reforming reality is not a materialist." Malinowski (1935) also holds the same viewpoint that "ultimately the meaning of all words is derived from bodily experience" (see Halliday & Hasan, 1985: 7). Lakoff & Jonson (2002: 249) strengthens the role of human experience by stating that "mind is embodied, meaning is embodied, and thought is embodied in this most profound sense." Because human body parts are more highlighted than other things, people tend to use their body experience to understand and produce language. Words concerning body parts are thus frequently used as the references of metonymy. (Zhang, 2010: 107-112) The following examples illustrate such N.-V. conversions in both Chinese and English:

（1）樟木县，这是一个山城，所有人背山而住，只有几条街，呈 Z 字形。

（2）"今谁掌其权?"（李商隐：《行次西郊作》）
掌嘴、掌管、掌握、掌权、掌航等。

（3）目送、目测、目击等。

（4）指鹿为马；指摘、指责。

（5）The men *armed* themselves with sticks and stones.

（6）He *backed* the car out of the garage.

（7）He couldn't help *eyeing* the cakes hungrily.

（8）We found a man *nosing* around in our backyard.

（9）Gary sat *fingering* his beard, saying nothing.

（10）Who will be *footing* the bill for the party?

（11）They are just *mouthing* empty slogans.

（12）He *elbowed* his way through the crowd.

(cf Zhang, 2010; Tan, 2011)

From the above examples, we see that some demonimal verbs indicating body parts get new structural meaning of "to … by means of …" via metonymical mappings, such as example 3, 4, 6, 7, 8, 9, 11, 12; others are transferred to their functional verbs via metaphorical mappings, such as example 1, 2, 5, 10. As N.-V. conversions of body part words are more popular in ancient Chinese than in modern Chinese, and most of such expressions in modern Chinese have been regarded as entrenched ones, such as "目送, 目语, 目击, 指责, 掌管, 掌握, 掌权, 掌航", etc. Their metonymical usages are rarely thought about. Since most words concerning body parts in English can be used as verbs, troubles will be met in translation. As it is difficult to find a corresponding expression, the translator would accomplish CCE through conversions between the concrete and the abstract.

Sometimes the translator is apt to use concrete expressions to translate those abstract concepts so as to make the translation more vivid and succinct. Such concrete expressions usually integrate the prototypical image of the body part, the state and action of the subject, as well as the result of the action, etc. For instance:

1. 赶紧加快足步转过坡去，天空忽然开朗，一大片平整的山地现了出来。(Ai ,1999: 139)

TT₁: As I quickened my pace, *turned around and walked over* the hill, the sky suddenly cleared, revealing a large strip of hillside fields planted with rice shoots, all over a foot tall. (possible literal translation provide by the author)

TT₂: As I quickened my pace and *headed across* the hill, the sky suddenly cleared, revealing a large strip of hillside fields planted with rice shoots, all over a foot tall. (tran. by William Bishop,   Ai 1999: 138)

TT₃: As I quickened my pace and *headed over* the hill, ... (revised from TT₂ by the author)

In the source text, the expression "转过" suggests two successive actions "转身" (suggesting the manner) and "走过" (action), which are integrated via what Shen (2006a: 6) called *Dajie* blending (blending the first and last Chinese character of both phrases). If the ST is translated literally into English, we will probably get TT₁, which is not succinct. In TT₂, "转过" is translated into "head across", which is also an integration of the concepts in ST. When "head" is converted to verb, it means "move toward a specified direction" (*OAED*). This meaning comes from metonymical and metaphorical mappings, in which the top part of the body is first transferred into the direction-decision part, and then transferred into "moving to a specific direction". The converted verb "head" integrates such image features as the body part, the agent's action, state and moving direction. It is an effective way to use such converted verbs in translation. Nevertheless, I do not think it is right to translate "转过坡去" into "head across the hill".

"Across" is not appropriate to be used here because it means "from one side to the other side" (*OAED*). When putting together with "head", it means "going from one side of the slope to the other side directly without the upward movement". How can a person go across the hill directly without turning around or climbing over it? So I think the expression "head over the hill" is better because "head" means "to move toward" and "over" expresses the upward and downward motion towards the other side, which is more appropriate in this context. The cognitive process of TT$_3$ can be illustrated in figure 4-1.

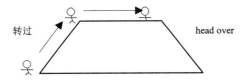

Figure 4-1 Cognitive schema of "head over"

2. 只有何大学问认定不打不成材，非但不怪罪老秀才学规森严，而且还从旁给老秀才呐喊助威。（Liu, 1999a：29）

The grandfather, however, stoutly maintained that beating produced talent and he *backed* the old scholar. (tran. by Alex Young, ibid: 28)

In the source text, the concept set "呐喊助威" contains the manner-indicating concept "呐喊" and action-indicating concept "助威". "呐喊" means "to help or support somebody to encourage him to gather strength by waving the flag and screaming loudly", which is cognitively implied in the sememes of "助威". On the other hand, the meaning of "助威" is "to help or support somebody so as to encourage him to gather strength" (cf *New Oriental Dictionary*[1]) ."从旁" refers to the indirect manner of help or support. So the conceptual meaning of "呐喊" is integrated into "助威" in translating, which contains the same sememe of "help" or "support" as the verb "back" does.

"Back" originally refers to the broad and flat part of body, which can be relied on steadily. Later, it is converted to verb, meaning "to help or support somebody or something by using money or words." (*OAED*) Such a N.-V. conversion is from metonymical mappings. In this translation, the translator omits "非但不怪罪老秀才学规森严" and integrates "还从旁给······呐喊助威" into one word "back". Even though "back" can not generalize all those meanings, it implies that the grandfather does not blame the old scholar for his strict disciplines. The sentence structure of "非但不怪罪" presupposes the following expression "而且还帮助", so in cognitive context the two balanced sentence structures can be integrated into one cognitive frame or conceptual schema "support". The schema of the ST is implied in the SL, which calls for the translator to dig and reconstruct in the TT (see Wang, 2009: 157). In this example, the translator uses "back" to translate the whole sentence so as to make the expression more succinct. Although the linguistic form is not equivalent to the source expression, the meaning is equivalent in cognitive context. What is more, "back" integrates the prototypical image feature of the body part, and the manner of the grandfather. The reasoning process of CCE can be illustrated in figure 4-2.

---

[1] 《新东方辞海》，http://tool.xdf.cn/ch/.

(LF=linguistic form; CC=cognitive context)

Figure 4-2 CCE between "从旁呐喊助威" and "back"

The above exemplification shows the integration of the conceptual set "从旁呐喊助威" in the source text into the concept "back" in the target language to achieve cognitive equivalence.

3. 现在又突然冒出一个地委院里的人，并且排在他前面，这不明着表示陆洪武看不起他？(Liu,1999b: 179)

And now somebody had emerged, seemingly from the woodwork, and *muscled in ahead of him*. Surely this must mean that Lu Hongwu didn't appreciate him. (tran. by Paul White, ibid: 178)

In the source text, the literal meaning of "排队" is "forming a line or queuing up according to the order. (*Xin Hua Dictionary*)" But "排……" is mapped by the action "冒出" (indicating a quick and unexpected manner) in this context and acquires the contextual meaning "joining in in front of him unexpectedly by means of disordering action or physical strength", so the literal translation of "queuing up ahead of him" is not appropriate. "Muscle in" means "to use your power to get involved in or take control of something that someone else was doing" (*Longman Contemporary English Dictionary*), or "joining in something when one has no right to do so, for one's own advantage"(*OAED*), which is equivalent to the original meaning in cognitive context. "Muscle" originally refers to the part of human body and is the reflection of strength and power. When this feature of body part is mapped onto human domain via metonymical mapping, a man of muscle is endowed with the conceptual sememe of "strong or powerful man". This semantic feature is further projected into human action domain and forms the expression of "muscle in".

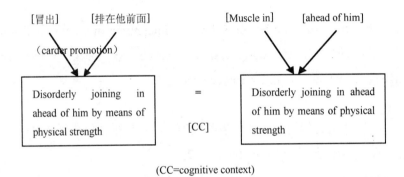

(CC=cognitive context)

Figure 4-3 CCE between "排在他前面" and "muscle in ahead of him"

The source context is about the promotion of carders, and the hero is worrying about the possibility of being replaced by some others in promotion. The Chinese expression "排在他前面" has the implied meaning of "joining in in front of him by some inappropriate action", and "muscle in" can express this implied meaning of making illegal efforts to forcefully get ahead of him on the authority's candidate list for promotion (see figure 4-3). Besides, such a translation is more succinct and aesthetic as "muscle in" also integrates the prototypical image of the human body part, and the imposing manner of a strong man.

4. 便有，也只怕他们未必来理我们呢！（Cao,2003: 168）

Even if I had, they'd most *likely cold-shoulder* us. (tran. by the Yangs, ibid: 169)

The dotted part of the source text contains such conceptual sets as "未必" (may not, indicating uncertainty), "来" (come, indicating the manner), "理会" (contact, indicating an action) and "我们" (us). Its cognitive contextual meaning is "behaving unfriendly to us or show that they do not care about us". *Cold shoulder*, when converted to verb, means "to behave towards somebody in an unfriendly way, to show that they do not care about somebody or they want somebody to go away" (*Clings Advanced English Study Dictionary,* 5th edition), which is corresponding to the original meaning in cognitive context.

"Shoulder" originally refers to part of human body, which is usually used to carry things. It is easy to be connected with "bearing the responsibility or burden" through metonymical mappings. When putting together with "cold", the emotional feature of cold (unfriendly) is projected to the domain of "shoulder", and finally forms the blended meaning that "treat somebody unfriendly" (see figure 4-4). So we have the above dictionary explanation of "cold shoulder". Such usage integrates the prototypical image feature of human body part, state and function of the body part, as well as the speaker's manner. Although the linguistic form of the TT is not equivalent to the ST, the communicative meaning is equivalent in cognitive context.

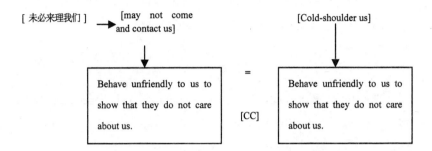

Figure 4-4 CCE between "未必来理我们" and "cold-shoulder us"

From analyses of the above examples, we deduce such an empirical rule:

$$S(x) + VP (Act + M_{+1}+I_0) \longrightarrow S + VP (DV +M_0+I_{+1})$$

ST   TT

(S= subject; VP= verbal phrase; x= agent or actor; M_{+1}= manner; DV=denominated verb; I_{+1}=Image; $_0$ = zero; arrow = integrated in)

This formal empirical rule is explained as follows:

English denominated verbs concerning body parts can be used to translate the abstract Chinese act. As the denominated verbs integrate the agent's acts and manners, suggesting the prototypical images of the original noun, they can make the versions more succinct and vivid.

As there are many such N.-V. conversions in English, the translator is apt to change the abstract to the concrete expressions in C-E translation. However, N.-V. conversions are less popular in modern Chinese, so they are rarely used in E-C translation. When meeting with such expressions in English text, the translator tends to transfer the concrete expression into abstract concepts or descriptions according to the context. For instance:

5. Simon Wheeler *backed me into* a corner and *enclosed* me there with his chair, and then sat down and reeled off the boring story which follows this paragraph.

TT: 在西蒙•惠勒推推让让之下，我后退到一个角落里。他把椅子搬来横在我面前，坐定之后便滔滔不绝，给我讲述起这段文字之后的那个单调乏味的故事。（Wang 2005）

In this example, the author uses the denominal word "back" to express a dynamic scene where the narrator "I" was pushed and forced to move backward by Simon Wheeler into a corner. It is easy for the reader to build a mental picture of the original scene, but it is hard to express the scene with similar Chinese words as we do not have such denominal verbs in Chinese. So what the translator can do is to express such a mental scene into proper Chinese.

From the above examples, we see that such N.-V. conversions have the grammatical function of both verb and noun, and both conceptual meanings are blended in expressions, which makes the version move succinct in form and rich in connotation. Although N.-V. conversion in form plays the grammatical function, it is in fact an integrating process of conceptual metonymy or metaphor. Such an integration can make the images and conceptual sememes more vivid and richer. Through exploring the semantic shifting process of denominal verbs, we find that the meanings of denominal verbs are closely related to the prototypical features of those source objects. So we state that the prototypical feature of the source object is the basic motivation of verbalization. Langacker (1999: 10) thinks that the denominal verbs of body-part words are activated by metonymic cognition and the prominent principle of cognition plays a restrictive role. Only those interactive, functional and visible human body parts can be used as viewpoint to activate the cognitive domain of the relevant verbs. Shen (2010: 6) also holds the similar view that concepts of action must rely on the relevant objects, so it's impossible to imagine an action and think of the relevant objects simultaneously. N.-V. conversions of body part words provide available methods for translation especially C-E translation, and the translator is likely to choose N.-V. conversions to improve the aesthetic effect.

4.2.1.2 CCE in Demonimal Verbs Concerning Natural Phenomena

As we know, one of the basic principles of cognitive linguistics is to recognize the order of reality—cognition—language (Wang,2007: 273). That is to say, language is regarded as the reflection of cognition, and cognition comes from sensation of the real world. As Johnson (1987) states, "Human probably named themselves, their body parts and their immediate environment early in the development of language. As today, the human body, and the space surrounding it, presumably formed the basis of further meaning extensions." Our Chinese ancient philosophy also takes such points as "we know and describe things from the ones near or close us" (*Jin qu zhu shen, Yuan qu zhu wu*). Natural phenomena, as the real existence that human beings experience everyday, are closely related to language. Traditional Chinese Medicine (TCM) may be the best reflection of the relationship between human being and the environment. TCM holds the view that human body should keep *Yin* and *Yang* balance with the change of seasons, and the five elements of the universe such as metal, wood, water, fire and earth represent five human internal organs respectively, which promote and control each other (Pellatt & Liu,2010: 72-74). TCM reflects the harmonious relationship between human and environment. We live in the world, embody the world and then represent the world in our language. "There is no such thing as a neutral, disembodied, omniscient, or uninvolved observer. An observer's experience is enabled, shaped, and ineluctably constrained by its biological endowment and developmental history (the products)—phylogenetic and ontogenetic—of interaction with a structured environment." (Langacker,2000: 203) With the extension of human cognition, the description of natural phenomena is closely related to human being and vice versa, thus words to describe one domain are used to describe the other domain, so is the conversion of such words to verbs. Wang (2008: 37-59) analyzes different reasons to form denominal verbs, such as limitation of original expression, pursuit of economical and novel expression, prominence of certain aspects of expression, etc. Nevertheless, denominal verbs make the expression vivid and novel.

According to my incomplete statistics, almost all English words concerning natural phenomena can be used as verbs, while such expressions are less popular in modern Chinese. In translation, we also find that translators like using denominal verbs concerning natural phenomena to replace certain abstract concepts especially in C-E translations.

6. 打枣, 这就是童年的节日, 童年的欢乐的不可逾越的高峰! "劈里啪啦" 竹竿在上面打, "稀哩哗啦", 枣子往地上掉。(Wang,1999: 275)
Beating down dates was one of the treats of childhood. From the boughs beaten with bamboo poles *the dates came raining down*. (tran. by Gladys Yang, ibid: 274)

In this example, the translator uses "the dates came raining down" to translate "稀里哗啦, 枣子往地上掉", which is not corresponding in linguistic form in that the sound and manner of "稀里哗啦" and the place "on the ground" are integrated into the image schema of "raining". The original expression contains such conceptual sememes as "dates, falling down, continuously, intensively, on the ground, slapping", which can be inferred in cognitive context. The image schema of "raining" also contains such cognitive elements as "rain drops, falling down, continuously, intensively, on the ground, slapping", so it is easy for the translator to build a mapping relationship between the schemata of "beating dates" and "raining". The cognitive operating process of the translator can be described as follows:

When the translator experiences cross-space mapping and integrating, the similar schemata are activated first in his cognition. Those corresponding elements will be mapped and then projected to the blend space and produce emergent structure. In the blend space, the emergent structure experiences composition, completion and elaboration and forms the final translation. The whole process is controlled by a variety of contextual parameters. In this example, the features of those beating down dates are mapped onto the raining space/domain. Such cognitive sememe features as dates, falling down, continuously, intensively, on the ground, slapping, etc. are mapped onto those of the raining schema, then such elements are projected into the blend space, and finally a novel structure "dates come raining down" is produced, which means "dates following down like rain drops". Although the linguistic forms of the ST and the TT are not equivalent, their cognitive sememe features are equivalent. The process of conceptual integration between schemata of dates beating and raining is illustrated in figure 4-5 and their equivalence in cognitive sememe features is shown in figure 4-6.

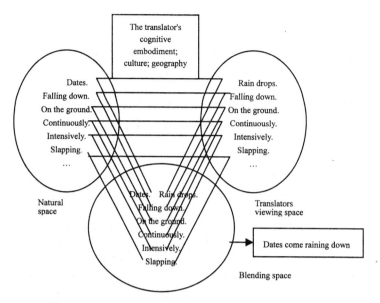

Figure 4-5 Integration between beating dates and raining

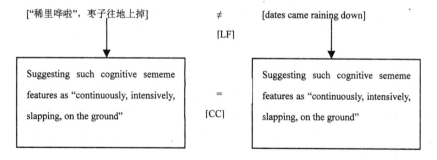

Figure 4-6 CCE between "唏哩哗啦，枣子往地上掉"

and "dates come raining down"

Why the schema of raining rather than the schema of snowing is activated in the translator's cognition? We can explain it with the contextual parameters. As what we have discussed, raining shares more similarities with dates falling down than snowing, such as the slapping sound and bouncing up state when falling on the ground. What is more, the translator may also be influenced by the cultural and geographical parameters. For example, date trees are very popular in the north area of China but rare in many western countries. People who haven't seen date tree can hardly picture the scenario of beating dates down from the tree, to say nothing of the happiness in the activity. Meanwhile, rain is a very common natural phenomenon and can be experienced by every one, so the translator is apt to replace the scene of beating dates with that of raining. Chinese classical literary theories state that language is used to show image and image is used to express meaning[1] (see Liu, 2005: 160). The same is true with English in using vivid language to express meaning. Although the form in this translation is not equivalent to the source text in that the sound and the ground are omitted, its communicative meaning is equivalent to the ST as the rain falls down the ground with certain sound in the cognitive context. (see figure 4-6)

The integrated version is more concise and vivid in form and complete in meaning. Actually, the happiness of the children in beating dates may not be reflected from the scene of raining since people in different areas have different feelings with rain, which is the lost thing in cultural translation. Although it is very hard to pursue complete equivalence, the translator intends to do so in his cognition.

7. 天天有人举报，不是写信，就是打电话。(Liu, 1999b: 123)

Every day he was *snowed under* with these reports, either in the form of letters or as phone calls. （tran. by Paul White, ibid: 122)

---

[1] 王弼在《周易略例·明象》中说："夫象者，出意者也；言者，明象者也。尽意莫若象，尽象莫若言。"

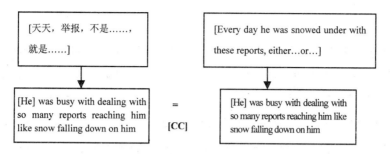

Figure 4-7 CCE between "天天有人举报" and "be snowed under"

In this example, the source text implies such conceptual sememes as "everyday there are so many reports coming to him" by using such words as "天天", "不是，就是" which connotatively suggest a large number of the same things reaching him. The translator does not give the word for word translation; instead, he uses the denominal word "snow" to express the connotative meaning. Used as verb, snow means "falling down like snow". In this translation, the feature of snow is mapped onto the domain of human action and human action is endowed with the features of snow—coverage, overwhelming, press, besiege, etc. Then elements of the two spaces are projected into the blend space and then such an emergent structure is produced as "There are so many reports by means of letters or phone calls like snow falling on the receiver and overwhelm him."(see figure 4-7) The translation is, therefore, equivalent to the source expression in the cognitive context. This translation integrates features of snow, social phenomena, the state and personal feeling of the agent.

8. 这时候，少奶奶常常取笑了五魁的一些很憨的行为后就自觉不自觉地看着五魁，五魁心里就猜摸，她一定是在为自己改做的裤子合适而得意吧。但是，女人那么看了一会儿，脸色就阴下来，眼里是很忧愁的

神气了。(Jia，1999: 125)

Today the young mistress indulges in some good-natured ribbing, teasing Wukui about his naive little eccentricities. That's not all she indulges in: He catches her looking at him. Consciously or not, her eyes have been glued to his form. At first he figures she's savoring the sight of her handiwork, the pants of perfect proportions displayed to greatest advantage. But then her face *clouds* over. Anxiety *floods* her eyes. (ibid: 124)

Cloud and *flood* are both natural phenomena. When clouds cover the sky, we say that the sky is not clear or it is cloudy. With the expansion of its semantic features, cloud is used as verb to refer to the state that cloud has, such as "to show sadness or worry (of sb's face)" (*OAED*), which is via metaphorical mappings. When *flood* is used as verb, it means that the place is filled or covered with water. In this translation, the features of cloud and flood are mapped onto human domain, and the state or action of human being is endowed with the same feature of cloud and flood: cloudy and spreading into or covering something suddenly respectively. When the face domain is connected with the sky domain, and the features of cloud and flood are mapped onto the face domain through analogy, then the face takes the same features of clouds and floods. In Chinese, we have the expression "脸色阴" (suggesting feature of the face) and in English we have the corresponding expression "the face clouds over". Such expressions integrate the prototypical image feature of cloud and the state of human facial expression. "眼里是很忧愁的神气" (indicating the feature and manner of the eyes) is translated into "anxiety *floods* her eyes" which also means "anxiety spreads into his eyes suddenly". The translation shares the similar meaning with the source expression "his eyes are filled with anxiety", so we say that the translation is equivalent to the source expression in connotative meaning rather than in linguistic form. What is more, this expression is more vivid and succinct. Zhang (2006) states that viewing from semiotics and pragmatics the most ideal linguistic expression is using the most succinct linguistic form to transmit the most sufficient and vivid information, and he regards N.-V. conversion as the best reflection of the linguistic economy or efficiency principle.

It seems that almost all these words concerning natural phenomena in English can be used as verbs to show certain features of human being, while such usages are less popular in modern Chinese. So in C-E translation, the translator may use these expressions so as to make the translation more vivid and succinct, while in E-C translation, the translator would better transfer the concrete expressions to abstract concepts.

From analyses of the above examples, we deduce such an empirical rule:

$$\underbrace{S+ VP\ (Act + M_{+1}/_{F+1}/P_{+1}+I_0)}_{ST} \longrightarrow \underbrace{S + VP\ (DV +M_0/_{F0}/P_0+I_{+1})}_{TT}$$

(S= subject; VP= verbal phrase; M= manner; F= feature; P= place; I=Image; DV= denominated verb; $_{+1}$=containing; $_0$ = without; arrow = integrated in)

The above formal empirical rule is explained as follows:

When denominal verbs concerning natural phenomena are used to express the abstract human act, they endow human act with the prototypical image of the natural phenomena. Such denominal verbs can be used to translate the Chinese verbal phrases containing manner, feature or place, with the manner, feature or place integrated and prototypical image exposed.

4.2.1.3 CCE in Denominal Verbs Concerning Animal Names

Both Chinese and English have words concerning animal names

converted from nouns to verbs. Their animated features are mapped onto the verbs and make the verbs more concrete and vivid. In certain context, such animated features can be further mapped onto certain abstract concept by means of metonymical mappings, and cause meaning shift. If the metaphorical meanings of such N.-V. conversions have been accepted as a schema, then in translating, such animated features can be mapped directly through metonymical mapping. For example, fox (欺诈), wolf (狼吞虎咽), pig (好吃懒做), parrot (机械地模仿), snake (蜿蜒爬行), etc. can easily be connected with each other only because the semantic features of the words have direct relevance with the prototypical features of these animals. In Chinese, we also have such expressions as "蛇行，鼠窜，牛饮，狐疑，雀跃，蜂拥，鱼贯，蚕食，鲸吞，蜗居"，etc., which are using animal action to express the manner or action of human being. What is more, we also use concepts concerning animal names to describe human action or manner directly. For instance:

(1) 他猫下身子，藏在土墙后面。

(2) 他在屋角猴着。

(3) Don't *monkey* with my PC.

(4) The highway *snaked* through the valley. (examples cf Jing,1985; Mao, 2007: 263)

In these examples, such concepts as cat, monkey and snake are contextualized into human action and manner in our cognitive structure. Tan (2011), in talking about the features of the first two examples, states that certain features of cat and monkey are used as metaphor to refer to human features and then used as metonymy to refer to the relevant human action. Tan's view can also be understood in this way that the features of cat and monkey are first mapped onto features of human being through metaphorical mappings, and then through metonymical mappings they are used to denote certain actions relevant to such physical features. In translation, when such animal words are used to refer to human behavior, their relevant features are activated and human being is endowed with the corresponding features of the animal. The translator often uses such expressions to pursue succinctness and vividness. In the following instance, the concept "worm out" not only expresses the connotative meaning of the ST but also suggests an image.

9. 今打听得都中奏准起复旧员之信，他便四下里寻找门路，忽遇见雨村，故忙道喜。（Cao,2003：58）

Having just *wormed out the information* that a motion put forward in the capital for the reinstatement of ex-officials had been approved, he had been dashing about ever since, pulling strings and soliciting help from potential backers, and was engaged in this activity when he unexpectedly ran into Yu-cun. (tran. by Hawkes,1973: 84)

In this example, the Chinese phrase "打听……之信" literally means "to ask/inquire about the information", but in the source context it cognitively contains the sememe features such as "inquire about the information here and there from different people by different way", which suggests the long time and clever tactic needed. The social relations in *A Dream of Red Mansions (Hongloumeng)* is a hierarchical one and the social status are unstable, in which situation each official cares about his own social position, and those secret information is impossible to be heard about casually by others, so the dictionary explanations of "打听" are not appropriate to express the sociocultural connotation of the ST. Using "worm out" is a better choice in that the image of worm is mapped onto its action domain and forms the meaning "moving slowly in a twisting and turning way, especially to move through a narrow or crowded place". "Out" refers to the successful result of the movement. Such semantic features are then mapped onto human social communication domain and the meaning "inquiring by every way" is produced. In the translating process, the translator may first change the abstract concept "打听" into "inquiring with every way", then find the corresponding abstract concept, and finally transfer it into the concrete expression. The concrete expression integrates the agent's action, feature and manner, etc. Coincidentally, "worm something out (of somebody)" means "to make sb. tell you sth., by asking them questions in a clever way for a long period of time" (*OAED*), which corresponds to the source text in cognitive sememe features. Thus the research states that such an expression has been accepted as a kind of cognitive schema, and the translation is equivalent to the source expression in cognitive context. The reasoning process can be shown in the following figure:

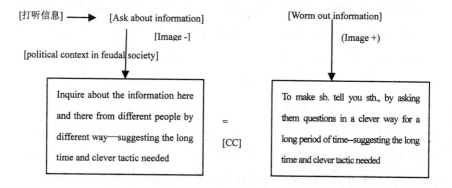

Figure 4-8 CCE between "打听信息" and "warm out information"

10. 然后，就钻进茂草中，轻柔地吹着口哨，含一片草叶学鸟叫，引诱树上的和树丛里的鸟儿下树出窝，觅食上钩儿。（Liu 1999a: 61）

After this he *ducked into* the bushes to keep watch, plucking a young leaf or two with which he imitated the cries of birds, to entice them to his traps. (tran. by Alex Young, ibid: 60)

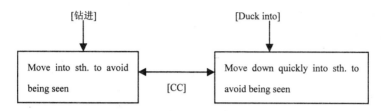

Figure 4-9 CCE between "钻进" and "duck into"

In this example, the literal meaning of "钻进" may be "drilling into, going into or breaking through", all of which are not appropriate in this context. The source context is about a naughty boy of 7 or 8 years old named He Manzi who is trapping birds in the bushes. The boy's action and aim are reflected by a series of verbs such as "钻", "吹", "学", "引诱", "下", "出", "觅", "上", etc. In order to entice the birds to the traps, the boy needs to hide himself in the bushes and imitate the voice of birds. So "钻进" in this context means "to move into sth. to avoid being seen". Both the semantic feature and image feature of "duck" fit the situation as duck has long neck and tends to bend its head when looking for food. When the body feature of duck is mapped onto its action domain, we can get such cognitive semantic feature as "bend down one's head". This semantic feature is then expanded to such semantic feature as "to bend down avoiding being seen by others" through pragmatic functional mapping, and then the semantic feature is mapped onto human action domain, as a result, human gets similar feature as an animal. According to the dictionary, "duck" can be used as a verb, which means "to move (esp. one's head) down quickly, to avoid being seen or hit" (*OAED*). In this example, "duck into" is equivalent in cognitive semantic feature to the source expression (see figure 4-9). Moreover, such translation integrates the image feature of duck, the action of duck, the manner and aim of the person, so it is more vivid. The following two examples show the same usage.

11. 走入里屋，见小姨躺在炕上，一副气息奄奄的样子。(from Liu 2002: 520)

I *ducked into* the inner room, and there my aunt, lying limply on the kang. She did indeed seem near death. (tran. by Liu Shicong, ibid: 521)

12. 喝了几口酒，刘世吾的脸微微发红，他坐下，把肉片夹给林震，然后斜着头说……(Wang, 1999: 91)

Liu's face became flushed as he drank. He sat down and gave Lin some pork. *Cocking his head* to one side, he said… (tran. by Bailey & Murray, ibid: 90)

In example 11, the source text "走入里屋" contains such cognitive semantic feature as "moving down one's head so as to avoid hitting the head of the doorframe", which suggests a low doorframe and poor life. The translation "duck into" also contains such semantic feature as "moving down one's head so as to avoid being hit" *(OAED),* so it is equivalent to the ST in cognitive context. "斜着头" in example 12 means "to cause one's head to tilt or slant", and the English expression "cock one head" also has the meaning item "causing one's head to tilt or slant", so the translation is equivalent to the ST in cognitive semantic features. Apart from their correspondence in semantic features, both translations in the above two examples contain the image of a fowl, so they are more vivid.

From the above examples, we see that N.-V. conversions of words concerning animal names are commonly used to translate the abstract concepts of the source text. Sometimes, when such words are also used as

N.-V. conversions in the source text, the translator may use the same or other words concerning animal names to replace the source one in order to suit the target culture. We can form such an empirical rule:

$$\frac{S + VP\,(Act + O+I_0)}{ST} \longrightarrow \frac{S + VP\,(DV + O+I_{+1})}{TT}$$

(S= subject; VP= verbal phrase; O= object; I=Image;
DV= denominated verb; $_{+1}$=containing; $_0$ = without)

Such empirical rule is explained as follows:

Denominal verbs concerning animal names such as cock, snake, duck, worm, monkey, mouse, etc. integrate the prototypical images and actions of the animals, and can be mapped onto the action and manner of human, so they are chosen to make the translation of human act more concise, vivid and humorous.

Such cases can also illustrate the nature of artistic creation in literary translation by using some vivid concepts or expressions in the TT to express or reproduce the conceptual meaning of the ST. Mao (2007: 263) states that almost all words concerning animal names can be used as verbs, sometimes to get similar shape, sometimes to get similar spirit, and sometimes to get both. Knowing the image features of different animals, the translator may use the N-V conversions of words concerning animal names to express relevant abstract concepts. In translation teaching, the teacher can also use this empirical rule to teach students how to convert between languages and cultures. Such empirical rule can not only improve students' translation skills and cognitive ability but also expand their vocabulary. By means of this empirical rule, we try to translate the former examples as follows:

（1）他猫下身子，藏在土墙后面。

He *ducked* behind the wall.

（2）他在屋角猴着。

He is *monkeying* in the corner of the house.

（3）Don't *monkey* with my PC.

别猴翻我的电脑。

（4）The highway *snaked* through the valley.

公路在山谷中蜿蜒蛇行。　(tran. by the author)

However, not all animal names in Chinese can be used as verbs, so in E-C translation, most of the time the translator may translate the connotative meaning of the animal name instead of using the similar denominal animal names. For instances:

13. The publisher was *cowed* into withdrawing his book.

出版商吓得不敢出版他的书了。

(吓得: indicating a manner or state)

14. The burglar *moused* about for valuables.

撬窃贼鬼鬼祟祟地四处搜寻值钱的东西。

(鬼鬼祟祟地搜寻: indicating a manner/feature +act)

15. He *craned* his head around looking for his pals in the crowd.

他探头四望，在人群中寻找伙伴们。

(探出: indicating a manner or state)

16. The baby was *cocooned* in blankets.

婴儿紧紧地裹在毯子里。

(紧紧地裹: indicating a manner/state+ act)

17. He *beetled* up the ladder.

他笨拙地爬上梯子。

(笨拙地爬: indicating a manner + act)

18. I *hared* up to London, left my book with the publishers and went to

my flat.

我飞快地赶到伦敦，把书稿交给那些出版商就回到了我的住所。

（飞快地赶: indicating a manner + act)

(examples cf. Lu Gusun 1993; Pan 2005: 54)

In the above examples, all the verbalized animal names are converted to manner/feature/state + (act) in their Chinese translations. That is to say, the implied prototypical images and features of the animals can only be described in Chinese.

4.2.1.4 CCE in Denominal Verbs concerning Object, Position and Other Things

Using a noun form to express an event is to reflect an abstract action into a concrete and vivid action, which is the most important step in metaphorical structuring. This is a typical metaphorical thinking process, which is to replace the abstract by the concrete (Liu,2000). Slobin (1979: 65) holds the viewpoint that language often expresses abstract sense via metaphorical expansion. So the objectification of abstract concepts is the basic way to know the world (see Liu 2000).

There are many denominal verbs expressing object, position and other things in both English and Chinese, which contain integration of both metonymical and metaphorical mappings. For instances:

（1）裘千仞道："老弟春秋正富，领袖群雄，何不乘此时机大大振作一番？出了当年这口恶气，也好教你本派的前辈悔之莫及。"（金庸:《射雕英雄传》）

（2）当时北桥河上游两岸为农田，下游两岸多鱼塘，每于台风或暴雨过后，河水上涨，常有渔民在河中罾鱼。

（3）船一靠码头，大家七手八脚锚好船，收拾一下就上岸了。

（4）但是，他对妙斋越来越冷淡，他想把妙斋"冰"了走。（老

舍:《老舍短篇小说选》)

（5）昨天工作得很辛苦，所以晚上几个朋友小资了一把。

（6）他的思想感情相当平民化，既不杨子荣也不座山雕，他与他的读者完全拉平。（王蒙:《躲避崇高》）

（7）Mr. Smith *UA'd* to Los Angeles. (UA: United Airlines)

（8）Laura *Forded t*o New York while Leila *Chevied* to Chicago. (Ford and Chevy are both brands of cars)

（9）Whenever she goes back home, she will *soap-and-water* her hands.

（10）My sister *Houdini'd* her way out of the locked closet. (Houdini is the name of a famous magician)

（11）The stain on the wall was *papered* over.

（12）They *touristed* through the East Coast.

（13）Their technique includes a fluttering of hands *cupped* around the harmonica.

（14）We *wheeled* the cage to the center of one wall. (examples cf Zhang, 1988, 1999; Gao, 2008; Liu, 2000; Gao & Xu, 2000; Wang, 2001: 79)

From the above examples, we see that when the nouns are converted to verbs, the expressions become more vivid, imaginable and sensible. That is to say, those abstract and general concepts are changed into visible and concrete expressions. According to cognitive linguistics, concepts are not innate but come from pre-conceptual experiences. For instance, Lakoff substitutes what he calls an empiricism philosophy for the objectivist (and subjectivist) one. Briefly, this suggests that we have certain pre-conceptual experiences, such as experiences of body movements, the ability to move objects, perceive them as a whole and retain their images. Certain image schemata will recur in our everyday body experience, such as containers, paths, balance, up and down, part and whole, front and back, etc. Lakoff claims that abstract concepts arise from these pre-conceptual physical experiences partly by metaphorical projection (Lakoff,1987: 267-268). So those abstract concepts can be reverted to the pre-conceptual experiences, which lay the foundations for translators to use concrete images to express abstract concepts. In order to make the analysis clearer, the following examples will be discussed according to the different kinds of integration.

a. Integrating the prototypical image of the object, place, and the process of the activity (the path of the activity is like…)

19. 环湖路上，连那位抗癌明星的身影也不见了。

As he *skirted* the lake shore, he didn't see the cancer-battling celebrity. (cf Liu & Li,2009: 379-385)

In this example, the source text "环湖路上，连那位抗癌明星的身影也不见了" is translated into "As he skirted the lake shore, he did not see the cancer-battling celebrity". The forms are not equivalent and the concepts are changed while what they express are the same event. Concepts such as "环", "路", "上", "身影" in the ST are omitted and concepts such as "he" and "skirt" are added, so we see that the translator experiences the process of conceptual integration in his cognitive operation. (see figure 4-10)

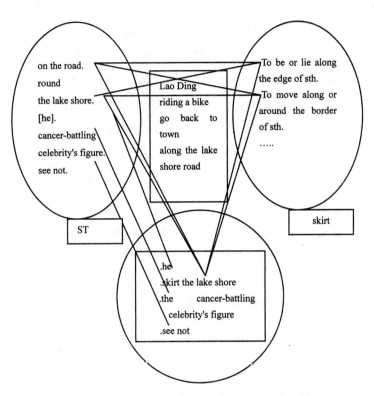

As he skirted the lake shore, he didn't see the cancer-battling celebrity.

TT blend space and the blended version

Figure 4-10 Integration between "skirt" and "road"

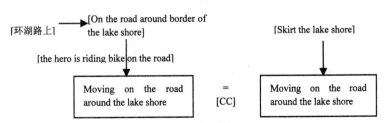

Figure 4-11 CCE between "环湖路上" and "skirt"

First the action domain of the "skirt" schema is perspectivized or highlighted and relevant features are activated and projected to the source text domain to find mapping relation. In the action domain of the "skirt" schema, two semantic features are activated, one is "to be or lie along the edge of something" and the other is "to move along or around the border of something" *(OAED)*. They are mapped onto the source text domain of "moving around the lake", and elements of both domains are mapped onto each other. Then elements in both domains are projected into the blend space, and finally produce the emergent structure (shown in the box of the blend space)—"skirt the lake shore". To adapt to English grammar and syntax, we need to add a subject to the emergent structure to form a complete and appropriate sentence, so the conceptualized meaning is mapped back to the input space (source text space) to find rationale. But the visible context (co-text) is not available in providing such information, so the translator needs to use the invisible context, which are those appeared in the former part of the text and having become the cognitive context as is shown in the middle rectangular. Those contextual parameters are involved in the source text space, among which the hero "Lao Ding" appears to be the agent "he" in the translator's cognition. Then the agent "he" is projected into the blend space and complete the emergent structure. In the blend, the emergent structure will be further revised according to the English expressive and syntactic convention and finally form the TT. Although such translation blurs the concrete way of movement in the ST—riding the bike, it is equivalent in the cognitive context because skirt contains all ways of movement. (see figure 4-11)

Here we can infer such an empirical rule:

Since denominal verb such as "skirt" integrates concepts of "go or move, around, the edge or the border", we can translate actions concerning such implied concepts by using such converted verbs to reach CCE.

This rule can be applied to translating examples 20 and 21 as follows:

20. 他们避开热气腾腾的馄饨锅，在墙角的小桌旁坐下来。(Wang, 1999: 89)

They *skirted round* the stove and sat down at a table in the corner. (tran. by Bailey & Murray, ibid: 88)

21. We *skirted (round)* the field and crossed the bridge. 我们沿着田边走，经过了那座桥。(cf *OAECD*)

b. Integrating the prototypical image and function of the object, the state and manner of the agent (doing something like... or in a state of...)

22. 他不说话，独自托着腮发愣。(Wang 1999: 93)

Silent, he stared blankly, his chin *cupped in* his hands. (tran. by Bailey & Murray, ibid: 92)

In the source text, "托着腮" is the simultaneous manner of the state "发愣" and is used to modify"发愣". The translation put the simultaneous manner after the state as an absolute structure according to the English syntax. The abstract concepts "托着腮" are transferred into "his chin cupped in his hands", with "cup" expressing the concrete image. Such expression changes the perspective of observation from the hero's chin to his eyes. When "cup" is used as a verb, its function domain is highlighted through metonymical mappings. Then the relevant elements of the function domain are mapped onto human action domain, so we get the integrated expression----"cup something in one's hands", which means "to make your hands into a round shape like a cup to hold something" (*OAED*). The translation is more vivid than "hold his chin in his hands" though they carry the same information and are equivalent in cognitive context (see figure 4-12). Such converted words integrate the image of the prototypical object, the function of the object, and the subject's manner and state, so they can be used to express human state or manner.

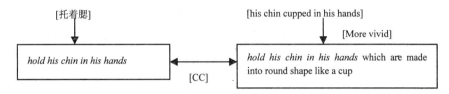

Figure 4-12 CCE between "他托着腮" and "his chin cupped in his hands"

The following example witnesses the similar usage:

23. 许年华按照习惯性动作，将两条胳膊摊在桌边上，身伏下，头搁在手上，与金全礼说话。(Liu 1999b: 195)

Xu leaned forward in his usual manner, with his elbows on the table and his face *framed* in his hands, and talked to Jin. (tran. by Paul White, ibid: 194)

The word for word translation of "头搁在手上" may be "his head is held in or put on his hands" which is not appropriate. Paul White translates it into "his face framed in his hands" which expresses the agent's simultaneous state vividly. When "frame" is used as a verb, the function domain of its schema becomes the prominence and is mapped to the human action domain. Those relevant elements are projected into the blend space with involvement of contextual parameters and produce the new expression "face framed in one's hands", meaning "hands put under the face like a frame" (*OAED*). Such translation is equivalent in communicative meaning to the source expression in cognitive context and very vivid.

c. Integrating the prototypical image, state and result (is like…)

24. 原是一带静寂的山，淡淡抹着向晚烟霭的，也在谷里反送出强烈的回声。(Ai 1999: 139)

The former tranquility of the mountain, *enveloped in* fine evening mist, was shattered by a violent echo resounding through the valley. (tran. by William Bishop, ibid: 138)

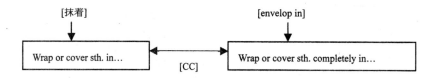

Figure 4-13 CCE between "抹着" and "envelop in"

In the ST, the writer uses "抹着" to describe the tranquil mountain in fine evening mist, which shows readers a mountain picture of Chinese wash painting. The possible literal translation may be "covered or wrapped in". The translator uses "enveloped in" to translate it, which contains more sememes. "Envelop" originally refers to an object to contain letter or other things. When it is used as a verb, it means "to cover or wrap something or someone up completely" (*OAED*). Although the form is not equivalent to the source text, the aesthetic effect is equivalent in cognitive context. The reasoning process of its CCE is shown in figure 4-13. We can also use "wrap in" to replace "envelop in", but it brings us different image sensation.

d. Integrating the prototypical image, function, and location (put...in....)

25. "她是一只水鸟儿，我不想把她关在笼子里。"（Liu,1999a: 159）

TT₁: "She's used to her freedom. I haven't the heart to *cage* her."
(tran. by Alex Young, ibid: 158)

The literal translation of "把她关在笼子里" is "to put or close her in the cage" while the translator uses "to cage her" to make the version more succinct. When "cage" is used as a verb, its carrying function becomes salient and perspectivized. It means "to put something in the cage". In the source text, the expression contains two conceptual metaphors. The first metaphor is "she is a water bird", which means she is as free as a water bird. The second metaphor is "marriage is the cage of life for her", which explains why he does not want to marry her. To her (the female opera singer), marriage life is like putting her into the cage of family life. The translation explicates the first metaphor into "she's used to her freedom", while keeps the metaphorical image of the second metaphor. In my opinion, the image and connotation of water bird can be understood by both Chinese and English readers, so we can keep the image in translation. The translation can be revised into the TT₂.

TT₂: She's used to *be free like a waterbird*. I haven't the heart to *cage* her. (tran. by the author)

From analysis of the above example, we deduce the following empirical rule:

Converted verbs such as cage, net, box and pocket, etc. mean "putting something in the cage, net, box or pocket", which integrate the prototypical image, location, function, and result of the object, so they can be used to express the corresponding activity.

The empirical rule can also be applied to the following three examples.

26. 喝了酒，揣上二十块现大洋，陈小手告辞了……

Having drunk the wine and *pocketed* his twenty gold pieces, Small-Hands Chen rose to take leave. (tran. by Goldblatt)

27. They *netted* a good haul of fish. 他们捕了满满一网鱼。*(cf OAECD)*

28. She hates *being boxed up* in an office all day. 她讨厌整天关在办公室里。*(cf OAECD)*

e. Integrating the prototypical image, material, and attendant element   (using something to do…, or doing something with…)

29. 他们到县上来，咱们桌上桌下招待；咱们到他们这开个会，他们顿顿让咱们吃大锅菜！(Liu,1999b: 3)

When they come down to our place we *wine and dine them* like nobody's business, but when we come here for a conference they make us scrabble for every meal in the public trough! (tran. by Paul White, ibid: 2)

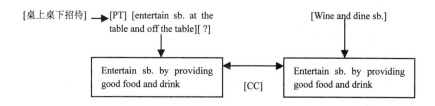

Figure 4-14 CCE between "桌上桌下招待" and "wine and dine somebody"

In this example, the possible word for word translation of "桌上桌下招待" is "to entertain somebody at the table and off the table" which will make the target reader confused. According to the source context, the hero was complaining of the simple meals he was provided with, so "桌上桌下招待" in this cognitive context should refer to "entertain somebody by providing him with good food and drinks". The translator uses the concrete images of "wine and dine" to specify the content of entertainment. When *wine* and *dine* are put together, their functions as reception and entertainment are highlighted, which integrate the action of reception and the materials used. However, this expression is to use part of the materials to refer to the whole things the host provide to entertain the guests. As is explained in the dictionary, "wine and dine (sb)" means "to entertain somebody by buying them good food and drinks" (*OAED*). So the translation is equivalent in communicative meaning to the source expression in cognitive context (see figure 4-14). Such an empirical rule can be deduced:

When the source expression is constructed by the structure of action (verb) +object + attendant element (with) + material, we can translate it into the corresponding converted verb that integrates the material and attendant element.

f. Integrating the profession and action of the profession (working as..., or acting as)

30. 何满子的父亲，十三岁到通州城里一家书铺学徒，学的是石印。（Liu,1999a: 11）

Manzi's father had been *apprenticed* at the early age of thirteen to a bookseller in Tongzhou to learn the art of lithography. (tran. by Alex Young,

ibid: 10)

When "学徒" is used as a noun, it is converted from the verb "study (学) as an apprentice". When it is used as a verb in this example, its action feature is highlighted which means "working or acting as an apprentice". So the English translation is meaning equivalent to the source text, and it integrates the profession and action.

However, if the expression is specific in one culture without correspondence in the other culture, the translator needs to think of a way to keep the image.

31. 莲丫头进你家门十二年，给你家当了十二年的牛马，……（Liu, 1999a: 201）

Wang Ri Lian has *slaved* for you all these years. (tran. by Alex Young, ibid: 200)

The possible literal translation of "给你家当了十二年的牛马" is "she has acted as cattle and horse for your family for twelve years", which can not express the original cognitive semantic feature because the image features of cattle and horse are different between Chinese and English. In China, cattle and horse were traditionally used to plow the field and pull the cart, so we have many expressions to show the low status of both animals, such as "做牛做马", "牛马不如", "老黄牛", "孺子牛", etc. Nevertheless, the western countries lack such expressions because of their higher mechanization. The source context is about the oppression that Wang Rilian has suffered in Du Si's family. Wang Rilian was bought by Du Si and Dou Yehuang at her early age as a young daughter-in-law, and she was treated very cruelly. When Du's son died, they wanted to sell Wang Rilian to a bad man. Aunt

Yi Zhangqing played a trick on Du Si to free Wang Rilian. This sentence is said by Yi Zhangqing to state the sufferings of Lian, and the semantic feature of "当牛做马" is "being dominated by the master without freedom". The translator uses the verbalized "slave" to express the cognitive semantic feature of "being dominated without freedom", which keeps the semantic feature of the original expression, and such translation is more accurate and vivid.

Generally speaking, there are more N.-V. conversions in English than in modern Chinese. When translating from English to Chinese, if the translator can not find the corresponding concrete expressions, he can only change the concrete expressions into abstract concepts.

32. It took him all day to take the refrigerator apart, piece by piece, to *doctor* the malfunction and then put it back together.

他花了整整一天时间把冰箱零件一个个拆下来，检测故障，最后组装起来。(Mao, 2005: 106)

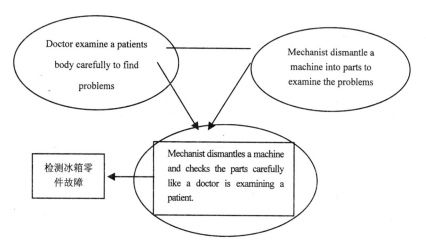

Figure 4-15 Cognitive reasoning between "doctor" and "检测"

In this example, "doctor" in the source text is used as a verb to highlight the action feature of a doctor, which is via metonymical mappings. The action feature of a doctor is "be able to conduct medical and technical examination to the parts of a human body for finding the problems" while the action feature of a mechanist is "be able to dismantle a machine for technical examination of parts of a machine for finding the problems". When the action feature of a doctor is mapped onto that of a mechanist and both are projected into the blending space, such new meaning is produced: "He is dismantling the refrigerator and examining the parts carefully for finding the problems just like a doctor is examining the parts of a human body". The translation "检测" contains two concepts "检查" and "测试", which also expresses the implied meaning of "examine carefully". From the analysis, we see that the equivalence of the translation is achieved at the levels of technical manner and purpose in cognitive context. (see figure 4-15)

The conversion from noun to verb provides selective methods to translation. By corresponding replacement, image transference, and shift between the abstract and concrete, the translation can become more vivid and effective. Since N.-V. conversion integrates the prototypical image, function, state, method, result, and so on, such translation is also very succinct. Viewing from the Semiotics and Pragmatics, the most ideal expression is to use the most succinct words to express the most sufficient and vivid information, so N.-V. conversion is the best reflection of such "economy or efficiency principle of linguistic expression" (Gao & Xu,2000: 8).

4.2.2 Cognitive Contextual Equivalence in Adj.-V. Conversion

In Chinese, many adjectives can be used as verbs, such as "高, 大, 富, 黑, 红, 好, 强, 重, 稳, 静, 亮, 厚, 容易, 高兴", etc. In English there are also some adjectives used as verbs, such as clean, dirty, glad, empty, wet, clear, etc. According to Shi & Bai (2006), about 70 percent adjectives can be used as verbs in Chinese while only 15 percent in English. Different conceptualization between Chinese and English adjectives decides their ways of conversion. For example, English adjectives are seldom converted to verbs. Even though some are converted to verbs, their converted meanings are related to the original adjectives. For instance, "yellow" also means "to become yellow" or "to make something become yellow". When such converted words are used in translation, they can make the version more vivid and succinct in realizing cognitive contextual equivalence. For instances:

33. 他玩了一天, 跑得乏了, 免不了尿炕, 周檎也不声张; (Liu,1999a: 89）

Sometimes, after a specially tiring day, Manzi would *wet* the brick bed, but Zhou Qin never said anything …. (tran. by Alex Young, ibid: 88)

"尿炕" in the source text can be literally translated into "urinate when in bed and asleep". In the target text, "wet" is converted to verb, which means "to make something wet". When "wet" is put together with "bed", it gets the idiomatic meaning "urinate when in bed and asleep" (*OAED*). So the translation is meaning equivalent to the source expression in cognitive context. The converted word "wet" integrates the action (urinate), result of the action (become wet), and the time (in sleep).

34. 在她料理这些事情的时候，常常撩一撩自己的头发，正像那些能干而漂亮的女同志们一样。(Wang,1999: 3)

As she did this, she kept *smoothing back* her hair with her fingers, in the way that pretty and able young women comrades often do. (tran. by Bailey & Murray, ibid: 2)

The Chinese expression "撩一撩自己的头发" refers to the habitual action of the woman, whose manner is to make her own hair back by using fingers rubbing back and forth and the result is making the hair smooth. When the English word "smooth" is used as a verb, it means "to make something smooth or flat", which exactly reflects the concrete action of the woman. So the translation is equivalent to the source expression at the level of communicative meaning in cognitive context.

4.2.3 Cognitive Contextual Equivalence in Adv.–V. Conversion

As there are many adverbs acting as prepositions in English, the distinction between prepositions and adverbs is not clear-cut, such as up, down, in, over, etc. Some experts categorize adverbs such as back, down etc. into directional verbs. Since such words belong to more than one category, we just choose the one we need to illustrate this research. Such phenomenon is probably caused by the close relation between adverbs and prepositions in their origin. Plummer explores the origin of prepositions from the development of Latin. He states that linguistic signs tend to be weakened while speakers are pursuing clear and strong expressions; as a result, small adverbs such as in, ex, ab, etc. are supplemented to interpret the meaning of the cases. Later when people find that these small adverbs can control certain cases, those once independent adverbs are converted into prepositions

(Plummer 1983: 58, tran. by the author). Apart from the adverbs contained in the examples of prepositions in the later section, this section shows an example to explain such usage in translation.

35. 吸完面条，大家移到会议室。（Liu,1999b: 77）

When the noodles had all been *downed* they adjourned to the meeting room. (tran. by Paul White, ibid: 76)

The source expression "吸完面条" implies the human body organ "mouth", the manner of eating "sulking in" and the result "completely finished the noodle". The translator transfers the perspective from the subject to the object, so "noodle" is used as the theme and the verb is acted by "down" in the TT. When "down" is converted from adverb to verb, it means "to drink or eat something quickly" (*OAED*), which is meaning equivalent to the source expression in cognitive context. The translation integrates the action (eat), manner (quickly) and direction (downward).

4.2.4 Cognitive Contextual Equivalence in Numerals–V. Conversion

In modern Chinese, numerals are rarely used as verbs, and the same is true in English except for "second". However, when they are put together with other words in English, the numerals can act as verbs, which generally belong to slang. According to Zhang (1995), numeral-V. conversions mainly appear in the 1950s and 1960s. Because of their vividness and easy usage, they were welcomed by the common Americans and then collected into dictionary. According to my incomplete statistics from dictionaries, the following expressions composed by numerals act as verbs:

(1) *Deep-six* means "to decide not to do or use something that you

had planned to do or use". For example:

Plans to build a new mall were *deep-sixed* after protests from local residents.

(2) *One-up* means "to get the better of; succeed in being a point, move, step, etc., ahead of (someone)". For example:

They *one-upped* the competition.

(3) *Two-time* means "to deceive a person you have a relationship with, especially a sexual one, by having a secret relationship with somebody else at the same time". For example:

Are you sure he's not *two-timing* you?

(4) *Zero in on* means "to give one's full attention to sth". For example:

Many of the other major daily newspapers have not really *zeroed in on* the problem.

(5) *Second* means: a) to refuse to serve (an undesirable or unwelcome customer) at a bar or restaurant; to reject; discard; b) to attend (a duelist or a boxer) as an aide or assistant; to promote or encourage; reinforce.

(cf *Random House Webster's Unabridged dictionary*; *American Heritage Dictionary*)

Although not very popularly used, such expressions can be found in C-E translation. Just because they are not popular, they can add some strangeness and vividness to the expression.

36. 小毛"哈哈"笑了："这就是了，这就是了，会上您主讲，我敲边鼓！"（Liu 1999b: 45）

Xiao Mao chortled with delight. "That's right. That's the way to do it. You'll be in the speaker's chair, and I'll *second* you." (tran. by Paul White,

ibid: 44)

In this example, the Chinese expression "敲边鼓" is a metaphorical use, which means "to speak or act to assist somebody". "边鼓" is a kind of drum serving as the main foil in musical instrument ensembles. The purpose of beating "边鼓" is to highlight the main instruments. When such semantic feature is mapped onto the domain of human action, it gets the metaphorical meaning of "highlighting" the object. In this context, "我敲边鼓" means "I will support or assist you by beating the drum", which implies the image of drum. In English, when the concept *second* is converted to verb, it means "to state officially at a meeting that you support another person's idea, suggestion, etc." *(OAED)* So the translation "I'll second you" is equivalent to the source expression at the level of communicative meaning in cognitive context though the image of drum disappears. When "second" is converted from the ordinal numeral to verb, it also experiences the cross domain mappings.

4.3 Cognitive Contextual Equivalence in Re-lexicalization of Motion Words

Talmy (2000: 21) classifies the elements between semantic meaning and surface expression. According to him, semantic elements include *Motion, Path, Figure, Ground, Manner,* and *Cause*, while surface elements include *verb, adposition, subordinate clause*, and what he characterizes as *satellite*. He states that the relationship between semantic elements and surface elements is not simply one-to-one, but one-to-many or many-to-one. That is, a combination of semantic elements can be expressed by a single surface element, or a single semantic element by a combination of surface elements. By the same token, semantic elements of different types can be expressed by the same type of surface element or the same type by several different ones. As different nations have different ways of conceptualization, their ways of lexicalizing the motion words are different. Talmy classifies and illustrates the different ways of lexicalizing motion words in different languages. He states that "In a Motion-sentence pattern, the verb expresses at once both the fact of Motion and a Co-event, usually either the manner or the cause of the Motion. A language of this type has a whole series of verbs in common use that express motion occurring in various manners or by various causes. Both English and Chinese belong to this type" (Talmy 2000: 27). He classifies English verbs into different kinds of conflation, such as: 1) Motion + Manner; 2) Motion + Cause; 3) Motion + Path; 4) Motion + Figure; 5) Motion + Ground (ibid: 27-67). Such characteristic of lexicalization in English sheds light to C-E translation which is regarded as the process of re-lexicalization. The following part explores the realization of CCE in three kinds of integration: Motion + Manner integration, Motion + Cause integration, Motion + Path integration. Since the last two kinds of Talmy's classification are implied in the N.-V. conversions we have discussed in the former section, we will not re-classify and discuss them in this section.

4.3.1 Cognitive Contextual Equivalence in Motion + Manner Integration

Talmy (2000: 27-28) further classifies this kind into two subcategories, and the first kind is "Be-located + Manner". For examples:

(1) The lamp stood/lay/leaned on the table. = [the lamp was located on the table] **with the manner of** [the lamp stood/lay/leaned there]

In Chinese, we have the similar expression: 油灯立/放/靠在了桌子上.

The second kind is "Move + Manner". For examples:

(2) The rock slid/rolled /bounced down the hill. = [The rock moved down the hill] **with the manner of** [the rock slid/rolled/bounced]

Such expressions are *Non-agentive*. The corresponding Chinese expressions should highlight the manners: 岩石缓缓地滑下/翻滚着下/滚荡着下了山.

(3) I slid/rolled /bounced the keg into the storeroom. = [I moved the keg into the storeroom] **with the manner of** [I slid/rolled/bounced]

Such expressions are *Agentive*, and they can be corresponding with the Chinese "把 ba" expression：我把桶滚进了储物间.

(4) I ran / limped / jumped / stumbled / rushed /groped my way down the stairs. = [I went down the stairs] **with the manner of** [I ran / limped / jumped / stumbled / rushed / groped]

Such expressions belong to *Self-agentive*, and have Chinese correspondences: 我跑/蹒跚着/跌跌撞撞地/冲/摸索着下了楼梯.

There are fewer integrated verbs in Chinese than in English, so the corresponding Chinese expressions should add and explicate the manner. Talmy (2000: 272) states that "mandarin is a strongly satellite-framed language, regularly using its satellites to specify path, aspect, state change, some action correlation, and much realization." The reason is "perhaps the majority of its agentive verbs are of either the moot-fulfillment or the implied-fulfillment types—requiring a satellite for their realization—with the latter apparently more strongly represented" (ibid: 272). Such differences are also reflected in C-E translation. The following part is the further classification of this kind illustrated by C-E translations.

4.3.1.1 CCE in Motion + Manner Integration

There are many words in English expressing the motion "walk" or "move" with certain manner, to name a list: dawdle (to take a long time to walk somewhere), stroll (to walk somewhere in a slow relaxed way), straggle (to move slowly behind a group of people that you are with so that you become separated from them), shuffle (to walk slowly without lifting your feet completely off the ground), slink (to move somewhere very quietly and slowly, especially because you are ashamed or do not want to be seen), steal (to move secretly and quietly so that other people do not notice you), slip (to go somewhere quickly and quietly, especially without being noticed), tiptoe (to walk using the front parts of your feet only), stagger (to walk with weak unsteady steps), totter (to walk or move with weak unsteady steps), waddle (to walk with short steps, swinging from side to side, like a duck), creep (to move slowly on your hands and knees), trudge (to walk slowly or with heavy steps, because you are tired or carrying something heavy), wade (to walk with an effort through something, especially water or mud), stride (walk with long steps in a particular direction), stalk (to move slowly and quietly towards an animal or a person, in order to kill, catch or harm it or them), hurry (to move quickly in a particular direction), rush (to move or to do something with great speed, often too fast), bound (jump or spring; run with jumping movements), sprint (to run a short distance at full speed), etc. (all the above explanations are from *OAED*) Such words integrate the motion and manner of the subject, so they are commonly used in Chinese to English translations.

37. 一位瘦小精干的少年立即去打来了水，一壶热，一壶冷，……
(Jia 2006: 129)

A slim, nimble young man *bounded up with* two vacuum bottles of water, one hot and one cold. (tran. by Goldblatt 1991: 207)

In this example, the source concepts "立即，去，打，来" are all integrated into the English phrase "bound up with". According to the dictionary, "bound" means "jump or spring; run with jumping movements (in a specified direction)" (*OAED*). It implies the motions "jump and run", manner "with jumping manner" (showing quickly). The original set of concepts indicating two directional actions "go and come" are implied into "movements" with the past tense expressing "了". Combined with the direction word "up" and the accompanying word "with", the meaning of the ST is completely expressed in the TT. The realization of CCE of "bound up with" can be shown in figure 4-16. What is more, the vividness of the immediate motion of the slim and nimble young man is shown.

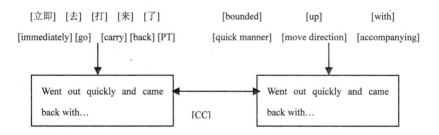

Figure 4-16 CCE between "立即去打来了" and "bounded up with"

(PT=past tense; CC= cognitive context)

38. 贾瑞如得了命，三脚两步从后门跑到家里。（Cao, 2003: 320）

At the word of command Jia Rui bounded out of his hole and *sprinted* for dear life through the rear gate and back to his own home. (tran. by

Hawkes 1973: 249)

The source text "三步两步" is to express the hurriedness of Jia Rui to escape from the plight, and the translator uses "sprint" to correspond with it. "Sprint" means "to run a short distance at full speed" (*OAED*), which integrates the motion "run", manner "at full speed", as well as the "short" distance from Jia Mansion to Rui's home. Such expression is suitable for the source context. "For dear life" is the implied meaning in the source text. According to the context, Jia Rui was punished by Wang Xifeng's deception. He was horrified and drenched by cold slops while waiting under the steps in darkness for escape, so once the rear gate open, he would certainly "sprint for dear life". Because English is hypotaxis while Chinese parataxis, the Chinese expression "三脚两步从后门跑到家里" is very clear for Chinese readers but incomplete for the English readers. So the translator adds "…bounded out of his hole" to make the expression logical. Although the translation is not equivalent to the source text in linguistic form, it is equivalent at the level of communicative meaning in cognitive context.

From the analyses of the above examples, we deduce such an empirical rule:

$$\frac{S(x) + VP\,(Act + M_{+1})}{ST} \longrightarrow \frac{S + VP\,(Act + M_0)}{TT}$$

(S= subject; VP= verbal phrase; x= agent or actor;
M_{+1}= manner; $_0$ = zero; arrow = integrated in)

The formal empirical rule is explained as follows:

If the Chinese expression is constructed by subject + act + manner, such as walk (走), run (跑) plus concrete modifiers to describe its specific manner of walk or run, they can be translated into the corresponding English motion words or phrases with the manner-indicating words integrated so as to make the translation more succinct.

4.3.1.2 CCE in Motion + Manner + Image Integration

Some English verbs not only integrate motion and manner, but also suggest an image. Used in C-E translation, they are very succinct and vivid. For instances:

39. 人们慢慢地向前动着，要上楼去换 7 号线。（Ju,2002: 34）

People *inched forward*, intending to change to Route 7. (ibid: 36)

The Chinese expression in the ST is "slowly moving forward", while the English translation is "inch forward". "Inch" means "to move or make something move slowly and carefully in a particular direction; advance slowly, as if by inches" (*OAED*), which integrate the motion "move" and manner "slowly"; what is more it also has the implied motion image of "moving by inches". So it is meaning equivalent to the source expression in cognitive context. (see figure 4-17)

Figure 4-17 CCE between "慢慢地向前动着" and "inch forward"

40. 本来，在我们这种情形里，如果大家真的规规矩矩地呆看着银幕，那还有什么意味！(Shi 1999: 51)

For people in our situation it would be unutterably dull just to *sit glued to the screen all the way through.* (tran. by Paul White, ibid: 50)

The literal translation of "规规矩矩地呆看着银幕" may be "sitting there quietly for a period of time and staring at the screen" which is neither vivid nor succinct. The translator translates it into "sit glued to the screen all the way through", which is better. "Glued to" means "to give all the attention to" (*OAED*). When combined with "all the way through", it expresses the duration of the time. So the translation is meaning equivalent to the source expression in cognitive context. Moreover, the English expression integrates the motion "stare at", manner "with all the attention", and the image "glue". Such version is more vivid and succinct.

From analyses of the above two examples, we deduce such an empirical rule:

$$\frac{S(x) + VP\ (Act + M_{+1} + I_0)}{ST} \longrightarrow \frac{S + VP\ (Act + M_0 + I_{+1})}{TT}$$

(S= subject; VP= verbal phrase; x= agent or actor; M= manner;
I=Image; $_{+1}$= containing; $_0$ = zero; arrow = integrated in)

The formal empirical rule is interpreted as follows:

If the source expression is composed of the agent + act + manner, and there is a corresponding English verbal phrase or verb indicating an image and containing the same or similar sememes, the translator can choose such English expression to make the translation more vivid and succinct.

4.3.1.3 CCE in Motion + Manner + Sound Integration

Some English verbs integrate the motion of the subject, the manner and sound of the action, so in C-E translation they are commonly used.

41. 我低头吃饭，故意把汤喝得哗哗响。

I kept my head down, eating, deliberately *slurping my soup*. (cf Liu & Li 2009: 379-385)

42. 他咕哝着说他想睡觉。

He *murmured* that he wanted to sleep. (*OAECD*)

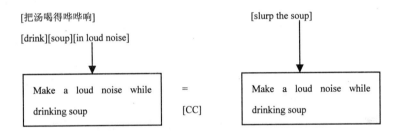

Figure 4-18 CCE between "把汤喝得哗哗响" and "slurp the soup"

In example 41, the dotted Chinese expression "把汤喝得哗哗响" implies such concepts as "喝(act), 汤(object), 哗哗响(sound and manner)", while the translation "slurp my soup" implies such concepts as "slurp (motion verb), my (attributive), soup (object)", thus they are not corresponding in linguistic form. But analyzing the sememes of "slurp", we will find that they are equivalent in cognitive context. "Slurp" means "to make a loud noise while you are drinking something (*OAED*)", which contains such sememes as "loud noise, drink". When combined with the object "soup", the sememes of the expression "slurp my soup" implies similar sememes with the source expression (see figure 4-18). Example 42 belongs to the same usage as example 41 in that "咕哝着说" also consists of two concepts: "咕哝"(manner + sound) and "说"(speak). "Murmur" in the TT means "to speak in low continuous indistinct sound", which also contains such sememes as "speak (verb), low continuous (manner), sound".

From analyses of the above two examples, the author deduces such an empirical rule:

$$\frac{S(x) + VP\,(Act + M_{+1}+S^1_{+1})}{ST} \longrightarrow \frac{S + VP\,(Act + M_0 + S^1_0)}{TT}$$

(S= subject; VP= verbal phrase; x= agent or actor; M= manner;
S^1=sound; I=Image; $_{+1}$ = containing; $_0$ = zero; arrow = integrated in)

This formal empirical rule is explained as follows:

If the Chinese expression contains an act or speak +manner +sound, and there has corresponding English verbal phrase or verb which integrates the manner and sound, the translator can choose such corresponding English expression so as to make the translation more concise and succinct.

4.3.1.4 CCE in Motion + Manner + Reason Integration

43. 英国现在兴高采烈地庆祝自己的 "胜利"，不是太早了吗？（Ju 1998: 4）

Isn't it too early yet for Britain to *crow*? (ibid: 5)

The Chinese expression "兴高采烈地庆祝自己的'胜利'" consists of several concepts such as 兴高采烈地(indicating the manner), 庆祝(act), 自己的(attributive), 胜利(indicating the reason). The translator translates these concepts into one English word "crow". According to the dictionary, *crow* means "to express gleeful triumph (about one's success, etc)" (*OAED*). The dictionary explanation for "gleeful" is "full of high-spirited delight", so the word "crow" integrates the act "express", manner "full of high-spirited delight", and reason "because of triumph".

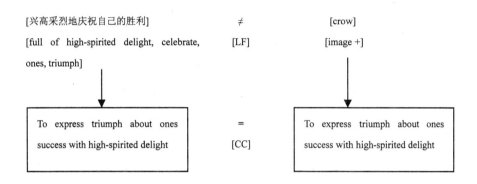

Figure 4-19 CCE between "兴高采烈地庆祝自己的胜利" and "crow"

According to the translator's explanation, the source text is from one of the international section of *People's Daily* in November 1982. It is a sarcastic essay, which represents Chinese government's attitude to Britain's occupying the Malvinas of Argentina. The source text criticizes the disgraceful action of Britain and implies that such action is not worth celebrating (ibid: 5).The translator tries to keep the sarcastic mood of the ST and chooses such a derogative word. From the above analysis, we see that the translation is not only meaning equivalent to the ST in cognitive context, but also vivid and succinct. (see figure 4-19)

4.3.1.5 CCE in Motion + Manner + Purpose Integration

44. 他一次又一次地向自己提出这样的问题，百思不得其解。(Wang 1999: 187)

Time and again he *puzzled over this question*. (tran. by Gladys Yang,

ibid: 186)

In this example the succinct English expression "puzzle over this question" is used to replace the source expression "向自己提出这样的问题, 百思不得其解". "Puzzle over/about something" means "to think hard about something in order to understand or explain it" (*OAED*). "向自己提出问题" means "to think about the question", "百思" refers to "think hard", and "不得其解" is implied in "hard to understand", so all these concepts are implied in the sememes of "puzzle over". Therefore, the translation is meaning equivalent to the ST in cognitive context (see figure 4-20). What is more, it is more succinct in that "puzzle over" integrates the motion "think", manner "hard", and purpose "in order to understand or explain it".

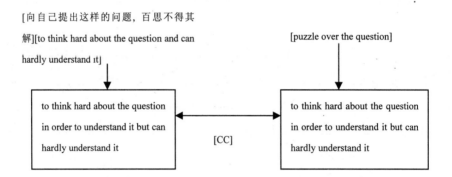

Figure 4-20 CCE between "向自己提出这样的问题, 百思不得其解" and "puzzle over the question"

4.3.1.6 CCE in Motion + Manner + Path Integration

45. 她跑向海涂深处，……

she *waded* deeper into the seaweed, ... (cf Liu & Li,2009: 379-385)

The Chinese concepts "跑" and "向" mean "run toward" in English, which describes the character's hardness and struggle in the muddy and sandy seaweed in the cognitive context. If it is translated literally into "she ran into the sea", it will not fit the situation. "Wade" means "to walk with an effort (through water, mud or anything that makes walking difficult)" (*OAED*), which is appropriate in the cognitive context. The translation integrates the motion "walk", manner "with an effort", and path "through water or mud", and reaches CCE, though it is not equivalent to the original linguistic form. This case shows that the original meaning of the concepts or set of concepts in ST does not simply refer to the surface meaning of the concepts; instead, it usually stands for the contextual meaning which is to be interpreted by the reader or translator accordingly. It is for this reason that we can be safe to say that equivalence exists in the cognitive context.

From analyses of the above examples, We can deduce the following empirical rule:

$$\frac{S(x)+VP(Act+M_{+1}+R_{+1}/P_{+1}/P^1_{+1})}{ST} \longrightarrow \frac{S + VP (Act +M_0+R_0/P_0/P^1_0)}{TT}$$

(S= subject; VP= verbal phrase; x= agent or actor; M= manner; R=reason; P=purpose; P^1=path; $_{+1}$= containing; $_0$ = zero; arrow = integrated in)

Such formal empirical rule can be interpreted as follows:

If the Chinese sentence structure is composed of "subject + act + manner + reason/purpose/path" and there exists a corresponding English verb which integrates the manner, reason, purpose or path, the English verb can be used to translate the Chinese verbal phrase so as to make the translation more succinct and vivid.

4.3.2 Cognitive Contextual Equivalence in Motion+Cause Integration

Talmy (2010: 28) explains the type of motion + cause conflation. For example:

The napkin *blew off* the table. (Nonagentive) = [the napkin *moved off* the table] *with the cause of* [(something) *blew* on the napkin]

In Chinese we have such corresponding expression "餐巾被吹下了桌子".

I *pushed/threw/kicked* the keg into the storeroom. (Agentive) = [I *moved* the keg into the storeroom] *with the cause of* [I *kicked* the keg]

In Chinese we have such conceptual set as "我把桶推进了/扔进了/踢进了储物间". Chinese sentence patterns such as "…把…" and "…被…" can correspond to the English "motion + cause" conflation. But translation is more complex in that meaning is often implied in the surface expression. The following part discusses the realization of CCE in different kinds of motion + cause integration.

4.3.2.1 CCE in Motion + Cause Integration

46. 他两腿猛踏自行车，游蛇似的在人群中左钻右突，似乎心里有啥事等着要办。（Ju 1998: 23）

He *pedaled his bicycle hard*, threading his way through the crowd, as if he had some urgent business to attend to. (ibid: 24)

The Chinese expression "两腿猛踏自行车" contains such concepts as the source of the strength "two feet", the degree of the action "hard", and the manner "press the pedals". The English version uses "pedal his bicycle hard" to correspond to the source expression, in which the body part and the manner are integrated. The dictionary explanation of *pedal* is "to ride a bicycle (by pressing the pedals)" (*OAED*), which contains the manner "by pressing the pedals". And in the cognitive context, the action of pressing the pedals is often done by the feet. Although the linguistic form is not equivalent, the meaning is equivalent in cognitive context. Besides, such translation is more succinct as "pedal" integrates the motion "move the bicycle" and the cause "by pressing the pedals" (see figure 4-21).

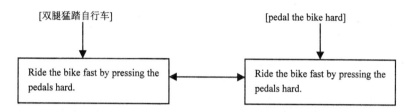

Figure 4-21 CCE between "双腿猛踏自行车" and "pedal the bike hard"

47. 说着，将文具镜匣搬来，卸去钗钏，打开头发，……（Cao, 2003：546）

'All right,' said Musk, and fetching her toilet-box with the mirror on top she proceeded to take off her ornaments and *shake her hair out*. (tran. by Hawkes,1973：404)

Example 47 is similar to example 46 in usage. In this example, "打开头发" can be literally translated into "open and spread the hair" which is an ordinary action without emotion in it. The translation "shake her hair out" is more dynamic and vivid than the literal translation as the translator uses the empirical thinking to show the original situation. If a girl with long hair banded by ornaments wants to spread her hair, she will first take off the ornaments and then shake her head to open and spread the hair. According to the dictionary, "shake something out" means "to open or spread something by shaking" (*OAED*), which contains all the sememes of the source expression, so it is meaning equivalent to the source expression in cognitive context. Apart from this, it also implies the cause "by shaking her head".

4.3.2.2 CCE in Motion + Cause + Result Integration

48. 招娣家最小的孩子，来娣死了。死在距离海涂地不到一百米的海里。

Her youngest child, her precious Boy at Last, was dead. She had *drowned* in the shallows just beyond the seaweed beds, less than a hundred metres from shore. (cf Liu & Li,2009: 379-385)

The source expression "死在海里" implies the cause of her death "drown by the sea water", and the translator uses "drown" instead of "die" to translate it. "Drown" means "to die because you have been underwater too long and you cannot breathe" (*OAED*), which integrates the result "die" and the cause "by drowning". As a result, "drown" is meaning equivalent to the source text in the cognitive context.

49. 幸亏是皮底鞋，不然一定湿透。

If I hadn't been wearing shoes with leather soals, my feet would have been *soaked*. (cf Zhou,2003: 469)

The Chinese expression "湿透" contains two concepts: manner or state "湿(wet)", and degree "透(thoroughly)". The English word "soak" also means "to become thoroughly wet by being in liquid or by absorbing liquid" (*OAED*), so it can be used to replace the phrase and reaches meaning equivalence. Moreover, this word integrates the result "become wet" and the cause "by absorbing liquid."

4.3.2.3 CCE in Motion + Cause + Place Integration

50. 她们看见不远的地方，那宽厚肥大的荷叶下面，有一个人的脸，下半截身子长在水里。

Not far away under a broad lotus leaf they saw a man's head—the rest of him was *submerged*. (cf Zhou, 2003: 465)

The source text "下半截身子长在水里" means that the man's rest part of the body below the neck is under the surface of water. The English word "submerge" means "to go under the surface of water" (OAED), which is equivalent in meaning to the source expression. In this translation, the motion "standing", cause "by going under", and place "in the water" are all integrated into "submerge".

From analyses of the above examples, the author deduces such an empirical rule:

$$\underset{\text{ST}}{\underline{S(x)+VP(Act+C_{+1}+R_{+1}/P_{+1})}} \longrightarrow \underset{\text{TT}}{\underline{S + VP (Act +C_0+ R_0 / P_0)}}$$

(S= subject; VP= verbal phrase; x= agent or actor; C= Cause;
R=result; P= place; $_{+1}$= containing; $_0$ = zero; arrow = integrated in)

This formal empirical rule can be interpreted as follows:

Those English words containing sememes of motion+cause+result/ place can be used to express the relevant Chinese phrases. Even though their linguistic forms are not corresponding to each other, they are expressing the same meaning in the cognitive context.

4.3.3 Cognitive Contextual Equivalence in Motion + Path Integration

Although Talmy does not regard English as a typical language in conflating motion and path, he illustrates many English words, which integrate motion with path such as enter, exit, ascend, descend, cross, pass, circle, advance, proceed, approach, arrive, depart, return, join, separate, part, rise, leave, near, and follow (Talmy,2000: 52). Those words listed by Talmy are very clear in direction, or they are clearly one-directional. In fact some other words can also express the path with more complicated directions, such as zigzag, wind, wobble, echo, etc. For examples:

(1) The narrow path *zigzags up the cliff.*

这条狭窄的小径曲曲折折地向峭壁伸延。

(2) She *wound her way through* the crowds.

她绕来绕去穿过了人群。   (cf *OAECD*)

In these two examples, both "zigzag" and "wind" integrate the motion and irregular direction of the path. Such usages are often borrowed by translators in C-E translation. For instance:

51. 他两腿猛踏自行车，游蛇似的在人群中左钻右突，似乎心里有啥事等着要办。（Ju,1998: 23）

He pedaled his bicycle hard, *threading his way through the crowd*, as if he had some urgent business to attend to. (ibid: 24)

In this example, the translator uses "thread one's way through the crowd" to translate "游蛇似的在人群中左钻右突", which changes the image of "snake" into "thread", nevertheless the meaning of the source expression is kept. According to *OAED*, "thread one's way through something" means "to go carefully or with difficulty through (something)", which corresponds to the original expression. Of course, we can also translate the Chinese expression into "snaking his way through the crowd", which can both keep the original image and express the meaning. Both "snake" and "thread" integrate the state and path of the movement.

Apart from the above examples, "path" is sometimes implied in manner in some words or expressions. For instance:

52. 车从这里的地铁爬上天桥，颤颤巍巍地从又乱又脏的街区开过去，往下一望，有时会突然看到一栋破极了的大楼的窗子里，有一些脸色神秘的东方人，穿着日式的大黑衣服，在练拳。(Ju,2002: 34)

The train is to climb up and onto the overpass and *wobble its way through this dirty and messy block*. Peering downwards and into the windows of some extremely dilapidated building, passengers may sometimes see some mysterious-looking orientals dressed in Japanese-style dark suits practicing karate. (ibid: 36)

In the source text, "颤颤巍巍地从又乱又脏的街区开过" implies such concepts as "颤颤巍巍 (manner), 从……(path), 开(motion)", so the English expression "wobble its way through" can be used. The dictionary explanation of "wobble" is "to move from side to side in an unsteady way" (*OAED*), which implies such semantic sememes as "move (motion), from side to side (path), in an unsteady way (manner)". Anyway, the translation is meaning equivalent to the ST in the cognitive context.

Sometimes "path" is even more complicated, and the exact direction is not easy to identify, maybe concerning back and forth, up and down, or all direction, which can be illustrated by the following example:

53. （河水倾泼丈余，）鸡鸣犬吠满城中。

The town echoed with the sounds of cocks crowing and dogs barking. (cf Liu & Li,2009: 379-385)

The source text expresses a dynamic image schema. According to our experience in village, during the tranquil night certain sound would cause bark and crow. It seems that the entire village is filled with such sounds. This is the result of human audio and spatial experience. The translator changes the viewpoint and set "the town" as the viewpoint space and uses "echo of sounds of cocks crowing and dogs barking" to fill the space. Moreover, the town here acts as an open container, and sounds act as figure moving back and forth, up and down, as a result the whole container is full of such sounds. Such expression is not only equivalent in associative meaning to the source expression, but also more dynamic than "the town is filled with…"

4.4 Cognitive Contextual Equivalence in Re-lexicalization of Redundant Words

Redundancy, as an innate feature of language in communication, is paid more and more attention to by linguists after World War II with the proposition of information theory by Shannon. Information theory is to use the mathematical theory to study the measurement, transition, change, operation and store of information. One of its focuses is to measure the efficacy of certain communicative channel because information in transmitting is inevitably disturbed by noise source (see Gui,1980). Shannon (1949) illustrates the communication of information in figure 4-22.

Since its proposition, information theory has been applied to other research fields, such as psychology, literary and translation studies. Such concepts as channel, channel capacity, noise, redundancy, communication load, encoding and decoding, etc. have been used by western translation theorists as important theoretical terms to study the translation process, standards and effects (Liao,1996). According to the information theory, information is inevitably disturbed by noise in channel. In order to keep the correctness of information, the sender would repeat information when encoding, so the receiver will receive more information to help decode what the sender really sends, thus the information can be completely transmitted. That's the origin of redundancy (Wang & Wang, 2002). Redundancy is a very popular linguistic phenomenon. According to the statistics by Zhao (2004), the average of English redundancy is about 73 percent, Russian 70 percent, and modern Chinese 63 percent. Gui (1980) even thinks that without redundancy language will be colorless. But that is not to say the more redundancy the better. Gui states that too much redundancy will decrease the efficacy of communication and lead to error.

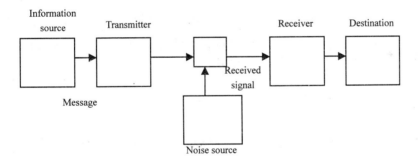

Figure 4-22 Communication of information (cf Gui 1980)

Chinese and English belong to different language systems and have different features. Influenced by their different cultural backgrounds, thinking modes and communicative conventions, people of either language are accustomed to their own way of expression. One positive statement in Chinese may be regarded as total negative by the westerners. So Liu (2005: 126) states that the study of discourse effect should distinguish absolute redundancy and effective redundancy. When translated from one language to the other, such redundancy must be suitably dealt with so as to make the communication smooth. If redundancy in one language is completely transferred to the other language, the target reader may find the translation awful or unreasonable. So how to deal with redundancy is an important task for the translator and the way to deal with redundancy is also an important topic for translation study.

Recently, studies on redundancy mainly concern the following fields: 1) the causes of redundancy in one's native language (Pan,1997; Wang & Chen, 2001); 2) redundancy in second language learning caused by the transferring influence of the mother tongue (Krashen,1983; Corder,1983; Faerch & Kapser,1986; Schachter,1983); 3) redundancy in C-E translations (Wen,1990; Liao,1996; Wang,2002; Zeng,2005, 2007c; Yin,2006; Zhou,2003; Zhang, 2001: 21-24; Lin,2001) . In discussing different kinds of translations, Zhou (2003) states that source information should be completely kept in literary translation, while in applied translation only useful information can be transmitted, and especially in overseas-oriented publicity translations useful information and expected effect should be paid more attention to. Zhang (2001: 21-24) takes similar viewpoint and proposes that different thinking modes and aesthetic senses should be first thought about in overseas-oriented publicity translations. Qian (1986) uses Iser's theory to explain the reason of literary works' containing more redundancy than non-literary works. He states that literary works are in descriptive language which contains many uncertainty and meaning gaps, so they leave space for the readers to fill according to their own interpretation; while non-literary works are in explanative language which needs certainty, so information should be effective and succinct. Based on their viewpoints, the following part mainly focuses on redundancy of non-literary works.

Zeng (2005) proposes the principle of information economy and succinctness in discussing overseas-oriented publicity translations. The principle of economy and succinctness contains two aspects: first, the translator tries to express more information with fewer words; second, the translator tries to let the reader get more fluent information with less time or energy. In order to complement the economy and succinct principle, Zeng adds five auxiliary principles: 1) the transmission of information should meet the needs of the receiver's native thinking mode; 2) the transmission of information should consider the receiver's culture; 3) the transmission of information should consider the receiver's expectation or special needs; 4) the transmission of information should consider the receiver's cognitive capacity; 5) the transmission of information should consider the features of the text itself, such as the length, style and deficiency, etc. He even summarizes ten operating rules from Pinkham (2000) to criticize one of our government's overseas-oriented publicity translations. The operating rules go like this: (1) to delete words providing no contents; (2) to delete or simplify unnecessary explanative words or shared knowledge; (3) to omit those can be derived from other words; (4) to delete the repetitive words in phrases; (5) to delete those modifiers whose meaning is implied in the modified noun or phrase; (6) to delete the category or attributive words when they are after the concrete words or species concepts; (7) when the superordinate and subordinate words are putting together, delete one of them; (8) try to use the lower or smaller linguistic units rather than the higher or bigger ones to express contents; (9) when one object is illustrated by many descriptive or evaluative words, delete or simplify those empty words; (10) when two or more same or similar information appear in the same or adjacent paragraph, try to condense the information. Zeng (2007c) puts these principles and operating rules into the theoretical construction of pragmatic translation system. Zeng's study is a relatively complete system in overseas-oriented publicity translations, which provides theoretical basis for further research.

Based on the former studies, this research regards re-lexicalization of redundant words in C-E translation as a kind of coincidental conceptual integration that the translator makes to reach equivalence in cognitive context. The nature of such integration is to identify the central meaning contained in the overlapped concepts and then find the corresponding concepts in the target language. Of course, contextual parameters are involved in the process of integration (see figure 4-23). The following part discusses CCE in re-lexicalization of redundancy from three aspects: CCE in repetitive redundancy, CCE in extensive redundancy, CCE in implied redundancy.

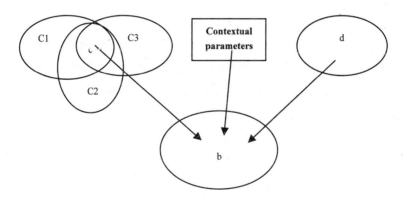

Figure 4-23 Integration of redundancy

4.4.1 Cognitive Contextual Equivalence in Re-lexicalization of Repetitive Redundancy

Repetitive redundancy here refers to the paired repetitions that appear together. Repetitive redundancy may be reasonable and effective in Chinese but unreadable in English because it adds burden to the target reader's cognition. Chinese expression features its symmetry and balance in structure so it is more repetitive in wording. That is why we have a lot of expressions with a pair of similar concepts putting together, such as 深仇大恨; 完美无缺; 街谈巷议; 神不知, 鬼不觉; 取之不尽, 用之不竭; 攻无不克, 战无不胜, etc. Such expressions are very natural and effective in Chinese. However, if they are directly translated into English, the version will be redundant and unreadable for English readers because they may regard such repetitions as "absolute redundancy" or "nonsense" (see Liu,2005: 126). Since one word is enough to express the similar meaning, the above paired repetitions should be integrated into the following English expressions: *deep hatred, perfect/impeccable, street gossip, stealthily/secretly, inexhaustible, all-conquering.*

Sometimes the corresponding English of the paired Chinese expressions contain the same semantic item, so they are naturally integrated into one in translation to reach meaning equivalence in cognitive context; on the other hand, those translations corresponding in surface meaning are incorrect ones. For instance:

54. 这是通往繁荣昌盛的唯一之路。

This is the only road leading to *affluence and prosperity.* (possible word-for-word translation)

In this example, the possible word-for-word translation of "繁荣昌盛" is "affluence and prosperity". In English dictionary, the concept "prosperity" refers to "the state of being successful or rich; good fortune", and "affluence" stands for "abundance of money, goods or property; wealth" (*OAED*). Since both words contain the same conceptual sememe "rich", they are redundant in meaning. The original four-character concepts can be integrated into the concept "prosperous" which is adequate to convey the meaning "繁荣昌盛". The translation can be revised into "This is the only road leading to prosperity" or even more concise into "This is the only road *to prosperity*" with "leading" cognitively integrated. Pinkham (2000: 64-65) states that the best way to deal with such redundant twins is simply deleting one of them or replacing both members of the pair with a new word that expresses the thought better than either of the original two. The cognitive reasoning process of this translation can be shown in figure 4-24:

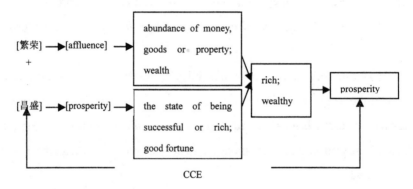

Figure 4-24 CCE between "繁荣昌盛" and "prosperity"

55. 我们就要有这个雄心壮志。

We must have this *ambition.*

Both "雄心" and "壮志" in this example basically refer to the same meaning, and the corresponding English is "ambition". They belong to what Pinkham (ibid: 63) called "redundant twins", and one of them should be deleted in translation.

56. 只要双方共同努力，双边关系就会继续发展壮大。

TT₁: So long as the two sides work together, bilateral relations will continue to *develop and grow*. (possible word-for-word translation)

In this example, the word-for-word translation may surprise the native English speakers as the two words are repetitive in meaning. The dictionary explanation of *grow* is "expand or gain; develop and reach maturity", which implies the paired word *develop*. The correct translation should be:

TT₂: So long as the two sides work together, bilateral relations will continue to *grow/expand*. (tran. by the author)

From analyses of the above examples, we deduce such an empirical rule:

If two concepts are putting together to express the same or similar connotative meaning, and one concept is integrated in the other in cognitive context, then choosing one of them to be translated is enough.

4.4.2 Cognitive Contextual Equivalence in Re-lexicalization of Extended Redundancy

Sometimes, we would use extended concepts or words to make the expression symmetrical and effective in Chinese. Some of the extended concepts contain no meaning, and we call them empty concepts. Some of the extended words are used as ornaments to the key information, which we call extended ornamental adjuncts. If such extended concepts or words are translated into English directly, the version will be Chinglish. Pinkham (2000: 170) makes the distinction between plain English and Chinglish as follows:

"Plain English is a language based on verbs. It is simple, concise, vigorous and, above all, clear. Chinglish is a language based on nouns—vague, general, abstract nouns. It is complicated, long-winded, ponderous, and obscure."

So in translating those extended redundancies, the translator needs to pay more attention and make some integration. This section mainly discusses how CCE is realized in the two kinds of integration: integration of empty concepts and integration of extended ornamental adjuncts.

4.4.2.1 CCE in Integration of Extended Empty Concepts

Empty concepts are very popular in Chinese phrases. If one phrase contains two or more concepts and only one of them carries meaning, then the translator needs to extract the valuable concepts and omit or integrate those meaningless ones.

57. 你知道白蚁之害吗？一座大厦如果有了白蚁，不加防治，不到十年时间，里面的地板壁板，都会蛀蚀一空。(Ju 1998)

In this example, the phrase "防治" contains two concepts "预防" (prevent/protect/safeguard) and "治疗/理" (possible equivalents such as treat/cure/heal/govern/control/administer). With the premise "有了白蚁", the concept "预防" becomes an empty one because "预防" presuppose that it has not been infested with termites. Only one concept "治" is extracted for use. As we know, *treat, cure* and *heal* are usually used in medical context, while *govern, control* and *administer* are used in political context. None of them are appropriate in such construction context. Restricted by the co-textual parameters such as *termites, building, floor, paneling, etc.*, 治 in this context means "to wipe out the termites". So only "wipe out" is projected into the blend space and forms TT₁. Although *wipe out* is not equivalent to 防治 in linguistic form, it is equivalent at the level of connotative meaning in cognitive context. The process of conceptual integration can be seen in figure 4-25, and the reasoning process of the cognitive contextual meaning is shown in figure 4-26.

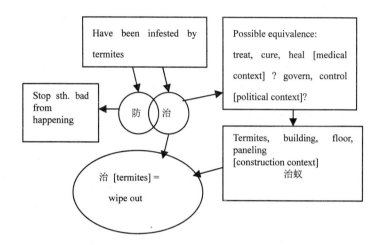

Figure 4-25 Conceptual integration of "防治"

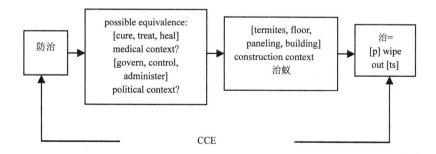

Figure 4-26 CCE between "防治" and "wipe out"
(p=people, ts=termites)

TT₁: Do you know how destructive termites are? If a tall building *is infested with termites and people do not wipe them out,* the floor and the wooden paneling inside it will have been eaten in less than ten years. (tran. by the author)

Or such empty concepts can be translated in a blurred way as follows:

TT₂: Do you know how destructive termites are? If a tall building *is infested with termites and nothing is done about it*, the floor and the wooden paneling inside it will have been eaten in less than ten years. (tran. by Ju Zuchun 1998)

Based on analysis of the above example, such an empirical rule can be deduced:

When a phrase contains more than one concept and its meaning is restricted by the premise of the co-text, then the translation of the phrase should rely on the premise of the co-text.

4.4.2.2 CCE in Integration of Extended Ornamental Adjuncts

In describing the scenery or introducing the history or culture of one place, we Chinese are apt to put many four-character phrases together as the ornamental adjuncts to make the expression effective and readable. However, English makes a feature of its succinct syntax and clear meaning, so in C-E translation, such extended ornamental adjuncts are often omitted or integrated into simple description. For instance:

58. 阿霸州风光秀丽，山河壮美。座座雪峰耸入云霄，原始森林遮天盖地，莽莽草原花团锦簇，叠溪遗迹神秘奥妙，瀑布溪流蜿蜒跌宕，高山湖泊灿若明珠，藏羌村寨别具一格，肥沃河谷瓜果飘香。

The *beautiful landscapes* of Aba Prefecture feature *towering snow-clad mountains*, *crisscrossing* rivers, and *boundless* forests and grassland. On this *fertile* land are *peculiar* geological ruins, *fantastic* streams and waterfalls, *alpine* lakes, and Tibetan and Qiang villages. (cf Zhang 2001: 21-24)

The ST is an introduction of the scenery, in which many four-character phrases are used as ornamental adjuncts to make the expression rhythmic and appealing. However, such beauty of linguistic structure can hardly be translated into English with the same effect. Some expressions are repetitive in form such as "座座" and "莽莽" while others are repetitive in meaning such as "秀丽/壮美", "遮天/盖地", "神秘/奥妙", "蜿蜒/跌宕".Such expressions are used to balance the structure rather than to provide valuable information. If they are translated literally according to Chinese expressive habit, the version will be redundant and unreadable, to say nothing of the equivalence in aesthetic feeling. Zeng (2007: 46) states that the value principle should be based on the audience's relation with the information value of the language. In order to achieve the best effect, the translator needs to obey the economy and succinctness principle to simplify those low-valued descriptive or pompous words so as to make the translation more acceptable. Zhang reorganizes the source information and translates it according to English expressive habit with the ornamental redundancy integrated.

4.4.3 Cognitive Contextual Equivalence in Re-lexicalization of Implied Redundancy

Implication refers to a kind of logic or semantic relationship, which can be expressed by the logic formula $p \supset q$. It means that concept p implies the semantic contents of concept q. According to its forms, implication can be classified into cognitive implication, lexical implication and structural implication, etc. (Zeng, 2005). Chinese and English belong to different language systems and people's thinking modes are also different, so the ways of expressing their thoughts are different. Suitable expression in one language may be unreasonable in the other because of the implied redundancy, and such redundancy should be avoided in translation to realize cognitive contextual equivalence. This section discusses the realization of CCE in integrating implied redundancy from the following aspects: meaning, intensifier, category, tense and plural.

4.4.3.1 CCE in Integrating Redundant Meaning

When the meaning of one concept is contained in the other, the translator should keep clear mind to escape redundant meaning in translation.

59. 中国今年农业获得了大丰收。

There have been *good harvests in agriculture* in China this year. (possible word-for word translation)

In this example, "丰收" in Chinese refers to "plenteous harvest in agriculture", so to plus "农业" before it is redundant. But Chinese readers are accustomed to such redundancy and they accept such expression naturally. However, if the source text is translated literally into English, it will be unacceptable. According to the dictionary, *agriculture* refers to "science or practice of cultivating the land and rearing animals; farming" (*OAED*), from which we can extract two cognitive schemata—cultivating land and rearing animals. The cognitive schema of cultivating land contains such elements as *farmers, land, seeds, sowing, shooting, fertilizing, maturing, grain, crops*. On the other hand, *harvest* refers to "the time of year when the crops are gathered in on a farm, etc.; the act of cutting and gathering crops" *(OAED)*. According to its dictionary explanation, we can extract such relevant cognitive elements as "farmers, land, seeds, sowing, shooting, fertilizing, maturing, grain, crops". Then, we can infer a cognitive schema of cultivating which is implied in the bigger cognitive schema of agriculture. As is demonstrated in figure 4-27, harvest is one of the activities of agriculture, and it equals to *harvest in agriculture* in the cognitive context, so "in agriculture" should be omitted in translation.

From analysis of this example, the author deduces such an empirical rule:

When a superordinate concept and a subordinate concept co-occur in one sentence, the sememes of the subordinate are implied in the superordinate. If the translator chooses the subordinate concept, then the superordinate concept becomes redundant and should be omitted.

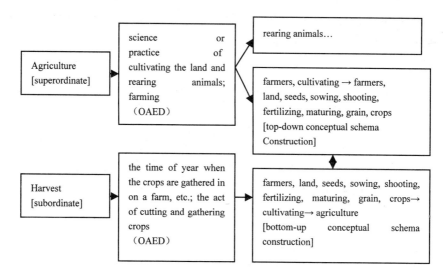

Figure 4-27 Cognitive schemata of agriculture and harvest

The following examples are also fit for this rule.

60. 绿色发展和可持续发展的根本目的是改善人民生存环境和生活水平。（Xi, 2010）

TT₁: The ultimate goal of green and sustainable development is to *improve people's living environment, better their lives and promote their comprehensive development.* (Beijing Review, April 22.)

The translation is redundant in using verbs containing similar meaning and nouns implied in each other. First, both "improve" and "promote" mean "better" or "to make better", so one word is enough. Second, according to the dictionary, "the environment" refers to "natural conditions, eg. land, air and water, in which we live" and "living standards" refers to "the way in which people live, for example how comfortable their houses are or how much money they have to spend on food and clothes"*(OAECD)*, so both words imply the subject—human being. We can revise the translation into the following succinct one to reach CCE:

TT₂: The ultimate goal of green and sustainable development is to *improve the environment and living standards.* (tran. by the author.)

61. 要呵护人类赖以生存的地球家园，……（Xi, 2010）

TT₁: We need to take good care of *planet Earth, our common home* … (Beijing Review, April 22)

"地球家园" is a very common expression in Chinese, which is symmetric in form with a warm feeling in tone. The English translation "*planet Earth, our common home*" contains two relevant concepts *planet* and *earth* which are repetitive in conceptual sememes. *Earth* means "the planet that we live on" (*OAED*), which implies the sememe of planet. So the two concepts can be integrated into one as in TT₂ to reach real equivalence in cognitive context.

TT₂: We need to take good care of *the Earth, our common home* ...
(tran. by the author.)

4.4.3.2 CCE in Integrating Redundant Intensifier

One of the features of Chinese governmental document is to use
evaluative adjuncts to strengthen the tone, such as "积极", "认真", "大力",
"自觉", "完全", "彻底" etc. Pinkham (2000: 36) calls them unnecessary
intensifiers, which will confuse the target readers if translated literally into
English. They may doubt that Chinese government is not active or serious in
dealing with such issues. Therefore, these unnecessary intensifiers should be
deleted or simplified in C-E translation.

62. 要以极其认真负责的历史责任感对待环境与发展问题，坚持走
可持续发展道路。（Xi, 2010）

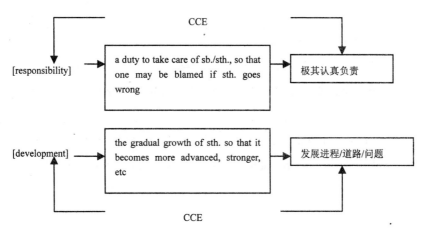

Figure 4-28 Cognitive contextual integration of "responsibility" and
"development"

TT$_1$: We need to handle *the issue of* environment and development *extremely seriously* and with a historic sense of mission, and need to adhere to *the path of* sustainable development. (*Beijing Review*, April 22.)

The translation is redundant in using intensifiers such as "extremely seriously", which have been integrated into "historic sense of mission" as *mission* in cognitive context is an official job must be treated seriously. Other redundancies include "the issue of" and "the path of", which are category words implied in environment and development respectively. *Environment* means "the physical conditions that sb./sth. exists in". *Development* means "the process of producing or creating something new or more advanced", which implies the conceptual sememes of issue or path in the cognitive context. So "the issue of" and "the path of" can both be deleted in translation (see figure 4-28). As people of different nations may form their own cognitive schemata through grasping semantic features of words or concepts, they will consciously compensate the defaulted values in their cognitive structure, and then compose and complete the relevant information (see Zeng, 2005: 6). We can revise the translation into TT$_2$.

TT$_2$: We should *take a historical responsibility* to the environment and development and adhere to sustainable development. (tran. by the author)

In this translation, *take a historical responsibility* implies the meaning of "*serious*" in cognition, and other redundancies are all integrated.

63. 要更加自觉地认识到，加快经济发展方式转变刻不容缓，必须在发展中促转变，在转变中谋发展，等等。（Xi, 2010）

TT$_1$: We *should be more soberly aware* of the urgency to speed up transformation of economic development mode, and make transformation and development mutually reinforcing. (Beijing Review, April 22)

This example contains the same problem as example 62. The source expression "要更加自觉地" is very typical Chinese, which is used to strengthen the tone and show the determination. But the literal translation "should be more soberly aware of" is unacceptable in English because of its redundancy. *Aware* means "realizing or knowing something" which is sober in cognition, so "more soberly" is unnecessary. In order to express its strong tone, we can use "must" to replace "should". Thus we get TT_2.

TT_2: We *must realize* the urgency to speed up transformation of economic development mode, and make transformation and development mutually reinforcing.

Other similar examples are shown as follows, in which intensifiers bracketed should be deleted to reach CCE rather than surface meaning corresponding.

      彻底粉碎——(completely) *smash* (*smash*: to destroy, defeat or put an end to something/somebody; destroy: destroy completely, damage irreparably)

      完全征服——(completely/totally) *conquer* (*conquer*: take possession of (something) by force; defeat; overcome. All imply the meaning of "completely")

(Explanations in brackets are from *OAECD*)

4.4.3.3 CCE in Integrating Redundant Category or Attributive Words

Dealing with concepts indicating category in C-E translation is a well-known phenomenon that has been recognized by many scholars. Zeng (2005) defines category-indicating concepts as generalized concepts with the same classification, which reflects the extension of things, or collections of elements with the same characteristic in extension. For example, *mood* includes happy, sad, depressed, and so on. Chinese is very popular in using category words to summarize or describe a situation. Common Chinese category words include "现象, 情况, 工作, 任务, 建设, 因素, 态度, 局面, 状况, 过程, 反应, 心理, 活动, 问题", etc. Attributive words refer to those that can reflect their own state, nature or feature, such as 性格, 特性, 圆形, 大型, 红色, etc. While in English, category or attributive words are often reflected by the same words or word's affixations rather than by adding lexical forms. So in translation, the difference between Chinese and English should be noted and the category-indicating concepts can be generally integrated into a concise concept which suggests the notion of the category itself through cognitive interpretation. For instances:

64. 我们党结束了那个时期的社会动荡和纷扰不安的局面。
Our Party put an end to *the social unrest and upheaval* of that time.

It is very common in Chinese expression to use "……的局面", while in English "the situation/state of…" must be omitted because it is integrated in "unrest and upheaval". According to the dictionary, "unrest" means "a political *situation* in which people are angry and likely to protest or fight", and "upheaval" refers to "a *state* of violent disturbance and disorder (as in politics or social *conditions* generally)" (*OAED*). Both words imply the category word "situation or state", and such category words should be integrated in translation to reach real equivalence in cognitive context rather than linguistic form corresponding.

65. ……加快经济改革的步伐……

…to *accelerate* (the pace of) economic reform…

The source expression "加快经济改革的步伐" can be translated into "to accelerate economic reform" instead of "to accelerate the pace of economic reform" since "accelerate" means "to increase the speed (pace) of", which integrates the category word. Therefore, equivalence is not the correspondence in linguistic form but conceptual sememe equivalence in cognitive context.

66. 依法严厉打击各种犯罪活动，坚决扫除黄赌毒等社会丑恶现象。

We must (seriously) *crack down* on all criminal activities according to the law and *eradicate* such *social evils* (phenomena) as pornography, gambling and drug abuse and trafficking. (Li 2004)

Since social evils such as pornography, gambling and drug abuse belong to social phenomena, the category word should be deleted in English. What is more, "crack down" and "eradicate" are both very strong in tone, so the intensifiers also need to be omitted. That is to say, although the linguistic form of the TT is not corresponding with the ST, the meaning is equivalent in the cognitive context.

Apart from those category nouns, there are also many category verbs. Li (2004: 279-287) summaries category words appeared in verbal phrases and points out that if such category verbs carry no meaning, they should be omitted or changed in other ways in translation. Such category verbs include "坚持……的原则", "采取……办法", "处于……状态", "发挥……功能/作

用", "实现……目标", "完成……任务", "采取……方针/政策", "实施……战略", "采取……态度", "处于……局面", "以……为中心", "以……为纲", "出现……现象", "走……道路", and so on.

67. 亚洲要保持经济良性发展势头，继续拉动世界经济增长，必须更加注重完善发展模式，走出一条符合时代潮流，具有亚洲特色的绿色发展和可持续发展之路。（Xi, 2010）

TT₁: To maintain the sound *momentum of* economic development *in the region* and boost world economic growth, we must *further* improve the development model, and seek *a path of* green and sustainable development *that is* with Asia characteristics and is consistent with the trend of our times. (*Beijing Review*, April 22.)

In this example, TT₁ keeps all the category words of the ST, which are in fact unnecessary redundancies. *Momentum* means "the ability to keep increasing or developing", so this word should be integrated in *development*. *Improve* means "to make sth./sb. better than before", which implies the meaning of "further" in cognitive context, therefore "further" should be integrated in "improve". As what has been talked about in the former section, "a path of" should be integrated in the sememes of "development". "In the region" is self-evident in this context with the appearance of "Asia", as a result it can also be omitted. We can revise the translation into a more succinct one as TT₂.

TT₂: To *maintain* a sound economic *development* and boost world economic growth, we must improve the model and *seek a green and sustainable development* with Asia characteristics and consistent with the trend of our times. (tran. by the author)

68. 我们必须坚持解决群众当前困难与长期发展相结合的原则。

We should try to solve people's immediate problems and at the same time to promote long-term development. (cf Li,2004: 279)

The source expression "坚持……原则" is not a real principle but an empty expression, so the translator omitts such category verb and changes the expression. Such translation keeps the basic meaning of the source expression and reaches meaning equivalence in cognitive context.

Apart from those category words, the attributive words should also be correctly dealt with in C-E translation considering the different thinking modes and lexical formations. For instances:

(1) 共同合作 (mutual) cooperation

(2) 红色 red (in color)

(3) 圆形 round (in shape)

(4) 大型 large (in size)

All these words in brackets are integrated in the English attributive words, so they must be omitted in C-E translation.

4.4.3.4 CCE in Integrating Time–Related Concepts

English and Chinese are also different in expressing tense. Tense change in English is reflected by changing word form while in Chinese it is reflected by adding words expressing time or adding auxiliary concepts such as "着, 了, 过" (see Xu 2007). So in C-E translation, Chinese time-related concepts such as "现在, 过去, 未来, 已经" etc. are integrated into the English word forms and should not be repeated in most cases except for emphasis. For instances:

69. 未来经济的发展，在很大程度上依赖于……

TT₁: The development of our economy *in the future will*, to a large extent, depend on……

In Chinese we use "未来" to express the future tense, while in English *will* means "used for talking about or predicting the future" (*OAED*). So when we use "will", the time-related concept "in the future" is integrated in our cognitive context and should not be repeated in linguistic expression. In this example, the translation is influenced by the Chinese thinking mode and expressing way and it is redundant. We can revise the translation into TT₂.

TT₂: The development of our economy *will*, to a large extent, depend on……" (tran. by the author)

70. 现在我们总比过去好得多。

Anyway, things *(at present/now) are* much better than before. (《邓小平文选》)

"现在" is used to compare with "过去" in the ST, and both concepts can be expressed by the concrete time-relating phrases. In English "is" and "are" are both used as the present tense implying the time-relating concepts of "at present" or "now". So "at present" or "now" is integrated in the cognitive context and should not be expressed in linguistic form.

71. 当前，全世界都在关注着我国的改革。

The whole world *is watching* the reforms in our country. (《邓小平文选》)

The present continuous tense reflected by "当前" and "在……着" is used in the Chinese expression, while the English expression "is watching" is also a present continuous which implies "at present", so it is unnecessary to express the linguistic form of "at present". Anyway, such concepts can be recognized by readers in cognition through grammatical markers.

72. 过去两个超级大国主宰世界，现在情况变了。

(In the past) The world *used to* be dominated by two superpowers. Now things have changed. (《邓小平文选》)

"Used to" refers to "something happened continuously or frequently during a period i*n the past*" (*OAED*), which integrates the time-relating concept "in the past". So in translation, "in the past" should not be expressed in linguistic form to reach cognitive context equivalence.

4.4.3.5 CCE in Integrating Redundant Plural Form

English and Chinese are also different in plural changes. English plural form is reflected by the inflection such as adding "-s" to the noun or irregular inner change of the noun, while Chinese plural form is accomplished by lexical method such as adding other plural concepts (see Zhang,2009: 157-160) . So in C-E translation, when Chinese plural concepts are implied in the English inflection, it is unnecessary to repeat them.

73. 要采取一系列措施来确保……

TT$_1$: We should adopt *a series of measures* to ensure that…

In Chinese, the word "措施" is fuzzy in number and its plural meaning requires other words or expressions such as "一系列" and "许多". However, "measures" in English expresses the plural form of "measure" by adding the suffix "-s", which implies "a series of", so it is unnecessary to repeat the plural form. The proper translation is:

TT$_2$: We should adopt *measures* to ensure that... (tran. by the author)

74. 在这一时期，多种物资的供应严重缺乏。

Throughout this period there was a severe shortage in the supply of (*a great variety of*) *goods*.

With the same reason as in example 73, "goods" in this example integrates the concept "多种" (a great variety of), so it is unnecessary to repeat it in English. All in all, those words containing similar concepts or concepts containing similar sememes should be integrated into one in translation so as to reach real meaning equivalence in cognitive context.

4.5 Summary

This chapter discusses how CCE is realized in different kinds of coincidental conceptual integration in translation. It is found that coincidental conceptual integration in translation is a phenomenon of re-lexicalization, which is fulfilled via metaphorical mapping, metonymical mapping, projection, and sememes extraction, etc. For instance, re-lexicalization of converted words is to integrate the prototypical features of the noun with the relevant action, behavior, manner, state, location, or function, etc. of the subject via metonymical and metaphorical mappings; re-lexicalization of motion words is in fact the integration of the subject's motion with the manner, cause or path, etc.; re-lexicalization of redundancy is the integration between implication, sub-super ordination and repetition.

By means of re-lexicalization, the redundant concepts are integrated in the cognitive context, so even though the number or form of concept is changed, the meaning is cognitively kept in translation. That is, although the linguistic expressions of the ST and TT are not equivalent to each other, the meanings are equivalent in the cognitive context. With analyses of different kinds of coincidental integration in translation, the research also deduces some empirical rules to guide the analyses of similar examples. What is more, the cognitive motivation of such operation is also explored in this chapter. The research finds that re-lexicalization is one of the cognitive mechanisms of the translator in realizing cognitive contextual equivalence in translation. Such cognitive mechanism is guided by the receptive-aesthetics-oriented translation principle for the pursuit of a more concise and vivid version.

Chapter 5

Cognitive Contextual Equivalence in Deviant Conceptual Integration

5.1 Introduction

Deviant conceptual integration refers to the phenomenon that the translation is deviant to the source expression in linguistic form while equivalent in meaning at certain level in cognitive context. Sometimes, when the source expression does not have a coincidental correspondence in the target language, or the dictionary explanations are not suitable in certain context, the translator needs to exert his cognitive experience to reconstruct or compensate the conceptual meaning according to the context. Such translations may be viewed as deviant conceptual integration. Translations of deviant conceptual integration are creative ones so they seem to be more novel and vivid in linguistic form that provides an attractive aesthetic effect. In translation, especially in literary translation, the translator is apt to use deviant conceptual integration to create new expressions so as to produce more readable versions. However, the translator's creativity must be restricted by the context; otherwise his translation will be too free or even becomes a rewriting. This chapter is an exploration of cognitive contextual equivalence realized in translations of deviant conceptual integration. According to the degree of deviance, this part mainly discusses CCE in three kinds of deviant conceptual integration: synesthetic image deviant conceptual integration, information deviant conceptual integration, semantic meaning deviant conceptual integration.

5.2 Cognitive Contextual Equivalence in Synesthetic Image Deviant Conceptual Integration

Image is very important in literary works, so its translation should also be cared about. In *American Heritage Dictionary*, "image" is defined as "a mental picture of something not real or present" or "a vivid description or representation" or "a concrete representation, as in art, literature, or music that is expressive or evocative of something else". According to *Ci Hai*, "Yixiang" (Chinese image) belongs to Chinese ancient aesthetics. "Yi" refers to the meaning in mind (Xinyi) and "Xiang" refers to the physical image (Wuxiang). So "Yixiang" refers to the mental picture formed by the blending of the object's concrete physical image and the observer's state of mind. Pound, deeply influenced by Chinese image poetry, states that image can be of two sorts: "Firstly it can arise within the mind. It is then 'subjective'. External causes play upon the mind perhaps; If so, they are drawn into the mind, fused, transmitted, and emerge in an Image unlike themselves. Secondly, the image can be 'objective'. Emotion seizing upon some external scene or action carries it to the mind; and that vortex purges it of all save the essential or dominant or dramatic qualities, and it emerges like the external original. (Zhao 1997:19)" His classification is in fact the same as the Chinese classification of *Yi* (subjective) and *Xiang* (objective). Viewing from these different explanations, this research states that both *Yixiang* and *image* share the similar connation, so image is used in this research to refer to both image in western literature and *Yixiang* in Chinese literature.

Image study in China has a long history. Liu Xie in his *Wenxin Diaolong* first applies *Yixiang* to the field of artistic creativity. He points out that the writer should combine the object's form with the subject's emotion before writing so as to form the aesthetic image. Zhu (1998: 6) regards image as the mental picture impressed by certain object. Jiang (2002) interprets image by means of the Gestalt theory, whose interpretation endows image with the feature of wholeness and completeness. Chen & Li (2008) regards the Gestalt image as combination of traditional image (cf Ma & Zhang,2010). Generally, image is closely connected with culture. Cultural image is first used as a concept by Xie (1999: 85). Xie points out that cultural image is closely related to the national legend and the primary Totemism, and both of them have fixed and distinctive cultural connotations, so cultural image consists of Physical image and Connotation. Other scholars share almost the same opinion in defining cultural image (Zhang,2004; Hou, 1998: 96-102) .

This research does not discuss image from the perspective of traditional studies but tries to explore the synesthetic image deviant conceptual integration such as synesthetic image-prominence in translation. Synesthetic image-prominent conceptual integration refers to those translations highlighting synesthetic images; that is, the translator tends to add or change a sense image in translation to adapt to the target reader's need. In talking about adding sense image in translation, we may first think of being loyal to the source text. So the research mainly discusses those cases with similar meaning but different images. The most popularly used of this kind is adding synesthetic images in translation, which can be hardly regarded as disloyal to the source text as mappings between different sense organs are very common. Since synesthesia is frequently used in literary writings to improve aesthetic effect, translators also use synesthetic images to make the translation more vivid and strange to increase the readers' interests.

Cognitive linguistics regards synesthesia as projection mapping between different sense organs. According to *Oxford English Dictionary* (2004), synesthesia refers to: 1) psychology. The production of mental sense impression relating to one sense by the stimulation of another sense, as in colored hearing; also a sensation produced in one part of the body by stimulating another part. 2) The use of metaphors in which terms relating to one kind of sense—impression are used to describe sense—impression of other kinds. Qian (2002: 64-65) points out that "sense organs such as vision, hearing, touch, smell and taste can be mapped onto each other. Color may have temperature, sound may have image, cool or warm may have weight, smell may have quality, etc. Shelley (2009: 88-93) studies the cross domain mappings between different sense organs. She makes a comparison between Chinese and English Visual Synesthetic Metaphors and finds that mappings between different sense organs are very common in both languages. Ullmann (1957: 280), based on his statistics of different literary works, summarizes the trend of image movement between different sense organs. He states that "transfers tend to mount from the lower to the higher reaches of the sensorium, from the less differentiated sensations to the more differentiated ones, and not vice versa." Their viewpoints of mapping between different sense organs provide motivation to the analysis of CCE in synesthetic image deviant conceptual integration. This section mainly discusses four aspects: CCE in visual image prominence, CCE in audio image prominence, CCE in taste image prominence and CCE in touch image prominence.

5.2.1 Cognitive Contextual Equivalence in Visual Image Prominence

Visual image prominence refers to the phenomenon that the translator highlights the visual image in translation so as to improve the aesthetic effect. For instances:

1. 说毕，携宝玉入室。但闻一缕幽香，竟不知所焚何物。（Cao,2003: 142）

TT$_1$: With that she led Baoy inside. Baoyu *smelt a subtle perfume* … (possible literal translation)

TT$_2$: With that she led Baoyu inside. *A subtle perfume hung in the air* and he could not help asking what incense was being burned. (tran. by the Yangs, ibid: 143)

The dotted part of the source text contains such concepts: "闻"smell (the subject's action), "一缕"a subtle (degree), and "幽香" perfume (object), which can be translated literally into TT$_1$. TT$_2$ by the Yangs changes the concepts into: a subtle (degree), perfume (subject), hung (state or manner), in the air (situation), in which "perfume" is changed from object to subject and the verb is changed from the subject's action to the object's state or manner with a situation added in the end. The literal translation of TT$_1$ does not contain any image, while TT$_2$ is a visual-image prominent one. Such visual-image prominent conceptual integration is to make the readers feel that the perfume can be seen by their eyes. The strangeness of such expression leaves aesthetic space to the reader.

Such expression belongs to the cross-space mapping between vision and smell. According to our daily experience, when something is burnt, smoke comes out of the burning object and assails our nostril and then we smell it. So the mapping between vision and smell is natural and reasonable. The source context is about Baoyu's traveling to the fairy land in his dream. The fairy lady led him to the Disenchant house, in which he enjoyed the songs of red mansions. When he was entering the room, Baoyu smelt a subtle perfume in the air. TT$_2$ leads the readers to imagine that Baoyu also saw the subtle smoke in the air. Such translation strengthens the vision and provides the reader a mental picture of a thread of subtle perfume in the air. Although the linguistic form is changed, the connotative meaning is kept in cognitive context (see figure 5-1). Yan Fu (see Luo 1984: 136-137), in talking about his operating principle in reaching expressiveness, states that he would sacrifice the linguistic form so as to get the real meaning in translation[1]. Yan's statement is a support for the equivalence realized in cognitive context rather than in linguistic form.

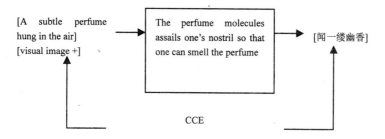

Figure 5-1 CCE between "闻一缕幽香" and "a subtle perfume hung in the air"

---

[1] 严复在《天演论》译例言中谈到"达旨"的操作原则是"取明深义,故词句之间时有所颠倒附益,不斤斤于字比句次,而意义则不倍本文"。

2. 一丈青大娘泼口大骂起何大学问。(Liu 1999a：41)

TT₁: Aunt Yi Zhang Qing *let loose a stream of abuse* about her husband. (trans. by Alex Young P38)

In this example, the dotted part of the source text contains such concepts as "泼" (suggesting the manner), "口" (indicating the place), "大" (indicating the degree), and "骂" (act, suggesting the sound), while the translation "let loose a stream of abuse" contains such concepts as "let loose" (act, suggesting a manner), "a stream of" (degree, suggesting the visual image) and "abuse" (sound). Such translation highlights the visual image of abuse in that abuse is endowed with the feature of a flowing stream, and the degree of abuse is also implied in it. Reading such version, the reader may form a mental picture of abuse flowing in the air and going into the ears of the husband. When the audio space is mapped onto the visual space, the degree will be strengthened and the reader will be touched more deeply. The cross-space mapping between the audio and the visual spaces is shown in figure 5-2.

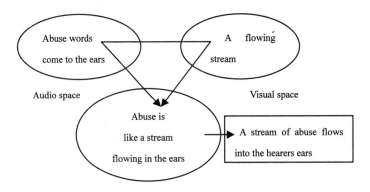

Figure 5-2 Cross-space mapping between the audio and the visual spaces

We can also translate the sentence into TT₂ to make the visual image of abuse become more prominent:

TT$_2$: *A stream of abuse from* Aunt Yi Zhang Qing *flowed to/enveloped* her husband. (trans. by the author)

5.2.2 Cognitive Contextual Equivalence in Audio Image Prominence

Sometimes audio image is also highlighted so as to make the translation more vivid and clearer. For instance:

3. 在一阵浪笑声中，五魁终于打问清了唐景的住处，钻出人窝就高高低低向山根高地上走去。(Jia 1999: 64)

Gales of laughter envelop the audience in renewed waves of good cheer, and Wukui soon finds someone who divulges the coveted information. He extricates himself from the jostling mass of humanity and plunges into the shadows beyond the reach of the theatre light. He heads toward a certain high spot at the base of the mountain. (ibid: 61)

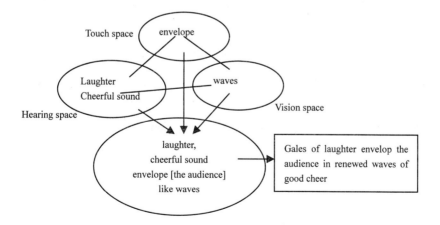

Figure 5-3 Cross-space mapping between different sense organs

In this example, the dotted part of the source text is a description of the cheerful villagers who were enjoying themselves by watching the vulgar performance celebrated in the night of the bandit leader's marriage to a beautiful woman who was robbed on the way to her wedding. The expression "在一阵浪笑声中" implies that the audience were indulged in the great cheer and shouted their laughter continuously which was like the waves of the sea. The translator uses "gales of laughter" to express the suddenness of the outburst loud laughter because "gale" means "a forceful outburst" *(AHD)* or "the sound of very loud laughter" *(OAED)*, and uses "envelop the audience" to show the touch image by changing the laughter into a visible entity that can envelop the audience; moreover, the translator also highlights the continuous frequency of cheer by using "renewed waves of good cheer", in which the invisible cheer is endowed with the feature of visible waves. When the senses of hearing, vision and touch are mapped onto each other, the degree of expression is strengthened. By means of synesthesia, the translation highlights the audio-image and it also helps the reader form a mental picture of the original scene, in which the audience's manner and state of laughing and cheering are vividly shown. The cross-space mapping between different sense organs can be shown in figure 5-3.

Sometimes, if the English word implies an audio image in itself, the translator needs to take care in using such expressions to avoid redundancy. For instance:

4. 女人叫道：“不要杀他，我跟你们走就是了！”落下来的刀一翻，刀背砸在五魁的长颈上，五魁就死一般地昏过去了。(Jia, 1999: 49)

TT₁: *The woman's scream splits the air*, "Don't! I'll go with you!" the falling knife flips and the back of its blade smashes onto Wukui's neck. For Wukui, everything goes black. (ibid: 48)

The literal meaning of "叫" contains no emotion, which can be corresponding to *call, shout, cry, scream,* etc. But in this example, "叫" contains a specific emotion in the cognitive context. The event happened on the way to the bridegroom's village, where the greeting team suffered the bandits. As the bandits wanted to carry the bride away, Wu Kui wanted to help the bride escape from the bandits and backed the bride for a long way but finally was caught by the bandits. The bandits wanted to cut Wu Kui's head and the bride was pleading for him. As to the bride, she was very appreciative of Wu kui's help, therefore she would utter such pleading words. But on the other hand, she was also scarred to death when meeting with such dangerous situation, so we can imagine that her voice is in a very loud, trembling and piercing way.

Checking dictionary, we find that *scream* is more appropriate than other words in this context. Its dictionary explanation is "giving a long piercing cry of fear, pain or excitement" (*OAED*), which contains an audio image of long piercing cry. But when thinking deeper about the semantic features of piercing, we find that it also contains a touch image. As the essential meaning of *pierce* is "to make a small hole in sth., or to go through sth., with a sharp object", *scream* is endowed with the feature of certain entity such as a sharp object to pierce the hearer's ears or the air which acts as a solid thing. TT$_1$ explicates the synesthetic image expression, yet it is redundant in conceptual sememes as *scream* integrates the touch image of "splitting the air". Therefore, we can revise the translation into the following.

TT₂ : *The woman screamed*: "Don't! I'll go with you!" the falling knife flips and the back of its blade smashes onto Wukui's neck. For Wukui, everything goes black. (tran. by the author)

5.2.3 Cognitive Contextual Equivalence in Taste Image Prominence

Sometimes the translator may use the image of taste to express the emotion, as a result the version will be more novel and attractive.

5. 宝玉恍恍惚惚，不觉弃了卷册，又随了警幻来至后面。但见珠帘绣幕，画栋雕檐，说不尽那光摇朱户金铺地，雪照琼窗玉作宫。更见献花馨郁，异草芬芳，真好一个所在。又听警幻笑道："你们快出来迎接贵客！"(Cao,2003: 140)

As if in a daze he left the registers and followed her past pearl portieres and embroidered curtains, painted pillars and carved beams. Words fail to describe those brilliant vermilion rooms, floors paved with gold, windows bright as snow and palaces of jade, to say nothing of the delectable fairy flowers, rare plants and fragrant herbs.

As Baoyu was feasting his eyes on these marvelous sights Disenchantment called with a laugh: "Come out quickly and welcome our honored guest." (tran. by the Yangs, ibid: 141)

The under-dotted source text "真好一个所在" is an evaluation made by Baoyu to show his emotion of enjoying such a good place, and it is also used as a summarization of the former description. If it is translated literally into English, the version should be "It is really a good place to live in". The Yangs' version uses a conjunctive sentence pattern to translate the evaluative information. The viewpoint is changed from the subjective evaluation of Baoyu to his self enjoyment, in which a taste image is highlighted. Judging from the linguistic form, we may think Yang's version is not corresponding to the source expression in linguistic form. But if considering the cognitive context, we will find that the translation is not only equivalent in communicative meaning but also much better than the literal one.

According to the source context, Baoyu was traveling in the fairyland and has experienced a lot of beautiful sceneries. After that he was led to the disenchantment's house to enjoy the fairy music and wine. The theme of the paragraph is about Baoyu's enjoyment in the fairyland and the subject is Baoyu, so the perspective is also from Baoyu. The translation "as Baoyu was feasting his eyes on these marvelous sights" not only makes the co-text coherent and cohesive, but also integrates the evaluative concepts of "marvelous sights", so we say that it is equivalent to the source text in cognitive context. "Feasting his eyes" is the synesthetic image between vision and taste, in which eye is endowed with the function of mouth and can eat the beautiful scenery. It belongs to the cross-space mapping between taste and vision. Such expressions are also common in Chinese, such as 秀色可餐, 大饱眼福, etc. So such deviation of image conceptual integration is acceptable in both languages.

Some English idioms contain the image of taste and they can be used in C-E translation. For instance:

6. 当五魁一次一次作驮夫的差事，他们是使尽了嘲弄的，现在却羡慕不已了。(Jia,1999: 13)

Every time he carries a bride, they always derive the greatest of pleasure from making fun of him. Today, though, they're *eating their hearts out*! (ibid: 12)

The source text "羡慕不已" contains such concepts as "羡慕" (admiration or envy) and "不已" (suggesting a strong degree), which can be translated literally into "admired or envied him very much". The source context is about the other carriers' reaction to Wu Kui who will carry a fairy-like beautiful girl to her wedding in another village this time. As these carriers can not get such a good business, they are longing for it and envious of Wu Kui in their minds. The English idiom "eat one's heart out for sb. or sth." means "to endure envy, longing, frustration, etc. in silence" *(OAED),* "endure" means "continue in existence", and "last" also suggest a long and strong degree, so the idiom meets the needs of the original semantic meaning. What is more, by using such an idiom, the translator also highlights the taste image and adds vividness to the translation.

5.2.4 Cognitive Contextual Equivalence in Touch Image Prominence

When an abstract thing is metaphorized into a human being and is endowed with the action of touch, we say that the touch image is prominent. Touch image prominence can also increase the aesthetic effect of literary translation.

7. 一丈青大娘见他们头也不抬，理也不理，气更大了，又吆喝了一声："都给我穿上裤子！"（Liu,1999a: 7）

When she saw this, *fury seized her* and she shouted again, louder, "Put on your trousers!"(tran. by Alex Young, ibid: 6)

The source expression "气更大了" is to show the emotion of Aunt Yizhangqing. The expression contains the concepts such as "气" indicating state of fury, "更" indicating comparative degree, and "了", a tense marker indicating the past. When it is literally translated, we can get such a version as "she was even more furious". Young translates it into "fury seized her", which personifies "fury" into a subject with the action of seizing somebody. Although it is not corresponding to the source expression in linguistic form, it is meaning equivalent in cognitive context. Such expression comes from the conceptual metaphor: angry is an enemy. The enemy seizes her and she is fighting back, so she is becoming more furious. In the cognitive context it has the same sense as the source text. Moreover, this touch-image-prominent translation is more vivid than the literal one in expressing the state and emotion of the subject. This synesthesia is the projection mapping between domains of touch and emotion. The cognitive reasoning process of its equivalence can be shown in figure 5-4.

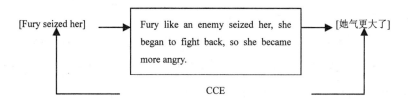

Figure 5-4 CCE between "她气更大了" and "fury seized her"

Such touch-image prominence is popularly used in C-E translations, in which the translator is apt to choose the metaphorical usages so as to make the expression stranger and more vivid. For instance:

8. ……如今一味好道，只爱烧丹炼汞，余者一概不在心上。（Cao, 2003: 44）

TT₁: ...He *loves/ believes in / is indulged in Taoism* so much that he takes no interest in anything but distilling elixirs. (possible literal translation)

TT₂: But *he's so wrapped up in Taoism* that he takes no interest in anything but distilling elixirs. (tran. by the Yangs, ibid: 45)

In this example, the possible literal translations of the under-dotted source text may be "He loves/believes in/is indulged in Taoism so much that...", which are common descriptions containing no image. The Yangs translate it into "He's so wrapped up in Taoism that..." which is a metaphorical usage containing an image of touch, and moreover the abstract concept "Taoism" is endowed with the feature of an entity which can contain things. According to the dictionary, "be wrapped up in sb./sth." means "have one's attention deeply occupied by sb./sth." or "be deeply involved in sb./sth." (*OAED*), therefore it is equivalent to the original expression in semantic meaning; moreover, such translation is more novel and vivid because it contains the image of touch.

From analyses of the above examples, we see that sense image prominence is a common method that translator uses to improve the aesthetic effect. Since all sense organs are closely connected and synesthesia frequently happens, the cross-space mappings between different sense organs are very ordinary. So it is also common for the translator to highlight certain sense image in translation. Qiu (2010: 176) states that synesthetic images make language stranger and more novel so they may add poetic value to linguistic expression. The same is true with the sense image prominence in translation. Although the linguistic forms are changed, their meanings are equivalent to the source expressions in cognitive context.

5.3　Cognitive Contextual Equivalence in Information Deviant Conceptual Integration

Information deviant conceptual integration refers to the translator's integration between the source text information and the target language expression with the involvement of different contextual parameters. In translating literary works, in order to fill the blanks and interpret the indeterminacies left by the writer, the translator will exert his or her creativity to condense or reconstruct the content of the source text information to adapt to the convention of the target expression or reader's aesthetic need. No matter how the content of information is deviant from the source text, the basic meaning is kept.

According to the aesthetics of reception, literary text is an open schematic structure to be completed by the reader. Iser stresses the blanks and indeterminacies of the text meaning. He states that meaning cannot be found in the text itself but be produced during the reading process. Literary texts possess numerous indeterminacies which constitute the most important element of literary works. Filling the blanks or indeterminacies is the realization of communication, for they exist in the interactions between text and reader. The premise is that the blanks or indeterminacies should be based on the common understandability of the readers, that is to say, the blanks or indeterminacies should activate the reader's cognitive schemata or world knowledge, otherwise the blanks or indeterminacies are meaningless (Zhang, 2010: 100).

During the translating process, the translator as the source text reader will first try to understand the source text, in which process he will have to interpret the blanks and indeterminacies according to his own understanding and imagination, after that he will express his understanding in the target language. The translator's understanding and expression are not free but controlled by various contextual parameters including cognitive schemata and co-textual parameters. The processes of understanding and expression belong to two different conceptual integrations, one is the integration between the source text information and the translator's cognitive schema, which produces the blended source information; the other is the integration between the blended source information and the target language, which produces the target expression. Contextual parameters involve in both processes. Since the cognitive schema of the target readers is different from that of the source readers, to fill or not to fill or how to fill the blanks becomes the cause of different translations (ibid).

Based on the different ways of conceptual integration, this section discusses CCE in information deviant conceptual integration from two aspects: CCE in lengthy information integration, CCE in thematic prominence integration.

5.3.1 Cognitive Contextual Equivalence in Lengthy Information Integration

Due to the different thinking modes and linguistic expressions between Chinese and English, some detailed descriptive information in the source text may be lengthy and unacceptable for the target readers, so the translator tends to integrate the lengthy information into generalized concepts. For example:

9. 半年多来，她几乎一个星期写一篇，然而回答全是"此稿我们暂不采用，现退还给你，请另行处理……" (Ju,1998: 62)

TT$_1$: For the past six months, she had written and posted almost one story a week, *but only received such answer letters as "We will not accept and use your story this time, and now return it to you. Please deal with it in other way..."* (possible literal translation)

TT$_2$: For the past six months, she had written and posted almost one story a week, *but what she received in return was the same polite rejection slip.* (Ju,1998: 63)

TT_1 is the possible literal translation of the source text, in which all these concepts are translated and the information is totally kept. But such translation is not really equivalent to the source text in meaning; moreover it is very lengthy and unreadable for the target readers because it does not fit for their thinking mode and expressive convention. The Chinese text intends to express the hard situation of the author's being rejected by highlighting the detailed information. Yet in English such information is regarded as lengthy and tends to be generalized into abstract concepts. TT_2 is following the convention of the English expression, in which the content of the letter is generalized into the abstract concepts---*the rejection slip. Slip* means "a small piece of paper, especially one for writing on or with something printed on it" (*OAED*). And *rejection slip* refers to a piece of paper with the rejection words printed on it, which is a reflection of the real situation. When modified by the manner concept *polite* and the frequency concept *again*, the source information is totally integrated into the short expression of TT_2. Although TT_2 is not corresponding to the ST in linguistic form, it is equivalent in the cognitive context.

The translator does not translate the source letter word-for-word so as to avoid the redundancy of linguistic expression. Instead he generalizes the content into the abstract concepts---"rejection slip" which is commonly used in English culture. Since the phenomenon it expresses is the same as the source context, he thinks that to borrow such expression is suitable. And in order to keep the politeness of the source expression, he adds "polite" before "rejection slip" (Ju,1998: 65).

Such phenomenon is very popular in literary translation, especially for those translators with great achievements. For instance, Howard Goldblatt, whose translations of Mo Yan won Nobel Prize for literature in 2012, makes a lot of adaptation and deletion in translating Chinese literary works into English. The following is one of his translation examples:

10. (张扣辩护道:) "谢谢审判长的提醒，我马上进入实质性辩护!近几年来，农民的负担越来越重!我父亲所在村庄，种一亩蒜薹，要交纳农业税九元八角!要向乡政府交纳提留税二十元，要向村委会交纳提留三十元!要交纳县城建设税五元(按人头计算)，卖蒜薹时，还要交纳市场管理税、计量器检查税、交通管理税、环境保护税，还有种种名目的罚款!" (莫言 2012:340)

"Thank you for reminding me, Your Honor. I'll get right to the point. In recent years the peasants have been called upon to shoulder ever heavier burdens: fees, taxes, fines, and inflated prices for just about everything they need."（tran. Goldblatt, Mo 2012: 268）

In this example, the source text is a detailed description of the peasants' burdens. Using Gallic planting as an example, the author shows various fees, taxes and fines that Gallic planters need to pay, and the inflation. Such detailed information is persuasive for Chinese readers in showing peasants' hard lives, but it is unnecessary for the English readers because they can not understand so many different kinds of fines and taxes, and moreover what they realy interest is the plot instead of the detailed laws and regulations, so the translator deleted a lot of detailed information of the source text and generalized peasants' burdens into several concepts: "fees, taxes, fines, and inflated prices". According to *OAED*, *fee* means "an amount of money that you pay for professional advice or services, or doing sth.", *tax* means "money that you have to pay to the government so that it can pay for public services", *fine* means "a sum of money that must be paid as punishment for breaking a law or rule", and *inflate* means "take actions to make the prices rise". Reading these words, the target readers can also understand Chinese peasants' heavy burdens and hard living in the novel. So although the translation is not corresponding in linguistic form, it reaches equivalent effect to the target readers in cognitive context.

From analyses of the above examples, we deduce such an empirical rule:

If the detailed information of the ST is lengthy, unnecessary, or unacceptable in literal translation, it can be generalized into abstract concepts according to the target linguistic convention.

Sometimes when the source expression is cultural specific and concept-defaulted in the target language, the translator will also have to generalize the detailed information into abstract concepts.

11. 桂林公园里阵阵桂香扑鼻而来，满树金花、芳香四溢的金桂；花白如雪、香气扑鼻的银桂；红里透黄、花多味浓的紫砂桂；花色似银、季季有花的四季桂；竞相开放，争妍媲美。进入桂林公园，阵阵桂香扑鼻而来。

TT₁: In the Osmanthus Park the fragrance of Osmanthus assails your nostril. There are *fragrant gold Osmanthus with full golden flowers, silver Osmanthus with snow white flowers, purple-grit Osmanthus in red and yellow flowers with strong fragrance, four-season Osmanthus with silver flowers.* All these Osmanthus are competing each other for full blooming. (possible literal translation)

TT₂: The Park of Sweet Osmanthus is noted for its *profusion* of Osmanthus trees. Flowers from these trees *in different colors* are *in full bloom* which *pervade the whole garden with the fragrance of these blossoms.*

（Zhang, 2000: 56）

TT3: The Guilin Park is noted for *a variety of* Sweet Osmanthus trees, *especially for a type with silver bloom all year round. When all the trees are in full blossom in autumn,* they present the visitors with *golder, silver, snow-white, and yellowy-red flowers* with pleasant fragrance pervading the garden. (Zeng,2012: 174)

The source text contains such concept sets: species-indicating concepts "金桂 (gold osmanthus), 银桂 (silver osmanthus), 紫砂桂 (purple-grit osmanthus), 四季桂 (four-season osmanthus)"; color-indicating concepts "golden, silver, white, red, yellow"; smell-indicating concepts "香(sweet), 芳香(fragrant), 浓香(strong fragrant)"; manner-indicating concepts "竞相 (compete each other), 争艳媲美(compete for blossom)"; state-indicating concept "blooming". If all these concepts are translated, we will get TT$_1$, which is lengthy and unreadable for the English readers. And those names of Osmanthus are meaningless for them. What the English readers care about is the colorful and fragrant phenomenon of the park rather than the detailed information of different species of Osmanthus. TT$_2$ breaks the order of the source expression and integrates the detailed information into some abstract concepts, such as species-indicating concept "profusion of Osmanthus trees"; color-indicating concept "different colors"; smell-indicating concepts "fragrance, sweet"; manner-indicating concept "in full bloom"; state-indicating concept "pervade". So TT$_2$ is very succinct in linguistic form. However, considering the information value and effect of publicity, Zeng (2012: 174) states that the thematic relevant information should be highlighted and some useful information should be added to remind the readers. Guided by such strategy, Zeng provides TT$_3$ which integrates the source information of type and color, and highlights the feature of Osmanthus in different seasons. Such translation is both succinct and informative for the readers.

From the above example, we can infer another empirical rule:

If the source information is expressed by detailed species-indicating concepts, such as colors, tastes, manners or states and those concepts are cultural defaulted in the target language, the translator may integrate such species-indicating concepts into their genus-indicating concepts.

5.3.2 Cognitive Contextual Equivalence in Thematic Prominence Integration

When the source text contains certain specific cultural connotation and literal translation can not be understood or accepted by the target readers, the translator may reconstruct the information according to the theme and theme-inclination of the text. Information reconstruction aims at transmitting the connotative meaning rather than the surface meaning.

12.　　　　　　　　我喝我的清茶

他饮他的花酒，我喝我的清茶。人生需要一种境界：自我安定。

面对别人的成功与荣耀，我喝我的清茶，我明白那掌声已有所属，匆匆忙忙赶过去，不会有成功等着你，还是自己再创造业绩吧，跟着别人永远只能摸着成功的尾巴。

凡事不逃避，我喝我的清茶。荷花居污泥而不染，若为怕水污而种在旱地上，它早就枯死了。人生也一样，避恶、避丑、避邪，只能说明自己心灵脆弱。一个自我安定的人是不怕环境污染自己的，而有力量影响他人。古代孟母三迁是为了怕孩子受坏影响，要为自己就没必要逃避了，后来孟子长大成人后也没有听说孟母再搬家。

自我安定可不是找一个安宁的所在，而恰恰是在紊乱的环境中保持安定的心境。"定"是一种境界，是居于多变之中的不动摇。只有达到这一境界才能掌握自己的方向，才能做到"他饮他的花酒，我喝我的清

茶。" (Written by Wang Shuchun, cf Ju,2000: 7)

Contenting Myself with Plain Tea

Human life, it seems to me, needs a placidity of mind. *While others may be wining and dining, I'm content with plain tea.*

Not dazzled by other people's aura of success and glamour, I'll indulge in my simple pleasure. Clearly aware where the credit goes, I won't join in the rush in the vain hope of accepting the prize to be handed to me on a plate. The best a blind follower can do is tailing after the winner. The only alternative is to create wonders of one's own.

I stick to the pureness of my pleasure, never escaping from reality. The lotus grows in the mud without being tainted. If, to avoid the dirt, one plants it on dry clean ground, it simply won't grow. The same holds true for human beings. Shrinking from what is ugly, vile and evil only proves the frailty of one's character. A person in full possession of mental serenity never stands in fear of being mentally contaminated by the filthy environment. On the contrary, he can exercise positive influences all around. Mencius's mother made three removals during his childhood to keep him away from bad influences, which did not pose any problem for her. History does not record any more of such removals after he grew up.

Enjoying the tranquility of mind does not mean hiding oneself in a haven. What is meant is the maintenance of such a mental state in the midst of chaos, i.e. moral immovability amidst kaleidoscopic changes. Only a person who has attained this plane can be a real master of his destiny, *contenting himself with the purest and simplest pleasure.* (tran. by Ju Zuchun, ibid: 8)

The source text is entitled with "我喝我的清茶" which is also the

argument of the essay. The whole text repeats such argument four times with sufficient grounds. The translator does not translate the argument literally into "I drink my plain tea"; instead, he integrates the concepts and explicates the conceptual sememes every time according to the theme and theme-bounded information. He integrates the acting process concept "drink" into the mental process concepts of "content with, indulge in, stick to, content oneself with". Tea, as a concept indicating the concrete physical image, is changed into the abstract emotional concepts such as "simple pleasure, pureness of pleasure, and purest and simplest pleasure" (Zeng, 2006: 5-30). Why does the translator operate in this way or is the translation reasonable? We need to explore the mental process of the translator.

The author repeats the argument four times to strengthen the theme-relevant conceptual sememe. But the conceptual sememe can not be induced from the surface meaning of the statement—*I drink my plain tea*. Zeng states that understanding the connotation of literary works needs a creative construction and the readers do not interpret the text according to its linguistic expression (ibid.). So in this example, we need to grasp the theme of the text first and understand the logical relation of the argument with the theme. The theme is a reflection of the intellectual's state of mind in the tide of economy after the reform and opening-up policy---to keep placidity in the unsteady environment. But such connotation can not be expressed literally, so the writer uses "I drink my plain tea" to reflect the theme vividly. As tea represents purity, calmness and simplicity in Chinese culture, so people who are content with plain tea symbolize those who enjoy or are satisfied with a plain and simple life. Such connotation is Chinese culture specific while defaulted in the western culture, so the translator needs to convey the connotative meaning rather than the surface meaning in translating such arguments. Sun (2001: 315) holds the similar view that "a translation should be capable of producing upon the readers an effect that is exactly like the original."

Apart from the theme of the text, the translator is also influenced by the theme-bounded information. In paragraph one "我喝我的清茶" is in contrast with "他饮他的花酒", which are two total different life styles. "饮花酒" represents indulging oneself by wining and dining, which is a luxurious life style while drinking plain tea is a representation of plain life. "喝" is translated connotatively into "be content with". "喝清茶" in paragraph 2 makes a contrast with "面对别人的成功和荣耀" in that plain tea represents a steady and plain life, and people who are content with plain tea do not peruse glory and fame. Restricted by the theme, "我喝我的清茶" represents the author's pursuit of a plain life, so the translator translates "喝" into "indulge in". In paragraph 3, "喝清茶" is in contrast with not escaping from the reality, so it gets the connotation "stick to the pureness of the pleasure", which is the strengthening of the former content. In the last paragraph "喝清茶" is in contrast with "饮花酒" again, which is the corresponding and deepening of the former information, so the translator uses the "purest and simplest pleasure" to deepen the meaning and "content one self with" to correspond with the meaning of the beginning part.

From analysis of the above example, such an empirical rule can be deduced:

When the source information is theme-bounded and the concepts in it are culture-specific and defaulted in the other language, the translator can explicate the connotative meaning of the concepts according to the theme and theme-inclination of the ST.

5.4 Cognitive Contextual Equivalence in Meaning Deviant Conceptual Integration

When the source expression does not have a corresponding expression in the target language and literal translation can not be understood by the target readers, the translator may change or reconstruct the meaning according to the context, which is meaning deviant conceptual integration. Through conceptual integration, the translator may widen, narrow, or even reconstruct the meaning to suit the target reader's understanding and acceptance. Such operations are creative for the translators, nevertheless the translator's creativity must be controlled to certain degree according to the context.

There are many researchers concerning meaning deviance in translation and most of them agree on meaning adjustment when conceptual categories are not corresponding in both languages. According to the statistics of Chen (2009), only 22 percent conceptual categories in English and Chinese vocabularies are corresponding with each other, while other 78 percent are not totally corresponding, either implied or defaulted in the other language. When correspondence can hardly be found, it's necessary for translator to adjust the meaning. Fang (2005) regards the translation of words as transference between different cognitive categories, including elevation, degeneration, correspondence, transference and activation of conceptual category. Liu & Li (2005) states that translator can actively operate between two different conceptual categories and use relevant translating strategies. Wang (2007) points out that since the conceptual categories are not always corresponding between the source and the target languages, the translator may use the different layers of the conceptual category to keep the key meaning of the source text. Their statements provide rationale for translation.

This research takes the view that in translating the translator is always doing conceptual integration between the source content and the target linguistic expression under the principle of CCE, in which process concepts of different categories will be integrated to suit the target text. This section mainly discusses CCE in meaning deviant conceptual integration from three aspects: CCE in conceptual integration of the same category, CCE in conceptual integration of the different categories, CCE in conceptual meaning reconstruction.

5.4.1 Cognitive Contextual Equivalence in Conceptual Integration of the Same Category

With the development of human cognition to the world, things are gradually classified into different conceptual categories. Things at same levels are classified into the same conceptual categories, as a result, those at the upper level are put in superordinate conceptual categories and those at the lower level are put in the subordinate ones. Since people in different culture or society are influenced by their specific natural environment, their ways of categorization are not always the same. For example, those superordinates in one culture maybe belong to the basic or subordinate level in another culture, and vice versa. Such differences in conceptual categorization make it difficult for translation. In order to make the version adapt to the target language and culture, translators have to shift the meaning in the same conceptual category. However, since such shifts happen in the same category, their general meanings are still kept. Those conceptual meaning upgrading, widening, downgrading, and narrowing all fall into this class.

5.4.1.1 CCE in Conceptual Category Upgrading or Widening

Although conceptual category upgrading and widening do not refer to the same thing, this research puts them together to illustrate meaning change between the superordinate and hyponym since the upgrading of conceptual category is also a reflection of conceptual category widening in translation.

13. 袭人看时，只见两个玻璃小瓶，却有三寸大小，上面螺丝银盖，鹅黄笺上写着"木样清露"，那一个写着"玫瑰清露"。(Cao, 2003: 938)

Eventually she returned with two little glass bottles, each about three inches high, which she handed to Aroma. They had screw-on silver tops and *yellow* labels. One of them was labeled 'Essence of Cassia Flower' and the other one 'Essence of Roses'. (tran. by Hawkes,1977: 162)

"鹅黄" in the source text is one of the traditional Chinese colors, which comes from the color of the gosling's mouth or fluff and belongs to light yellow. "鹅黄" is popularly used in Chinese literary works. In the poem written by Li She of Tang dynasty, there are "此花莫遣俗人看，新染鹅黄色未乾". Zhou Mi in Song dynasty writes in his Ci "别十姬，易服与花而出。大抵簪白花则衣紫，紫花则衣鹅黄" also describes such color. Chen Yi in his poem writes"沿河柳鹅黄，大地春已归". Apart from "鹅黄", we have many other sub-categories of yellow in Chinese color system, such as "橙黄，金黄，土黄，杏黄，棕黄，青黄，橘黄，粉黄" etc. However, we can not find the corresponding expressions in English vocabulary. Moreover, we are not sure which color is the prototype of yellow. If "鹅黄" is translated into "gosling yellow", the western readers will be confused. Hawkes upgrades the conceptual category and translates it into "yellow" to make it easy for the readers to understand. But in my opinion, since the Chinese people would like to use "浅黄" (light yellow) and "深黄" (dark yellow) to generalize those different degrees of yellow, what is more "light yellow" can be accepted by the western culture, we can translate "鹅黄" into *light yellow*, which is more adjacent to the source expression(see figure 5-5).

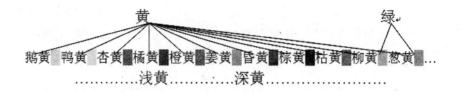

Figure 5-5 Class of Color System[1]

14. I buried my head under the miserable sheet and the rug, and cried like a child.

TT₁:我把头埋进痛苦的被单和毯子里，像个小孩似的哭了起来。

（possible literal translation）

TT₂: 我一头扎进被窝里，像个小孩似地痛哭起来。(provided by Zeng Lisha)

In this example, "under the miserable sheet and the rug" is a common expression in English. The possible literal translation of TT₁ is illogical in that "痛苦" does not refer to "被单" or "毯子", and moreover one should not bury his head in both the sheet and the rug. In English, *sheet, rug, blanket, and quilt* are all concrete covers used to keep people warm, and there is not a general or superordinate English word to include all these concrete word. But when both concepts of "the sheet" and "the rug" are put together as in this example, they should not refer to the concrete tools because a person can not bury his or her head under both the sheet and the rug according to our common sense. In the cognitive context, such expression is to show the

---

general usage of cover instead of its concrete meaning, so the two concepts can be integrated into a general and superordinate concept "被窝" in Chinese. What is more, the logical subject of misery should be "I" instead of "the sheet and the rug", so TT$_2$ is an appropriate translation. The relationship between "被窝" and other concrete coverlets is illustrated in the following figure:

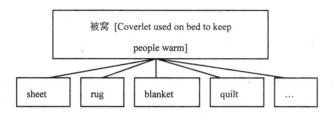

Figure 5-6 The relationship between different covers

5.4.1.2 CCE in Conceptual Category Downgrading or Narrowing

When literal translation is not appropriate in the target language or the conceptual meaning of the ST can correspond to that of the subordinate concept in the TL, downgrading or narrowing of conceptual category will be used. The aim of conceptual category downgrading or narrowing is to make the translation readable and acceptable in the target readers. For instance:

15. ——Yes? Buck Mulligan said. What did I say? I forget.

——You said, Stephen answered, O, *it's only Dedalus whose mother is beastly dead*. (Joyce, *Ulysses: Chapter 1*)

TT$_1$: ——怎么样？壮鹿马利根说。我说什么来着？我忘了。

——你说，斯蒂汾答道，咳，代达勒斯呗，他妈妈挺了狗腿儿啦。（tran. by Jin 1994:10）

TT₂："咦？"勃克·穆利根说。"我说什么来着？我可忘啦。"

"你是这么说的，"斯蒂芬回答道，"哦，只不过是迪达勒斯呗，他母亲死得像头畜生。"（tran. by Xiao & Wen: 42-43）

This is a conversation between Buck Mulligan and Stephen when Mulligan found Stephen was angry with him and he tried to know why. From the co-text and the tone of speech we know that Mulligan is a cynical medical student. In his eyes, human beings are like beasts because those dead people are dismembered like beasts in the medical laboratory. Mulligan's speech is a reflection of the cynical life style of the young Dubliners in the early 20th century. The source text "his mother is beastly dead" is translated literally into "他母亲死得像头畜生" by Xiao Qian and Wen Jieruo. This version is equivalent to the source text in linguistic form yet confusing in meaning as it presupposes that Stephen's mother died unnaturally maybe of certain accident or disaster, which does not fit for the story. Jin Di uses a dialect "他妈妈挺了狗腿" to translate it, which is very vivid and attractive. As we know, when dog is dead, its legs are like doornails. When such expression is used on human being, the cynical tone is expressed. Although the concept is downgraded and narrowed from beast to dog, the associative meaning is equivalent in the cognitive context, what is more, its aesthetic effect is similar to that of the ST.

Sometimes meaning changes along the history, so in translating historical works, the translator should understand its meaning according to the historical context.

16. So foul a sky clears not without a *storm*:

Pour down thy *weather*: how goes all in France?

(Shakespeare, *King John: Act IV*)

TT$_1$: 这样阴沉的天空是必须等一场暴风雨来把它廓清的；

把你的暴风雨倾吐出来吧。法国怎么样啦？（tran. by Zhu

Shenghao）

TT$_2$: 这样阴沉的天没有一场暴雨是不会放晴的：把你的暴雨倾吐

下来吧：在法兰西一切如何？（tran. by Liang Shiqiu）

The source context is about a messenger's reporting to King John that the army from France had arrived. Since he had ordered his man to kill young Arthur secretly, King John was terrified in facing the messenger and uttered such words. According to the dictionary, *weather* means: 1) The state of the atmosphere at a given time and place; 2) Adverse or destructive atmospheric conditions, such as high winds or heavy rain. Neither of the explanations can be used in such a context. If it is translated into "把你的坏天气倾吐下来吧", it is not reasonable as "坏天气" is too general and abstract. Mapped by the co-textual parameter—storm, "weather" is narrowed in the referential meaning and specified to "storm". So both Zhu Shenghao and Liang Shiqiu translate it into "暴风雨" instead of "坏天气".

All in all, conceptual category upgrading or downgrading happens when there is no corresponding concept to express the same object in the target language or there exists cultural default. In example 13, "鹅黄" can only be translated into "yellow" or "light yellow" instead of "gosling yellow" in order to make the readers understand and accept the version. The same is true to other expressions with different degrees of "yellow". Sometimes conceptual category upgrading or downgrading is caused by the translator's pursuing aesthetic effect, such as example 15, in which "野兽般死去了" is not as good as "挺了狗腿" in aesthetic effect. Other times the translator needs to consider the diachronic change of vocabulary, such as example 16, in which the meaning of "weather" has been extended from bad weather to all kinds of weather, so the translator needs to judge the meaning according to the co-text. Apart from these, there also exists vocabulary imbalance in expressing certain objects, for instance, "表哥, 表弟, 表姐, 表妹, 堂哥, 堂弟, 堂姐, 堂妹" in Chinese refer to different relatives, yet in English there is only one word "cousin" to represent all of them. In translating such appellation, conceptual category upgrading or downgrading is unavoidable and the specific meaning can only be inferred from the context. In a word, conceptual category upgrading or downgrading results from translator's integrating the source expression with the target language and culture. It is context-restricted and its purpose is to achieve CCE.

5.4.2 Cognitive Contextual Equivalence in Conceptual Integration of Different Categories

In translation, when meaning correspondence can not be found in the same category, the translator may try to find meaning correspondence from different conceptual categories. That is, the translator may use expressions in other categories to replace expressions in this category. Such strategies are usually found in translations of metaphor and metonymy.

5.4.2.1 CCE in Conceptual Integration of Metaphor

Metaphor is in fact the structure projection mappings from one domain to another. According to Fauconnier (1997: 9), "in order to talk and think about some domains (target domains) we use the structure of other domains (source domains) and the corresponding vocabulary." Metaphorical mappings have been studied by Reddy (1979), Lakoff & Johnson (1980), Turner (1986, 1991), Lakoff & Turner (1989), Sweetser (1990), Indurkhya (1992), Gibbs (1994), and so on. Ungerer & Schmid (2008: 49, 118) make a clear description of the way of mapping between different domains, which goes like this: when we talk in certain context, our cognitive representation of our pragmatic or sociolinguistic context is immediately associated with the related knowledge stored in long-term memory and form different cognitive models. Those familiar and concrete cognitive models are often used as the source model to help us understand those abstract and opaque target models. Lakoff & Johnson (1987: 417) state that the senses of a word are related to one another more or less closely by various means, one of which is conceptual metaphor. As Lakoff & Johnson (1980) observe, a metaphor can be viewed as an empirically based mapping from an ICM in one domain to an ICM in another domain. This mapping defines a relationship between the idealized cognitive models of the two domains. It is very common for a word that designates an element of the source domain's ICM to designate the corresponding element in the ICM of the target domain. The metaphorical mapping that relates the ICMs defines the relationship between the senses of the word. It is most common for the sense of the word in the source domain to be viewed as more basic (see Lakoff, 1987: 417).

Metaphor is very popularly used in commercial English to make the expression vivid and attractive, while its understanding and translating must rely on the context. The translator's role is first interpreting the writer's motivation of cross-space mappings and then expressing it with the target language, which is in fact a process of conceptual integration. For instance:

17. Microsoft rose 30 cents to $25.13 yesterday on the Nasdaq Stock Market. The shares have declined 18 percent this year. The company's *deep pockets* and the likelihood it will keep investing in Windows Phone 7 mean Microsoft may have an easier time luring developers than a smaller

company.[1]

In this example, "deep pocket" is a metaphorical use, which can not be translated into "深口袋". To interpret the inner meaning and give a suitable translation to the sentences, the translator needs to experience a series of mapping and integration. First, he or she needs to classify the words into different schemata or categories, such as stock market schema, company schema, and competing schema, etc. Elements in different schemata map onto each other, such as stock exchange, opening, close, capital, bear market, bull market, etc. in the stock market schema; investing, financing, developing, operating, promoting, marketing, etc. in the company schema; bid, succeed, failure, etc. in the competition schema. These elements either involve in the mapping and integrating directly or act as cognitive contextual parameters. Then, the translator is supposed to infer the metonymical meaning of "deep pocket". Here "pocket" is used to refer to things put in the pocket, and the thing put in it is capital as it is mapped by the investing schema. Restricted by the continuous acting parameter "keep investing", the meaning of "deep" is transferred into "abundant", thus "deep pocket" means "abundant capital". Then, mapped by the carrier function of "pocket", "deep pocket" is finally interpreted into "abundant capital resources". Translated into Chinese, it is "雄厚的资金资源" (see figure 5-7). In the next step, the former integrated meaning maps onto the competing schema and does further integration. Due to its abundant capital resources, Microsoft can easily defeat other small companies and lure more developers; as a result, its new products can win the biggest market share. With such integrated meaning, we get the following translation.

---

[1] http://www.indianmoney.com/news_n_updates_details.php?page_id=3&subcat=52&news_id=16686

TT: 昨日纳斯达克股票市场，微软股价收于 25.13 美元，上升 30 美分，今年该公司股价下跌 18%。不过凭借其雄厚的资金资源以及对 Windows Phone 7 手机操作系统的持续投资，微软比小公司更易吸引研发人员，从而在市场上抢占先机、博得头筹。(tran. by Zeng Lisha)

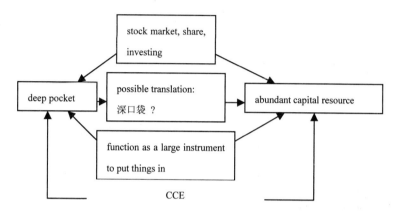

Figure 5-7 CCE between "deep pocket" and "雄厚的资金资源"

From analysis of the above example, the author deduces the following empirical rule of metaphor translation in commercial English:

Metaphors in the commercial context are mapped or restricted by its related schemata, such as stock market schema, fund schema, management schema, trade schema, import and export schema, negotiation schema, etc. The translator can first construct the related schema in his cognition and find the relations of the elements in the schema, and then judge the meaning of the metaphor according to the relations between each element.

Metaphors are also very popularly used in literary works, especially in proverbs or idioms. In translating such metaphors, the translator should not only consider the related mapping relations between elements of related schemata but also pay attention to the linguistic form of the proverb or idiom.

18.   ("I suppose three or four times: petty theft, drunkenness, nothing big or skillful. We were no help of him, you know. He needed a lot of attention from adults, not sisters who'd rather be doing something else.")

"Don't flog yourself, for heaven's sake. There are *bad apples*, and *handing them the barrel doesn't help*. Where is he now?" (Du, 2002: 39)

This example is from the talks between Anita and his boyfriend Clive about her nasty brother Jack who is a drunkard and came for money again. Jack is lazy, drunken, and always wandering everywhere, sometimes stealing or asking money from his sisters. In the eyes of Anita, Jack is a nasty man. So when Clive consoles Anita, he uses the English idiom which contains metaphors of *bad apple* and *barrel* to refer to Jack and his family. If such expressions are translated literally, the Chinese readers will be confused as they do not have such cognitive connection between apple, barrel and family. So the translator needs to explicate the implied meaning in some way. According to the co-textual parameters such as person "Jack", action "breaking the law", result "being arrested", evaluative parameter "awful", etc., we can decide their referential meaning. The metaphors in the idiom build the mapping relation between bad apple and bad person. The features of bad apple are mapped onto features of bad person as the two share many common features, for instance bad apple can be rotten while bad person can be vicious, and both are useless. Those common features are mapped onto each other first and then projected into the blend space to produce the emergent structure: *Jack is like a bad apple*. That is the completion of the first integration. If bad apples are put into the barrel, they will spoil the barrel. The same is true for human being. If a person is morally corrupt, he is no good to the family. So the mapping relation between the barrel space and family space is built up and projected into the blend space. Barrel and family share some common features, such as the similar function as container and same importance as necessities of life. When those elements are projected into the blend space, they produce such emergent structure: *the family is like a barrel*. That is the completion of the second integration. Then the results of the first two integrations experience the third time integration and produce the new meaning: *There are some bad persons; family help is useless to them*. Considering the linguistic form of Chinese idiom, we translate it into "烂苹果污桶，浪荡子败家". The whole expression can be translated into TT₂:

TT₂: "看在老天的份上，你就别自责了。俗话说：'烂苹果污桶，浪荡子败家'，他这会儿在哪儿？" (tran. by the author)

The conceptual integrating processes can be illustrated as follows:

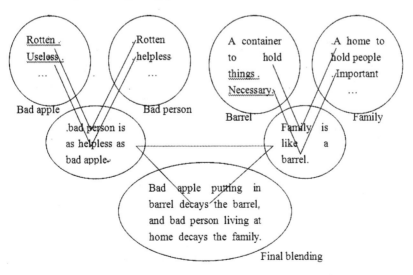

Figure 5-8 Multi-integrations between apple, people, barrel and family

5.4.2.2 CCE in Conceptual Integration of Metonymy

Metonymy belongs to pragmatic function mapping. According to Fauconnier (1997: 11), "The two relevant domains, which may be set up locally, typically corresponding to two categories of objects, are mapped onto each other by a pragmatic function. For example, authors are matched with the books they write, or hospital patients are matched with the illnesses for which they are treated." Fauconnier also proposes the Access Principle or Identification Principle, which goes like this: "If two elements a and b are linked by a connector F (b = F (a)), then element b can be identified by naming, describing, or pointing to its counterpart a. (1994/2008: 3)" The element named or described, a, is the *trigger;* and that the element identified, b, is the *target.* Metonymy and synecdoche are pragmatic function mappings. For example: *The mushroom omelet left without paying the bill.*

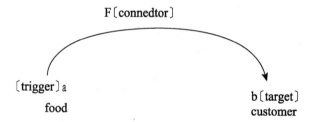

Figure 5-9 Pragmatic functional relation between food and customer （cf Fauconnier 1994/2008: 6）

According to the Access Principle, the customer and the mushroom omelet (the dish he wanted) build up a cognitive connection. That is, the customer who is the target can be identified by the mushroom omelet which acts as the trigger (see figure 5-9). If this sentence is translated into "蘑菇煎蛋卷没付钱就走了", it may mislead the reader and cause confusion because it disobeys our cognitive logic. But if it is translated into "点蘑菇煎蛋卷那人没付钱就走了", the confusion will be eliminated.

According to Radden & Kovecses (1999:17-59), metonymy can be classified into two main types viewing from its conceptual configurations in ICM: 1) Whole ICM and its parts; 2) Parts of an ICM. The first type can be further classified into several subtypes: (1) Thing-and-Part ICM; (2) Scale ICM; (3) Constitution ICM; (4) Event ICM; (5) Category-and-Member ICM; (6) Category-and-Property ICM. The second type also includes several subtypes: (1) Action ICM (has been talked about in the former chapter); (2) Perception ICM; (3) Causation ICM; (4) Production ICM; (5) Control ICM; (6) Possession ICM; (7) Containment ICM; (8) Location ICMs (cf Shu, 2008：180-184) . How to translate metonymy is decided by the translator's purpose and strategy, such as to keep the image of the source metonymy or to explicate the connotative meaning, etc. This research states that if the literal translation of metonymy costs the target reader's great cognitive effort in understanding, then the translator needs to explicate the metonymy. For instance:

19. Your invention is fantastic; you should *send it to Munich*.
    TT1: 你的发明真奇妙，你应该把它送到(慕尼黑的) (德国) 专利局。(cf. Li 1998: 120)

Munich is the capital and largest city of Bavaria in southwestern Germany. If the source text is translated into "你的发明真奇妙，你应该把它送到慕尼黑去", the Chinese readers will be confused since Munich can not activate their background knowledge of the patent office. In fact the source expression "Munich" is a metonymical use for the patent office of

Munich in Germany, in which the name of the place is used to refer to the function of the place. So the translator explicates it into "慕尼黑的德国专利局", which is much clearer for Chinese readers. However, if the context of situation is in other countries rather than in Germany or other adjacent countries, such translation is still confusing. Readers may wonder why the inventions of other countries be sent to the patent office of Germany? So this translation is still not a suitable one. We should regard the source expression "Munich" as a metonymical use, which refers to any patent office. Mapped by the thematic parameter "invention", its meaning is expended into any patent office. So we can explicate the integrated meaning as in TT$_2$:

TT2: 你的发明真了不起，应该去申请专利。(tran. by the author)

We can deduce an empirical rule of metonymy translation as follows:

If the corresponding linguistic form of the target language can not activate the reader's similar cognitive imagination as it is in the ST, the translator needs to explicate the metonymical meaning according to the target language convention.

Such empirical rule can be applied to example 20 and 21:

20. *Two heads are better than one.*
    两人智慧胜一人；三个臭皮匠胜过诸葛亮。
21. He's *all mouth* and no action.
    他这人光说不干。(cf *OAECD*)

The following examples show the process of conceptual integration and meaning generation of metonymy.

22. 她的账单一年比一年高。(cf Wang,2009: 26)

TT₁: Her *bills/accounts/account bills/statement of accounts* are *higher and higher* year by year. (possible literal translation)

TT₂: Her *debts mount up* year by year. (suggested by Zeng Lisha)

The source expression is a metonymical use in which "账单" refers to the debts that the female owes and "高" refers to the amount of debts that increase year by year. The possible literal translation of TT₁ is not appropriate as it does not fit for the meaning of the source context. For a working female, her "账单" should not be "bills" or "accounts" or "account bills" which are closely related with company finance. In cognitive context, "她的账单" should be the debts she owes others and "高" does not refer to the height of the pile of bills but the large amount of money. Such inference can be illustrated in the conceptual integration of mental spaces. "账单" and "高" build up a mental space of concrete concepts while "债" and "增多" build up another mental space of abstract concepts. Mapped onto each other and projected to the blending space, they finally form such novel meaning as "Her debts increase in amount year by year". Expressing in idiomatic English, it is TT₂ (see figure 5-10). Wang (2009: 26) regards this example as a compressed blending of human scale, in which "一年比一年高" is a change of objective scale viewing from the outside world but a compression of dissimilar things in the blending space.

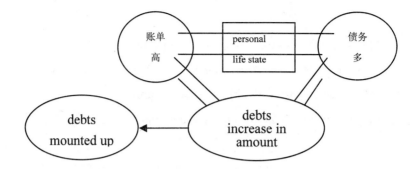

Figure 5-10 Cognitive reasoning between "账单高" and "debts mount up"

23. 大片大片的森林向车尾奔去。（cf Wang, 2009: 27）

TT₁: Vast tracts of forest rushed towards *the rear of the vehicle*. (possible literal translation)

TT₂: Vast tracts of forest rushed *backward*. （Suggested by Zeng Lisha）

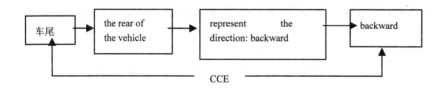

Figure 5-11 CCE between "车尾" and "backward"

In this example, "车尾" does not refer to the concrete part of a vehicle, instead, it refers to the backward direction, so literal translation of TT₁ is not correct. In our cognitive context, if the car or bus we are taking is rushing forward, we will find the woods on both sides of the roads moving backward. So viewing from the perspective of the vehicle, we may find that the woods are rushing to the rear of the vehicle. Of course this is caused by illusion. Such expression in Chinese can also be seen as a metonymical use in which

"车尾" is to replace the backward direction. So the translator can explicate it as in TT₂. The cognitive contextual equivalence between "车尾" and "backward" is illustrated in figure 5-11.

24. 布什打击萨达姆。（cf Wang, 2009: 37）

TT₁: Bush *attacked/hit/struck/cracked down* Saddam. (Possible literal translation)

TT₂: Bush *launched a war against* Saddam.（Suggested by Zeng Lisha）

In this example, if the source text is translated literally, we may get TT₁ in which the dictionary explanations of "attack, hit, strike, crack down" all contain the corresponding Chinese "打击". But if we check E-E dictionary, we may find that all these verbs imply the action between two persons. In the cognitive context, Bush does not represent himself but represent U.S. government and Saddam is also the representation of Iraq. So restricted by their identities and the historical background, we see that "打击" is not a personal action but one government or country's military operation to the other, and the military operation can be specified into the Iraq war the U.S. launched in 2003. So TT₂ is meaning equivalent to the source expression in cognitive context though it is not equivalent in linguistic form. The meaning inferring process is illustrated in figure 5-12.

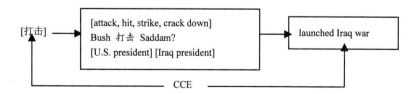

Figure 5-12 CCE between "打击" and "launch war"

5.4.3 Cognitive Contextual Equivalence in Conceptual Integration of Meaning Reconstruction

Leech (1981/1987: 13-33) divides meaning into seven kinds: conceptual meaning, connotative meaning, social meaning, emotive meaning, reflective meaning, collocative meaning and thematic meaning, in which the second to the sixth types belong to what he called associative meaning. Leech's division lays a good foundation for the choosing of meaning in translation. When there are many explanations of a word to be decided or none of the meaning items in dictionary is suitable in the specific context, the translator needs to reconstruct the meaning according to the contextual parameters. The following part discusses CCE in meaning reconstruction from five aspects: CCE in associative meaning reconstruction, CCE in blank meaning reconstruction, CCE in logical meaning reconstruction, CCE in empirical meaning reconstruction and CCE in coherent meaning reconstruction.

5.4.3.1 CCE in Associative Meaning Reconstruction

Based on Leech's division of associative meaning, this section mainly discusses CCE in collocative meaning reconstruction, social contextual meaning reconstruction and connotative meaning reconstruction.

CCE in collocative meaning reconstruction

One word may contain several different meanings and collocations in one language. When it is translated into another language, there is not a corresponding word with similar collocations to match it, and then the translator needs to decide the collocative meaning according to the context. For instance:

25. Little by little, until Henry grew accustomed to *the play of the kite, cord and wind*; until he felt the power to control it with his hands and fingers,

Henry let the red and white kite rise and ride the wind, the word HOPE lettered across its face in big, deep blue block letter the Carmella wanted. （cf Qiu, 2010：107）

　　TT₁: 渐渐地，亨利适应了那只风筝和线绳的摆动和微风的影响。直到他觉得自己的手指可以控制风筝的时候，他才让这红白相间的风筝迎风而起。那个用深蓝色大写英语字母写成的"HOPE"（希望）占满了风筝面，这是按照卡梅拉的意思写的。（ibid.）

　　TT₂: 渐渐地，亨利适应了风筝的摆动、线绳的松紧和风向的影响，他感觉自己已经能够灵活掌控，就放飞了这只风筝，红白相间的风筝面大写着深蓝色的"HOPE（希望）"，这是按卡梅拉的意思写的。(tran. by the author)

　　In the source text, "play" is a polysemy used to collocate with "the kite, the cord and the wind". When translating it into Chinese, we must pay attention to the collocative meaning of it. In TT₁, the sentence is translated into "亨利适应了那只风筝和线绳的摆动和微风的影响", which is not idiomatic Chinese. "Play" is translated into "摆动" to modify the kite and the cord, and translated into "影响" to modify the wind respectively. According to our experience of flying kite, we should continuously adjust the cord to make it tight or loose so as to adapt to the wind and keep the balance of the kite, and then we can fly the kite in the wind. So just using "摆动" is not a good way to modify both the kite and the cord in Chinese. According to the dictionary, "play" means "free and easy movement; activity; operation; interaction" (OAED) etc., and it can be chosen to collocate with different objects. According to the Chinese idiomatic expression, we can reorganize the source expression into TT₂ which is equivalent to the source expression in cognitive context.

CCE in social contextual meaning reconstruction

In literary works, the writer is apt to express meaning under certain social context, so the understanding and translating of such expressions should depend on social context, such as social status and social relations, etc. For example:

26. … and whenever any of the cottagers were disposed to be quarrelsome, discontented, or too poor she sallied into the village to settle their differences, silence their complaints and scold them into *harmony* and *plenty*. (*Pride and Prejudice*)

每逢村民们牢骚满腹，动不动就吵架，或者穷得活不下去的时候，她总是亲自赶到村里去调解他们的纠纷，封住他们的嘴巴，还把他们骂得一个个相安无事，不再叫苦叫穷。(tran. by Wang Keyi)

In this example, both the italic words in the source text refer to certain state, in which *harmony* refers to "a state of peaceful existence and agreement" and *plenty* means "a situation in which there is a large supply of food, money". If translated literally, the version will be "把他们骂得一个个和平融洽，生活富足", which is illogical because the result of scolding is not so. Wang Keyi translates it into "把他们骂得一个个相安无事，不再叫苦叫穷", in which the "state" concepts are transferred to "relation" concept "相安无事" and state-affair concept "叫苦叫穷". Although the linguistic form is different from the source text, the social contextual meaning is equivalent in cognition because this is the result of social relation mapping and conceptual integration. As the source readers do not understand the text only via the linguistic form and surface meaning; instead, they may consider all kinds of contextual information and put them into mental spaces to do cross-space mapping and conceptual integration so as to acquire the contextual meaning the writer intends to express, therefore, the translator also tries to express what the source text readers understand. In this example, the understanding of "harmony" and "plenty" should be connected with the contextual parameters such as "quarrelsome", "discontented", "too poor", "differences" and "complaints", etc. Then such relationship link between cause and effect can be built: because they were too poor→they complained about and be discontent of their poverty→they even quarreled with each other→she came→settled their difference, peaced their complaint→even scolded them→they did not quarrel or complain about their poverty. Finally, according to this relationship link, the translator can give an appropriate version.

CCE in connotative meaning reconstruction

Generally, literary works may contain some connotative meaning, which is the reflection of their specific culture and convention. Such connotative meaning should be translated; otherwise the implied meaning will be lost in the target text. For example:

27. 春蚕到死丝方尽，蜡炬成灰泪始干。（李商隐：《无题》）
Spring silkworm till its death *spins silk from love-sick heart,*
And candles but when burned up *have no tears to shed.* (tran. by Xu Yuanzhong)

These two lines are from the poem of Li Shangyin, a poet in the late Tang dynasty. Viewing from the linguistic expression, it seems to express two natural phenomena of spring silkworm's spinning and candle's shedding liquid. However, this couplet has its connotations which can not be translated literally. In other words, "丝" and "泪" are both slots that need to be filled in cognitive context by adding defaulted values. According to Ma (2009), the theme of the poem is "sorrow for departure" and the sub-theme of the two lines is "long for the beloved". The poet uses the metaphors of silkworm and candle to express his longing for his beloved. "丝" in the poem is the homophone for " 思 " which means "love-sick", and "tear" is the metaphorical expression for "longing tears" of the parted lovers. So in cognitive context, the Chinese expressions imply the connotations of "love-sick" and "longing" which need to be explicated in translation. In order to fill the blanks and explicate the connotative meaning, Xu Yuanzhong translates the couplets into "spring silkworm till its death spins silk from love-sick heart, and candles but when burned up have no tears to shed". Although his translation explicates the connotation of "丝", it keeps the blank of "泪" unfilled which is still a loss of the connotative meaning. Based on the analysis of the contextual parameters such as theme, sub-theme and historical culture, the author revises the translation into TT$_2$ which is more equivalent to the source text in connotative meaning. Wang (2009: 159) regards amplification or interpretation in translation as explication of the ST defaulted value, the purpose of which is to highlight its context, culture or understandability.

TT$_2$: Spring silkworm till its death spins silk from *love-sick heart;*

And candles till burned up have no *longing tears to shed.*

(Ma 2009)

5.4.3.2 CCE in Blank Meaning Reconstruction

Lakoff (1987: 116) thinks that there are slots in cognitive frames and each slot is equipped with many defaulted values. The activation of each defaulted value is decided by the context. In literary works, the writer is apt to leave some gaps for the readers to interpret, and usually the source text readers can understand the implied meaning easily according to the context. That's because those defaulted values are successfully activated in their cognitive frame due to the same context. However, when such gaps are kept in translation, the target readers will feel hard to understand as they do not share the same context. So the translator is supposed to fill the gaps and complete the meaning. In other words, the translator needs to explicate the defaulted values of the ST (Wang,2009: 159).

28. "*My family*," said Mrs. Micawber, who always said those two words *with an air*, though I never could discover who came under the denomination. (Dickens,2007: 149)

In this example, the italic parts are gaps that need to be filled. The context is about Mrs. Micawber's manner in talking about her parents' family with young David who was living at her home. Living hard life with Mr. Micawber, Mrs. Micawber used to talk about her good old days at her parents' home. Whenever she talked about her parents' home, she was very proud. So "my family" here does not refer to her present family with her husband and children but refer to her parents' home. The translator explicates this defaulted value into "my parents' family". "With an air" is another gap that needs to be filled. The dictionary explanation for "air" is "impression given; appearance or manner 给人的印象；外貌；态度" *(OAECD)*. If translated literally into Chinese, the version will be "⋯⋯米考伯太太说这几个字时总是带着一种印象/外貌/态度", which may confuse Chinese readers. The translator explicates the defaulted value according to the context and completes the meaning into "with an air of pride" so as to achieve the contextual equivalence through cognitive meaning reconstruction. The whole sentence is translated by Zhang Guruo as follows:

TT: "我娘家，" 米考伯太太说（她说 "我娘家" 这几个字的时候，老是很神气的（样子），不过我却从来没能发现，她娘家到底都是什么人。）(tran. by Zhang Guruo, ibid: 150)

Although the linguistic form of the translation is not corresponding to the source text, the translation is meaning equivalent to the source text in cognitive context.

Sometimes when the gaps are left at the structural level, it will be harder for the reader to understand and fill. Under such situation, background information can be used to form various relations so as to fill the blanks.

29. Ruth sighed with emotion: *"I'd rather a little of Bill than a lot of other man."*

In this example, both the propositional structure and meaning are incomplete, with some blanks left. The reader needs to replenish the defaulted parts and complete the structure in his cognition, which is the process of conceptual integration. First, some cognitive contextual parameters can be relied on in understanding this part, such as **social relationship**: husband (Billy Craham) and wife (Ruth); **social roles**: Billy Craham, a well-known American preacher who used to tour around the world for his missionary work most time of the year and had only very short stay with his wife who had to look after their young children and could not go together with Billy; **emotional relation**: Ruth had deep and constant love with her husband. Then two mental spaces can be built: one is Ruth's attitude to her husband—Bill; the other is Ruth's attitude to other man. Ruth's attitude to Bill is "would rather a little", and to other man's attitude is "would not a lot". Mapped by the contextual parameters marked in the rectangle, "a little" acquires the connotative meaning "a short period of time's stay", and "a lot" acquires the meaning "a long time's stay". Both the input spaces and the contextual parameters are projected into the blend space, and we get the integrated structure: Ruth would rather stay with Bill for a short period of time rather than stay with other man for a long time. Transferred into more suitable meaning and we get such expression as "I'd rather endure the very short union together with Billy instead of enjoying a longer stay with other man." Expressing it in idiomatic Chinese, we finally get the following translation:

TT: 露丝满怀深情地叹了口气："我宁愿与比利聚少离多，也不愿与他人长年厮守"。 (tran. by Zeng Lisha)

The cross-space mapping and integration between contextual parameters and mental spaces are illustrated in the following figure:

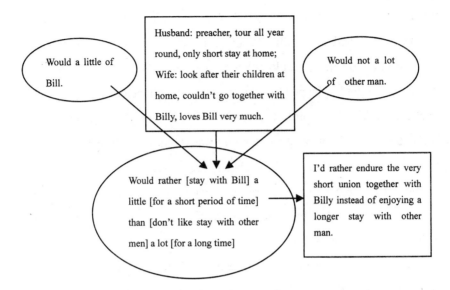

Figure 5-13 Conceptual integration of "I'd rather

a little of Bill than a lot of other man"

5.4.3.3 CCE in Logical Meaning Reconstruction

When the literal translation is illogical or the meaning items in dictionary do not suit the context, the translator can infer the logical meaning according to the context. Logical meaning inference can also be used to judge whether the translation is appropriate or not. For instance:

30.   "I suppose three or four times: petty theft, drunkenness, nothing big or skillful. We were no help of him, you know. *He needed a lot of attention from adults*, not sisters who'd rather be doing something else." (Du, 2002: 39)

TT₁: "我想大概有三四次吧，都是因为小偷小摸、酗酒，倒没有什么大事，也不是什么技能性犯罪。要知道，我们也没法帮他，他需要的是长辈对他的悉心照料，当姐姐的无法做到这一点。"（tran. by Hu

Hailan, ibid: 50）

TT₂: "应该有三四次吧：小偷小摸，酗酒滋事，倒没有犯过什么大案。你知道，这种事我们可无法帮他。父母早该对他严加管教，做姐姐的怎管得了他，做点别的什么还可以。" (tran. by the author)

This example is also from the talks between Anita and his boyfriend Clive about her nasty brother Jack, which has been introduced in the former section. When Clive asked how often he was inside, Anita began to describe her brother. Hu literally translates "he needed a lot of attention from adults" into "他需要的是长辈对他的悉心照料", which is illogical. According to the co-text, Jack is an able-bodied man and need not be taken care of by other adults. In the western culture self-reliance is taught from very young, so literal translation is confusing. "Needed" is in the past tense, so it should not be a present or usual condition. Instead, it can be understood as a subjunctive expression meaning "should need attention earlier" or "what if he had got attention earlier". The dictionary explanation of *attention* "noticing sth/sb" *(OAECD)* can be used here. Restricted by several co-textual parameters (family background parameter "Jack was spoiled in his childhood", action parameter "Jack always does bad deeds", cause parameter "Jack lacks discipline", result parameter "Jack has been inside the prison for several times"), *attention* gets the connotative meaning "管教" instead of "照料". Mapped by the collocation with "管教", *a lot of* can be translated into "严加" rather than "很多"(see figure 5-14). Due to the style of the source text, the author retranslates it into TT₂.

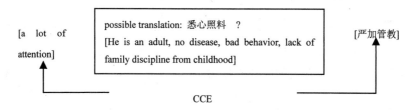

Figure 5-14 CCE between "a lot of attention" and "严加管教"

We can deduce such an empirical rule from this example:

If dictionary explanations are inappropriate or illogical in translating certain concept, the translator should not use the dictionary explanation directly; instead, he or she can infer the connotative meaning according to the dictionary and context.

The following example is an application of this empirical rule.

31. The town drunkard *stirs*, the clerks wake up, a furious clatter of drays follows, every house and store pours out *a human contribution*, and all in a twinkling the dead town is alive and moving. (Mark Twain: *Life on the Mississippi*)

TT₁: 镇上那个醉汉翻身起来，那几个店员也醒了，随后就是运货马车的一阵狂暴的响声，每户人家和每个铺子里都涌出一股人流。转瞬之间，这个死气沉沉的村镇就热闹起来了、活动起来了。(cf Qiu 2010: 123)

TT₂: 那酒鬼**一骨碌**爬起，店员们**蓦地**醒来，接货的马车**叮叮咣咣**疾驶而来，每家每户、每个店铺都倾巢出动、涌向码头，眨眼之间，死气沉沉的小镇变得**熙熙攘攘，生气勃勃**。(tran. by the author)

In this example, the source expression "pours out a human contribution" is difficult to understand and translate. If it is translated into "泼出一股人的

贡献", it is false equivalent because it is unacceptable to the target readers. So the connotative meaning can be infered according to the context. The source text is a description of the summer life on the west bank of the Mississippi river. According to the former description, "the white town drowsing in the sunshine of a summer's morning; the streets empty, or pretty nearly so; one or two clerks sitting in front of the Water Street stores; a pile of 'skids' on the slope of the stone paved wharf, and the fragrant town drunkard asleep in the shadow of them", we can see that the villagers live a very dull daily life. But the scene changes once a cheap, gaudy packet arrives upward from St. Louis and another downward from Keokuk. "Presently a film of dark smoke appears above one of those remote 'points'; instantly a Negro drayman, famous for his quick eye and prodigious voice, lifts up the cry, 'S-t-e-a-m-boat a-comin!' and the scene changes!" The cited part is a description of people's reaction to the coming of the steamboat. The first version is "涌出一股人流", which explicates the conceptual sememe but is a static description and not idiomatic Chinese expression. What's more the readers are still confused about the reason why people are pouring out.

Pour means "(causing people or things to) come or go in a continuous stream" (*OAED*), which in the source context refers to the large amount of people going out from home. When combined with "out", it means that all people in the houses and stores are out, so we can translate it into "倾巢出动". There is such an explanation for "contribution" in *OAED* as "an action or a service that helps to cause or increase something". Used in this context, it means that so many people pour out from home to the wharf so that the number of the crowd on the wharf is increased. So we explicate it into "涌向码头". "Moving" refers to the movement of the villagers on the wharf. And "alive" is caused by the movement of the villagers. So we readjust the sequence into "熙熙攘攘，生气勃勃". Apart from such inference of the logical meaning, TT$_2$ also tries to show the dynamic scene of the source text by adding dynamic attributes, such as "一骨碌", "蓦地", "叮叮咣咣疾驶". Fu Lei (1963) in talking about his viewpoint concerning translation states that he would rather strive for similarity in spirit rather than similarity in form (see Luo 1984: 558). TT$_2$ is a dynamic description which forms a contrast with the villager's everyday peaceful life and it is more attractive than TT$_1$. According to Liu (2005: 63), traditional Chinese translation theories are apt to express meaning with aesthetic sense, what Liu thinks is the feature of Chinese sense translation theory[1]. So even though TT$_2$ is not equivalent to the ST in linguistic form, it is equivalent at the level of logical meaning in cognitive context, and meanwhile it is more attractive than TT$_1$ in aesthetic effect.

5.4.3.4 CCE in Empirical Meaning Reconstruction.

Cognitive linguists state that we have certain pre-conceptual experiences, such as experiences of body movements, our ability to move objects, to perceive them as a whole and retain images of them (Lakoff, 1987: 267-268). Such pre-conceptual experiences act as image schema to guide our later understanding. In translating, the translator also needs to experience the source context and then re-organize the scene in proper target language. The following example may serve as a typical example to show one of the essential features of this aspect in translating process when it goes to render some abstract concepts from the English language to Chinese in terms of cognitive contextual equivalence.

32. A school of minnows swam by, each minnow *with its small,*

---

[1] 原文是 "中国传统译论一贯重视意义，重视在表现中将意义表述与审美嵌合、挂钩（即在审美意识参与下遣词造句）。这正是中国的翻译意义观的特色，......"

individual shadow, doubling the attendance, so *clear* and *sharp* in the sunlight. (White: *Once More to the Lake*)

TT$_1$: 一群米诺鱼游过，每条米诺鱼都带一个小小的单独的影子，使出席/到场的（？）数量翻倍，（？）在阳光下如此清晰和明显。(possible literal translation)

TT$_2$: 一群米诺鱼游过，鱼影随行，看上去鱼数倍增，在阳光下清晰可见。(tran. by the author)

In this example, the italic parts of the source text are difficult to translate. If translated literally as TT$_1$, it is incomplete in semantic expression and incoherent in logic because "doubling the attendance" is an abstract expression and there are some blank meanings that need to be decided (shown in question marks). The gaps left by the writer can be understood by the source text readers through their cognitive inference and meaning reconstruction while it is unacceptable to the target readers for they are unable to restrict the contextual meaning on their own, so it calls for the translator to fill the gaps by cognitively integrating the abstract concepts and restricting the contextual meaning so as to achieve the contextual equivalence. The translating process can be seen as two periods of transformation: the transformation of SL form to its prototype or deep semantic meaning, and the transformation of the prototype to TL form. The first period is called the understanding period, which belongs to the intralingual transformation—from the surface form to the deep meaning. The second period is called the expressing period, which belongs to the interlingual transformation—from the deep meaning to the surface form (see Qiu,2010: 73). Qiu regards the two periods as cognitive processes: first, extract deep information from linguistic expressions and form abstract conceptual representation; second, integrate the abstract conceptual representation with the TL form to get the TT (ibid). TT_2 is reconstruction of the scene in the mental space according to the translator's cognitive experience. The detailed operating process is described as *follows*:

The translator as the source text reader first takes the viewpoint of the writer and embodies the scenario of the source text. The described natural phenomena forms one input space and the observer's view forms another mental space. Then elements of the two input spaces experience mapping, projecting and blending, and form the blended source text concepts. Elements in the natural phenomena space such as *a* "the sun", *m* "school of minnows", *s* "shadows of minnows", *arrow* "the moving direction of the minnows" are chosen into the observer's view space and map onto the new elements, and then they are projected into the blend space and form the blended concepts. Contextual parameters in the frames also come into the spaces and play the role of restricting, mapping or referring. For example, we have such contextual parameters: **time** "before lunch of one August day", **place** "on the lake", **environment** "strong sunlight and clear water", **relation** "the sunlight shines on the surface of the lake", **the observer's feeling** "the lake surface is clear". In the blend space, the concepts experience composition, completion and elaboration, and form the blended source text semantic representation: a school of minnows swim by, and each minnow has a small shadow with it, so it seems that the fish number doubled; the water is so clear that the school of fish is clearly seen in the sunlight (see figure 5-15). Such semantic representation comes into the second period of integration, with such semantic units matching with the corresponding Chinese semantic units (see figure 5-16). Controlled by Chinese grammar and expression, the translator experiences the procedures of composition, completion and elaboration in mental spaces and finally forms the translation.

In TT$_2$, the translator explicates the object of "doubling attendance" as "the fish number", and specifies the object of "clear and sharp" as "the fish under the water". The attributive or relational or manner-indicating concepts such as "small", "individual" and "shadow" are integrated into a set of concepts in the target language such as "鱼影随行", indicating the manner of movement. By adding uncertainty concept "看上去", the translator makes the translation more accurate in this particular context. Of course, different readers may have different experience and interpretation, so they may produce different translations, but the real equivalence the translator pursues should be CCE. Wang (2002) points out that as long as the conceptual structure of the ST communicative event can reappear or be kept in the TT, the purpose of equivalence has been fulfilled. And the linguistic form is regarded by him as the natural result of grammar and conceptual integration.

Such an empirical rule can be deduced from analysis of the above example:

If a translator wants to fill the blanks left by the writer or make those abstract expressions more understandable and acceptable in translation, he can use cognitive experience to reconstruct the source scenario in his mental spaces and integrate the relevant concepts into suitable target expression. Since the process is restricted by contextual parameters, the translation will be equivalent to the source expression in cognitive context.

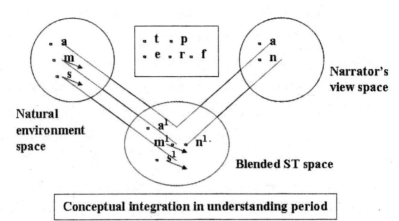

Conceptual integration in understanding period

[a-the sun; m-school of minnows; n-narrator; s_1-shadows of minnows; s_2-shadow of the narrator; t-time (before lunch in one summer day); p-place (on the lake); e-environment (clear water, sharp sunlight); r-relation (sunlight's reflection from water); f-feeling (sharp water surface); a^1, m^1, n^1, s^1, f^1 are blended source text meaning]

Figure 5-15 Conceptual integrating in the period of understanding

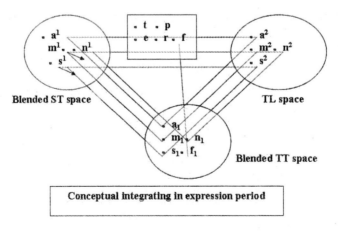

Conceptual integrating in expression period

Figure 5-16 Conceptual integrating in the period of expression

This empirical rule can also be applied in example 33.

33. In time my eyes *gradually shut up*; and, from seeming to hear the clergyman singing a drowsy song in the heat, I hear nothing, until I fall off the seat with a crash, and am taken out, *more dead than alive*, by Peggotty. (Dickens 2007: 13)

TT₁: 我这样想了一会儿，我的眼睛就慢慢地闭上了，起初还好像听见牧师在烘烘的热气中唱使人昏沉欲睡的圣诗，以后就什么都听不见了，以后就从座儿上砰的一声掉在地上，跟着坡勾提把我抱到外面，已经半死不活的了。（tran. by Zhang Guoruo, ibid: 22）

TT₂: 渐渐地我的眼皮开始打架了，教堂里热气烘烘，我恍恍惚惚听到牧师在唱一首令人昏昏欲睡的圣歌，也没听进去唱的什么内容，接下来就"砰"的一声从椅子上栽下去，坡勾提赶紧把我抱出去，我已是酣睡入梦。（tran. by the author）

This example is the description of young David's experience in church with his nanny Peggotty. Zhang translates "more dead than alive" into "半死不活" which is confusing and not fit for the embodiment. Malinowski points out that ultimately all meanings of all words are derived from bodily experience (see Halliday & Hasan,1985: 7). Lakoff & Johnson (2002: 249) states that mind is embodied, meaning is embodied, and thought is embodied in this most profound sense. If we experience the scene according to the context, we will get a more proper translation. As a little child, David felt sleepy in the dull atmosphere of the church. According to our experience, when a child is dozing off in a solemn condition, he will first try to open his eyes, and then gradually half open his eyes, and finally shut up his eyes and sleep soundly with his body falling off the seat. Such is the situation of young David. "半死不活" presupposes that the child is not healthy or something serious happens to him, and it is not proper in describing the child's state. Apart from this, "我的眼睛就慢慢地闭上了" implies that young David can control his behavior and close his eyes initiatively, which is also inappropriate to the source context. Liu (2005: 112), in talking about the differences between Chinese and English aesthetics, states that modern Chinese puts pragmatic social convention in the first place. In other words, modern Chinese should be accepted by the common audience no matter in literary writing or translation. TT$_2$ reconstructs the meaning according the cognitive experience, so it is logical and equivalent to the ST in cognitive context.

5.4.3.5 CCE in Coherent Meaning Reconstruction

Coherence is one of the basic principles of textuality (Halliday & Hasan, Hu,2002). Beaugrande & Dressler (1987: 4) maintains that "coherence concerns the ways in which the components of the textual world, i.e. the configuration of concepts and relations which underlie the surface text, are mutually accessible and relevant". When the expressions are incohesive, the coherence of meaning can only be constructed by the textual cognitive mechanism. The development of mental space theory lays a good foundation to the analysis of coherent mechanism (Fauconnier,1994; Fauconnier & Sweetser,1996; Wang,2005; Wu,2006; Su,2007); meanwhile it also provides descriptive methods to the study of coherence in textual translation (Wang ,2008). For instance:

34. Mike Veeck had begun his baseball career in 1976 as a ticket salesman with the Chicago White Sox[1]. By 1992 he was the owner of several minor-league teams [2] and had become well known for his *promotions*[3]. He put fans in rubber fat suits [4]and then had them sumo

wrestle at home plate[5]. He hired a blind announcer[6].

His outrageous *promotions continued with* Tampa Bay[1]. On the team's Lawyer Appreciation Night, each lawyer was charged twice the ticket price[2] and then billed again every half inning[3]. The proceeds went to Legal Aid[4].

TT₁: 迈克•威克的棒球事业始于 1976 年，当时他是芝加哥白索克斯队的一名售票员。到了 1992 年，他已经是几支乙级联盟队的所有人，并且因为他连连晋升而声名远播。//? 他曾让球迷穿上宽大的橡皮服装，并让他们在本垒板上相扑格斗。他还雇佣了一个盲人播报员。

他一再晋升的势头在转入坦帕海湾队后仍然继续。//? 在球队的律师晚间专场上，每位律师要支付两倍于票价的入场费，而后，每半局还要再收费一次。所得的收益全部都归入法律援助金。(Mao & Shen 2005)

This example is about the story of Mike and his family. When Mike's career of managing Baseball team is rising, his 7-year-old daughter is in danger of being blind because of disease. Mike, deeply influenced by his father Bill—a physical disabled man with strong and optimistic mind—left his job behind and began to accompany his daughter to enjoy the beautiful sceneries all over the country, which he believes will leave an impression to his daughter forever. The extracted part is about the development of Mike's baseball career. Here only discusses the translation of "promotion".

TT₁ translates it literally into "晋升" which is cohesive in the surface structure but incoherent because it causes the meaning gap between the former and latter sentences (marked in //?). According to the English textual principle, "promotion" is the theme of these two paragraphs which can be explained by the following statements. But in TT₁ "因连连晋升而声名远播" can not control the following statements, so we say it is not accessible in mental spaces.

The development of the text in mental spaces and co-text can be shown in figure 5-17 according to the Access Principle. (Fauconnier 1997: 39)

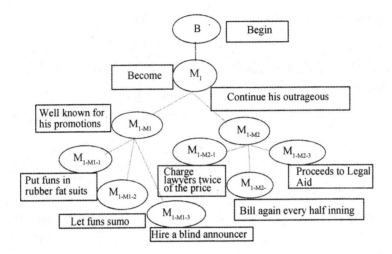

Figure 5-17 Development of the text in mental spaces and actual text

(∗Letters in the circles represent mental spaces; words in rectangles represent content of the actual text; dotted lines indicate development path of the text in mental spaces; B refers to Base space; M_1 and M_2 refer to focus spaces; M_1 and M_2 refer to sub-focus spaces; 1. 2. 3 after M_1 and M_2 represent view spaces below sub-focus spaces)

This integrated figure is to illustrate the mappings between the mental space frame and the co-text structure, as well as the coherent and accessible path of the textual development. The first sentence of paragraph 1 talks bout the beginning of Mike's baseball career, which is the base space; sentence 2 belongs to the focus space (M_1), talking bout Mike's development as the owner of several minor-league teams; sentence 3 belongs to the sub-focus space M_{1-M1}, which is about the fame of his promotions; M_{1-M1} controls the view spaces M_{1-M1-1}, M_{1-M1-2} and M_{1-M1-3}, marked by sentence 4, 5 and 6 respectively, the contents of which are putting fans in rubber fat suits sumo wrestling at home plate and hiring a blind announcer respectively. Sentence 1 in paragraph 2 is about the continuation of his outrageous promotions with Tampa Bay, so it should be the sub-focus space M_{1-M2} belonging to focus space M_1, which is at the same level with M_{1-M1}; The sub-focus space M_{1-M2} controls sentence 2, 3 and 4, forming three view spaces M_{1-M2-1}, M_{1-M2-2} and M_{1-M2-3} respectively, which are detailed information of Mike's outrageous promotions: on the team's Lawyer Appreciation Night, each lawyer being charged twice the ticket price; billing again every half inning; the proceeds going to Legal Aid. The development of the text must obey the Assess Principle and each space must be relevant to each other.

According to the above analysis we can infer the meaning of "promotion" in this context. There are four referent meanings in dictionary: 1) 提升，晋级；2) 促进，发扬，提倡；3) (企业等的) 发起，创建；4) (商品等) 宣传，推销；推销活动. (Lu 1993) Then we can define the contextual parameters concerned with "promotion": 1) theme of the paragraphs—promotion strategies; 2) methods—outrageous, well-known; 3) space—baseball field; 4) time--after 1992 (as owner of minor-league baseball teams), 1998 (as vice president of the sales and marketing for the Tampa Bay Devil Rays); 5) personal parameters: profession (managing baseball team), identity (boss), father's influence (successfully managing the major-league baseball teams). All these parameters are mutual relevant and mutual restrictive. The meaning of "promotion" can not be separately decided, but be inferred from the relations of these parameters. As "promotion strategies (P.S.)" acts as the theme parameter, it guides the inner development of the paragraphs. The following parts are extensive description of the P.S., which are relevant in the micro level to the larger level of textual functions. Thus the translator may construct a coherent and accessible text in his/her mental spaces. Restricted by contextual parameters, we can choose "宣传, 推销" as the basis of meaning decision. What is more, mapped by Mike's identity as a boss, we conclude that "promotions" refer to his unique "promotion strategies".

In short, we regard "well-known" (promotions) and "outrageous" (promotions) as the theme-triggering words, and view them as the evaluative parameters forming the evaluative and supportive relation with its sub-view spaces, marked as: M_{1-M1} { M_{1-M1-1}, M_{1-M1-2}} ; M_{1-M2} { M_{1-M2-1}, M_{1-M2-2}, M_{1-M2-3} }. We also view the abstracted meaning of "promotion strategies" as the theme of these paragraphs, which control or restrict the meaning relevance of the sentences or concepts on the micro level. Thus MST and CPT are integrated as in Figure 5-18 to show the relation between parameters under the guidance of textual coherence.

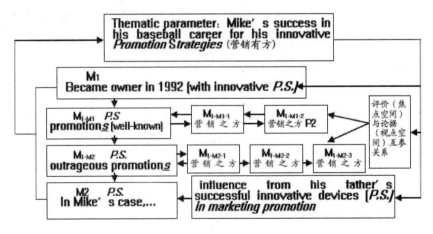

Figure 5-18 Relation between parameters under
guidance of textual coherence

The arrows in the left of the figure mean that the theme of the paragraphs is generalized in cognition from the theme-triggering words and their relevant parameters. Thus the research deduces such an empirical rule concerning textual coherence: *If a word of polysemy appears as the evaluative parameters (focus space), and the meaning of the word is confirmed by the following cases or statements, then the word and its following contents form the evaluative and supportive relation, and the meaning of the word can be generalized according to its thematic functions.*

According to the former translation, the theme of the paragraphs should be "成功连连晋升", but the key concept of "晋升" will make the readers confused in five aspects: first, according to conventional experience, tickets salesman can hardly be promoted to the leading position by his own boss; secondly, viewing from the relation between evaluative and supportive parameters, workers can hardly be famous only because of his being promoted to higher positions; thirdly, Mike's identity as the owner of several minor-league teams since 1992 determines that he could not "转入" the Tampa Bay as an ordinary worker; fourthly, there are some cross-paragraph corresponding parameters restricting the meaning from distance, such as the beginning sentences of the text "Mike Veeck had always dreamed of working for major league baseball team. Then, in August 1998, he was offered the position of vice president of sales and marketing for the Tampa Bay Devil Rays", and the contents of Mike's father as owner of the three major-league teams, so the correct translation should be "受命担任海湾队副总裁负责市场营销工作" instead of "转入……"

According to the above analysis, we make a revision of the former translation as follows:

TT$_2$: 1976 年，迈克•威克在芝加哥白索克斯棒球队销售门票，开始了他的棒球事业。到 1992 年，他已经是几支乙级联盟球队的老板，并因奇特的营销手法而闻名遐迩。他让球迷穿上充气相扑服在本垒板上参与比赛，还聘用盲人解说员现场讲解。

在受命担任坦帕海湾甲级队副总裁后，他的营销手法更加独出心裁。特辟了个晚间律师专场，门票价格是平时的 2 倍，中场休息还加收小费，其所得收益全部用于法律援助基金。

5.5 Summary

This chapter explores CCE realized in various deviant conceptual integrations in translation. Deviant conceptual integration is often used when there is no corresponding linguistic expression between the ST and TL, and then the translator needs to create new expressions according to the context. Sometimes the creation is made by the translator on purpose in order to get a more aesthetic effect or more readable version. However, this research holds the view that the translator's creativity must be restricted by the contextual parameters; otherwise his translation is improper. So in this chapter, all kinds of deviant conceptual integrations are discussed under the guidance of contextual parameters to realize CCE. By analyzing various examples, the author also deduces some empirical rules which are believed to be helpful in dealing with similar cases.

Chapter 6

Conclusion

This chapter mainly reviews the major findings, discusses the theoretical and practical implications, as well as takes up the limitations and directions for future studies.

6.1 Major Findings

The objective of this research is to explore the essential features and manifestations of contextual equivalence from the cognitive perspective. By viewing translating as a process of conceptual integration between the source content and the target language, this research demonstrates the variety of conceptual integration in translating process. It holds that equipped with the theoretical notions of cognitive contextual equivalence and co-work of identifying relevant contextual parameters, the translator may find different ways to achieve CCE at certain levels so as to achieve more acceptable versions.

The study begins with the definition of two working terms, in which CCE is defined to clarify the essential features of equivalence in translations when the translator's subjectivity or cultural and linguistic disparities are involved. CCE can avoid the debates caused by traditional terms of formal, functional and dynamic equivalence and it also redefines the standard of faithfulness to the source text in translating processes. Guided by the theoretical framework illustrated in Chapter 3, the research undertakes an example-based process analyses of translators' conceptual integration in translation and comes up with some major findings that are closely related to the research questions raised in Chapter 1.

First, equivalence or equivalence-attached faithfulness is a value-based principle, which is seemingly decided by the value of the source text but it is closely related to the recipients' value-perception according to their aesthetic needs. To be specifically speaking, if the source text has the value that can be consistent with the recipients' value orientations, then it is meaningful to achieve equivalence in the TT; otherwise, to purely discuss equivalence or faithfulness is theoretically meaningless. Based on this view, this research discusses equivalence more from cognitive context rather than linguistic form.

Second, translating is the process of conceptual integration between the source text and the target language under the guidance of contextual parameters. Cognitive contextual equivalence can be realized in the two types of conceptual integration in translation: coincidental and deviant. If the source expression has a correspondence in the target language with the change of concept number or form, the translator can choose such corresponding expressions. This is CCE realized in coincidental conceptual integration. Deviant conceptual integration is in fact reconstruction of image, information or meaning when there is not a correspondence in the target language. Through reconstruction, the translation becomes more readable and aesthetic while the communicative meaning is kept because the meaning construction is based on the translator's cognitive embodiment.

Third, contextual parameters include visible and invisible ones. Visible ones belong to those co-textual parameters which can be found in the co-text. Invisible ones refer to those that have become background knowledge or cognitive schemata. The set of parameters is an open and dynamic one, in which visible co-textual parameters can be changed into invisible ones with the development of the text. Contextual parameters play an important role in the whole process of conceptual integration in translation.

6.2 Theoretical and Practical Implications

Theoretically, there are four facets of implications:

First, the research broadens the dimension of translation study from the perspective of equivalence theory. This research puts forward the idea that equivalence can be studied from the cognitive context and proposes the term CCE, which helps to explore the essence of equivalence and avoid the traditional debates on terms.

Second, integrating theories of mental space and conceptual integration into the study of translating process makes analyses of the translator's conceptualization more descriptive and verifiable. Viewing translator's operating process as conceptual integration restricted by contextual parameters under the guidance of CCE will expand the scope of traditional translation studies. Meanwhile, the classification and analyses of different examples of conceptual integrations in translation can also make the study of MST and CIT more available and verifiable.

Third, introducing CPT into this study and viewing parameters as restricting factors in the whole operating process (including the translator's conceptualization and meaning reconstructing process) make the analysis of the translating process more descriptive and verifiable, and in return MST and CIT also compensate the study of CPT from the cognitive perspective.

Last but not least, to integrate MST, CIT and CPT into translation study provides implications for translation epistemology and methodology, which has enriched the study of translating process and extended the scope of CIT and CPT as well. Meanwhile, it also provides new theoretical evidences for the macro-construction of translation studies.

Practically, the theoretical framework constructed in Chapter 3 can serve as one of the analytic models for translation study. It can also be used as a model for translation teacher in teaching students evaluating textual coherence and inferring meaning in certain context. Moreover, the empirical rules formed in the study will be of great significance in guiding translating practice, translation research, and translation teaching at colleges.

6.3 Limitations and Directions for Future Study

Although the present study has obtained some significant findings, drawn satisfactory conclusions to the research questions, and accomplished the general research objective, it has, undoubtedly, not reached the point of satisfaction in many ways.

First, it is difficult to make qualitative analyses to those concepts and their relations. Although the aim of the research is to make a more objective study, the result is not satisfying.

Second, although the research has formed some empirical rules in analyzing examples, it is not enough to cover all translating phenomena.

Third, although the research tries to analyze the translating process in a descriptive way, the research, with no adequate or comprehensive data to show the translator's real thinking mode, is a subjective one to some extent.

The limitations of the present study indicate that future studies may be carried out in such directions as follows:

Firstly, qualitative analysis of the relations between different concepts still needs to be made and definitions of new concepts requires further exploration.

Secondly, more data need to be collected and analyzed so as to form a series of systematically related empirical rules which may offer a comprehensive view of all the possibility of achieving cognitive conceptual equivalence.

Finally, if possible, other methods such as interviews and retrospection can be made to learn more about the translator's real thinking process in translation, which can serve as the supportive factors in the theoretical research.

References

Adams, V. *An Introduction to Modern English Word-formation* [M]. London: Longman, 1973.

Bache, C. *Constraining Conceptual Integration Theory: Level of Blending and Disintegration* [J]. Journal of Pragmatics, 2005: 1615-1635.

Baker, M. *Contextualization in Translator-and Interpreter-Mediated Events*. In Jacob L. Mey & Sarah Blackwell (Eds.). Journal of Pragmatics (38) [C]. Elsevier, 2006: 321-337.

Baker, M & G. Saldanha. *Routledge Encyclopedia of Translation Studies* (2nd edition) [C]. Routledge, 2009.

Bassnett, S. *Translation Studies* [M]. London and New York: Routledge, 2002/2005.

Beaugrande, Robert-Alain & de. W. U. Dressler. *Introduction to Text Linguistics* [M]. London and New York: Longman, 1981: 4.

Bell, R. T. *Translation and Translating: Theory and Practice* [M]. London and New York: Longman, 1991: 29, 43-60.

Brandt, L. & P. A. Brandt *Making Sense of a Blend* [J]. Apparatur, 2002 (4): 62-71.

Brandt, P. A. *Mental Spaces and Cognitive Semantics: A Critical Comment* [J]. Journal of Pragmatics, 2005: 1578-1594.

Butler, C. S. *The applicability of systemic theories*[C]. Australian Review of Applied Linguistics, 1985 (1): 1-30.

Calzada Perez, Maria (Ed.). *Apropos of Ideology: Translation Studies on Ideology-Ideologies in Translation Studies* [C]. Manchester: St. Jerome Publishing, 2003: 1-22.

Cao, Xueqin. *A Dream of Red Mansions*[M]. Tran. Yang Xianyi and Gladys Yang. Beijing: Foreign Languages Press, 1994.

Cao, Xueqin. *A Dream of Red Mansions*[M]. Tran. Yang Xianyi and Gladys Yang. Beijing: Foreign Languages Press, 2003.

Cao, Xueqin. *The Story of the Stone*[M] . Trans. David Hawkes. Harmondsworth: Penguin Books, 1973, 1977, 1980.

Catford, J. C. *A Linguistic Theory of Translation: An Essay in Applied Linguistics* [M]. London: Oxford University Press, 1965: 20-27.

Chan, K. M. & James H-Y. Tai. *From nouns to verbs: verbalization in Chinese dialects and East Asian languages*. In J. Camacho and L. Choueiri (Eds.). Sixth North American Conference on Chinese Linguistics. NACCL-6. Volume II. Los Angeles: Graduate Students in Linguistics (GSIL), USC, 1995.

Chesterman, A. *Memes of Translation. The Spread of Ideas in Translation Theory* [M]. Amsterdam and Philadelphia: Benjamins, 1997.

Chesterman, A. *Semiotic Modalities in Translation Causality* [J]. Across Languages and Cultures 3 (2), 2002: 145–158.

Cicero, *De optimo genere oratorum*, Loeb Classical Library, transl. H. M. Hubbell (London: Heinemann, 1959). Bassnett, Susan. *Translation Studies* [M]. London and New York: Routledge, 2002/2005.

Clark, E. V. & H. H. Clark. *When nouns surface as verbs*. Language (4), 1979: 767-811.

Corder, S. P. *A role in for the mother tongue[A]*. In Gass and Selinker (eds.). Language Transfer in Language Learning[C]. Rowley, Mass.:

Newbury House, 1983.

Coulson, S. *Semantic Leaps: Frame Shifting and Conceptual Blending in Meaning Construction* [M]. Cambridge: Cambridge University Press, 2001.

Coulson, S. & T. Oakley. *Blending Basics* [J].Cognitive Linguistics, 2000(11): 175-196.

Coulson, S. & T. Oakley. *Blending and Coded Meaning: Literal and Figurative Meaning in Cognitive Semantics* [J]. Journal of Pragmatics, 2005: 1510-1536.

Dancygier, B. & E. Sweetser. *Conditionals, Distancing, and Alternative Spaces* [A]. In A. *Goldberg, ed., Conceptual Structure, Discourse, and language* [C]. New York: Cambridge University Press, 2005.

Delabastita, D. *Status, Origin, Features: Translation and Beyond* [A]. In A. Pym, M. Shlesinger, and D. Simeoni, eds., *Beyond Descriptive Translation Studies* [C]. Amsterdam, Philadelphia: Benjamins, 2008: 233-246.

Dickens, C. *David Copperfield* [M], shanghai: World Publishing Corporation, 2007.

Dik, S. C. *Functional grammar* [M]. Dordrecht: Foris, 1981.

Dinsmore, J. *Partitioned Representations* [M]. Dordrecht: Kluwer, 1991.

Dirven, R. *Can case grammar cope with conversion* [J]. Annales Universitis Scientiarum Budapestinensis Sectis Linguistica, 1986:17.

Encreve, P. "C'est Reagan qui a coule le billet vert" *Actes de la Recherche en Sciences Sociales*, 1988: 71-72.

Faech, C. & G. Kasper. *Cognitive dimensions of language transfer[A]*. In Kellerman and Sharwood Smith (eds.). Cross-linguistic Influence in Second Language Acquisition[C]. Oxford: Pergamon, 1986.

Fauconnier, G. *Mental Spaces: Aspects of Meaning Construction in Natural language[M]*. New York: Cambridge University Press, 1994/2008: preface 57-67, 3.

Fauconnier, G. Blending as a Central Process of Grammar [A]. In Adele Goldberg, (ed.), *Conceptual Structure, Discourse, and Language [M]*. Stanford: Center for the Study of Language and Information (distributed by Cambridge University Press), 1996.

Fauconnier, *G.* & E. Sweetser. *Spaces, Worlds, and Grammar* [M]. Chicago: University of Chicago Press, *1996.*

Fauconnier, G. *Mappings in Thought and Language* [M]. Cambridge: Cambridge University Press, 1997: 1-90.

Fauconnier, G. & M. Turner. *Conceptual Integration Networks* [J]. Cognitive Science vol. 22 (2) 1998, 133-187.

Fauconnier, G. *Conceptual blending and analogy* [A]. In Dedre Gentnet, Keith Holyoak, and Boicho Kodinov, eds., *The Analogical Mind*: *Perspectives from Cognitive Science* [C]. Cambridge, MA: MIT Press, 2001.

Fauconnier, G. & M. Turner *The Way We Think: Conceptual Blending and the Minds Hidden Complexities* [M]. New York: Basic Books, 2002: 23.

Fawcett, P. *Translation and Language Linguistic Theories Explained* [M]. Foreign Language Teaching and Research Press, 2001.

Fetzer, A. *Recontextualizing context: grammaticality meets appropriateness* [M]. Amsterdam, Netherlands; Philadelphia, PA: John Benjamins Publishing Company, 2004.

Firth, J.R. *Papers in Linguistics* [M]. Oxford: Oxford University Press, 1957.

Fraser, J. *What do real translators do? Developing the use of TAPs from professional translators* [A]. In S. Tirkkonen-Condit and R.

Jaaskelainen (eds.) *Tapping and mapping the processes of translation and interpreting: Outlooks on empirical research [C]*. Amsterdam and Philadelphia: John Benjamins, 2000: 113-120.

Gibbs, R. *The Poetics of Mind* [M]. New York: Cambridge University Press. 1994.

Givon, T. *Mind, code and context: essays in pragmatics* [M]. Hillsdale, NJ: Lawrence Erlbaum, 1989.

Givon, T. *Functionalism and grammar* [M]. Amsterdam; Philadelphia, PA: John Benjamins Publishing Company, 1995.

Givon, T. *Context as other minds: the pragmatics of sociality, cognition and communication* [M]. Amsterdam: John Benjamins Publishing Company, 2005.

Goatly, A. *The Language of Metaphors* [M]. New York: Routledge, 1997.

Gutt, E. -A., 1990. *A Theoretical Account of Translation-Without A Translation Theory* [J]. Target (2): 135-164.

Gutt, E. -A. *Translation and Relevance: Cognition and Context* [M]. Manchester: St. Jerome Publishing, 1991.

Gutt, E. -A., 1996. *Implicit Information in Literary Translation: A Relevance-Theoretic Perspective* [J]. Target (8): 239-256.

Gutt, E. -A., 1998. *Pragmatic Aspects of Translation: Some Relevance-Theory Observation[A]*. In: Hickey, Leo (Ed.), The Pragmatics of Translation [C]. Multilingual Matters, Clevedon: 41-53.

Halliday, M. A. K. *Language and Social Semiotic: the social interpretation of language and meaning* [M]. Baltimore, MD: University Park Press, 1978.

Halliday, M. A. K. & R. Hasan. *Language, Context, and Text: Aspects of Language in a Social-semiotic Perspective*[M]. Deakin University,

1985: 7.

Halliday, M. A. K. & R. Hasan. *Cohesion in English* [M]. London: Longman.

Harder, P. *Blending and Polarization: Cognition Under Pressure* [J]. Journal of Pragmatics, 2005 (37): 1636-1652.

Horace.On the Art of Poetry, in Classical Literary Criticism (Harmondsworth: Penguin Books, 1965). Bassnett, Susan. *Translation Studies* [M]. London and New York: Routledge, 2002/2005.

Hougaard, A. *Conceptual Disintegration and Blending in Interactional Sequences: A Discussion of New Phenomena, Processes vs. Products, and Methodology* [J]. Journal of Pragmatics, 2005 (37): 1653-1685.

House, J. *Translation Quality Assessment. A Model Revisited* [M]. Tubingen: Narr, 1997.

Hutchins, E. *Material Anchors for Conceptual Blends* [J]. Journal of Pragmatics, 2005 (37): 1555-1577.

Hymes, D. *Toward Ethnographies of Communicative Events* [A]. In P. P. Giglioli, ed., *Language and Social Context* [C]. Penguin Books. 1964.

Indurkhya, B. *Metaphor and Cognition* [M]. Dordrecht: Kluwer, 1992.

Jaaskelainen, R. *Tapping the process: An explorative study of the cognitive and affective factors involved in translating* [M]. University of Joensuu Publications in the Humanities no. 22. Joensuu, 1999.

Jakobson, R. *On Linguistic Aspects of Translation* [A]. R. Brower (ed.) *On Translation* [C], Cambridge, Mass., 1959.

Jespersen, O. A. *Modern English Grammar on Historical Principles [J]*. VI: Morphology. Gopenhagan: Mundsgaard, 1942.

Kade, O. *Zufall und Gesetzmassigkeit in der Ubersetzung* [M]. Leipzig: VEB

Verlag Enzyklopadie, 1968.

Katan, David. *Translating Cultures* [M]. Manchester: St. Jerome, 1999/2004.

Kelly, M. H. *Rule and idiosyncratically derived denominal verbs: effects on language production and comprehension* [J]. Memory and Cognition, 1998 (26): 369-381.

Kiparsky, P. *Word-formation and the lexicon* [J]. Proceedings of the Mid-American Linguistics Conference. Kansas: Lawrence, 1982.

Kiparsky, P. *Remarks on denominal verbs* [A]. In A, Alsina, J. Bresnan and P. Sells (eds.). Argument Structure[C]. Stanford: CSLI, 1997.

Koller, W.   *Einführung in die Übersetzungswissenschaft*[J], Heidelberg & iesbaden: Quelle und Meyer, 1979/2004.

Koller, W.   *Equivalence in Translation Theory* [A]. In Andrew Chesterman (ed.) *Readings in Translation Theory*[C], Helsinki: Oy Finn Lectura Ab., 1989: 99–104.

Kovecses, Zoltan. *Metaphor: A Practical Introduction* [M]. Oxford: Oxford University Press, 2002:145.

Krashen, S. & T. Terrell. *The Natural Approach* [M]. Oxford: Pergamon, 1983.

Krings, H. - P. *Was in den kopfen von Ubersetzern vorgeht: Eine empirische untersuchung zur struktur desübersetzungsprozesses an fortgeschrittenen franzosischlernern (What happens in the heads of translators: Empirical research on the structure of the translation process with advanced German learners of French (12))* [M]. Gunter Narr, Tübingen, 1986.

Krings, H. - P. *The Use of Introspective Data in Translation* [A]. Claus Farch and Gabriele Kasper, eds. *Introspection in Second Language Learning* [C]. Clevedon-Philadelphia: Multilingual Matters, 1987. 159-176.

Lakoff, G. *Women, Fire and Dangerous Things* [M]. Chicago: University of Chicago Press, 1987: 116, 267-268.

Lakoff, G. & M. Johnson. *Metaphors We Live By* [M]. Chicago: University of Chicago Press, 1980/2002.

Lakoff, G. & M. Turner. *More Than Cool Reason* [M]. Chicago: University of Chicago Press, 1989.

Langacker, R. W. *Grammar and Conceptualization* [M]. Berliin: Mouton de Gruyter, 2000.

Langacker, R. *Foundations of Cognitive Grammar*. Vol. 1[C]. Stanford, Calif.: Stanford University Press, 1987.

Langacker, R. *Foundations of Cognitive Grammar*. Vol. 2[C]. Stanford, Calif.: Stanford University Press, 1991.

Levy, J. *Translation as a Decision Process* [A]. in L. Venti (ed.) *The Translation Studies Reader* [C]. London, New York: Routledge, 1967/2000: 148-159.

Loscher, W. *Translation Performance, translation process, and translation strategies* [M]. Tubingen: Gunter Narr, 1991.

Malinowski. '*The Problem of Meaning in Primitive Languages*' supplement 1 to C. K. Ogden and I. A. Richards. *The meaning of meaning* [M]. London: Kegan Paul, 1923.

Mandelblit, N. *Grammatical Blending: Creative and Schematic Aspects in Sentence Processing and Translation*. Ph. D. dissertation, UC San Diego, 1997.

Marchand, H. *The Categories and Types of Present-day English Word-formation* (2nd ed.)[C]. München: Beck, 1969.

Martin, J. R. *Process and text: two aspects of human semiosis* [A], in J. D. Benson and W. S. Greaves (eds.), Systemic perspectives on discourse

[C], Vol. 1. Selected Theoretical Papers from the 9th International Systemic Workshop. Norwood, NJ: Ablex, 1985: 248–274.

Martin, J. R. *English text: system and structure* [M]. Philadelphia, PA: John Benjamins Publishing Company, 1992.

Martin, J. R. *Modelling context: the crooked path of progress in contextual linguistics*[A]. In M. Ghadessy (ed.)　Text and Context in Functional Linguistics [C]. 1999: 25-61.

McDonald, J. L. & P. A. Carpenter. *Simultaneous Translation: Idiom Interpretation and Parsing Heuristics* [J]. Journal of Verbal Learning and Verbal Behavior 20. 1981: 231-247.

Mo Yan. (Trans. by Goldblatt H.) *The Garlic Ballads*[M]. New York Arcade Publishing, 2012.

Munday, J. *Introducing Translation Studies: Theories and Applications* [M]. Routledge, 2001: 7, 11.

Newmark, P. *Approaches to Translation* [M]. Shanghai: Shanghai Foreign Language Education Press, 1981/2001.

Newmark, P. *A Textbook of Translation* [M]. Shanghai: Shanghai Foreign Language Education Press, 1988/2001.

Nida, E. A. *Toward A Science of Translating* [M]. Shanghai: Shanghai Foreign Language Education Press, 1964/2004.

Nida, E. A. & C. Taber *The Theory and Practice of Translation* [M]. Shanghai: Shanghai Foreign Language Education Press, 1969/1982: 12-32.

Nida, Eugene A. *Contexts in Translating* [M]. Amsterdam/Philadelphia: John Benjamins Publishing Company, 2001: 31-41, 112.

Nida, E. A. *Approaches to Translating in the Western World* [J]. Foreign Language Teaching and Research, 1984(2): 9-15

Nord, C. *Translation as a Purposeful Activity: Functionalist Approaches*

Explained [M]. Jerome Publishing, 1997.

Pellatt, V. & Liu, E. T. *Thinking Chinese Translation: A Course ir translation method* Chinese to English [M]. London and New York: Routledge, 2010:72-74.

Pinkham, J. *The Translator's Guide to Chinglish* [M]. Beijing: Foreign Language Teaching and Research Press, 2000: 1-36, 170.

Pym, Anthony. *Exploring Translation Theories* [M]. Routledge, 2010: 6-44, 71.

Quirk, R., S. Greenbaum, G. Leech, & J. Svartvik. *A Grammar of Contemporary English* [M]. London: Longman Group Ltd., 1972.

Quirk, R., S. Greenbaum, G. Leech, & J. Svarvik. *A Grammar of the English Language* [M]. London: Longman Group Ltd., 1985.

Reddy, M. *The Conduit Metaphor* [A]. In A. Ortony (ed.) *Metaphor and Thought* [C]. Cambridge: Cambridge University Press, 1979.

Schachter, J. *A new account for language transfer[A]*. In Gass and Selinker (eds.). Language Transfer in Language Learning [C]. Rowley, Mass: Newbury House, 1983.

Schleiermacher, F. *Ueber dieverschiedenen Methoden des Uebersezens* [A]. in H. J. Storig, ed., *Das Problem des Ubersetzens, Darmstadt: Wissenschaftliche Buchgesellschaft* [C]. 1813/1963: 38-70.

Scollon, Ron & Scollon, S. W. *Intercultural Communication* [M]. Blackwell, Oxford, 1995.

Shakespeare, W. *The Life and Death of King John.* 梁实秋译《约翰王》，中国广播电视出版社，2001.

Shelley Ching-yu Hsieh. *Embodiment in language (I): Human, animal and plant expressions* [M]. 台北：書林出版有限公司，2009: 88-93.

Slobin, D. I. *Psycholinguistics* [M]. Scott: Foresman and Company, 1979:65.

Snell-Hornby, M. *Translation Studies: An Integrated Approach* [M]. John Benjamins Publishing Company, 1995/2001: 15-22, 189-191.

Sperber, D. & D. Wilson. *Relevance: Communication and Cognition* [M]. Beijing: Foreign Language Teaching and Research Press, 1995/2001.

Sweetser, E. *Role and individual interpretations of change predicates.* Manuscript, University of California at Berkeley, 1989.

Sweetser, E. *From Etymology to Pragmatics: The Mind-as-Body Metaphor in Semantic Structure and Semantic Change* [M]. Cambridge: Cambridge University Press, 1990.

Takubo, Y. & S. Kinsui. *Discourse Management in Terms of Mental Domains*. Report for Monbusho grant No. 02300159, 1992.

Taylor, J. R. *Linguistic Categorization: Prototypes in Linguistic Theory (2nd edition)* [M]. Beijing: Foreign Language Teaching and Research Press, 1995/2001:126.

Tirkkonen-Condit, S. and J. Laukkanen *Evaluations — a key towards understanding the affective dimension of translational decisions* [J]. Meta, 1996 (1): 45-59.

Tommola, Jorma and Jukka Hyona. *Mental Load in Simultaneous Interpreting and Other Language Processing Tasks—A Pupillometric Study* [A]. Jorma Tommola, ed. *Foreign Language Comprehension and Production* [C]. Turku: AFinLA, 1990: 179-188.

Toury, G. *Descriptive translation studies and beyond* [M]. Amsterdam; Philadelphia: J. Benjamins Pub. , 1995: 10.

Turner, M. *Death Is the Mother of Beauty* [M]. Chicago: Chicago University Press, 1986.

Turner, M. *Reading Minds* [M]. Princeton, N. J.: Princeton University Press, 1991.

Ullman, Stephen. *The Principles of Semantics* [M]. Oxford: Basil Blackwell

& Mott Ltd., 1957: 280.

Ungerer, F. & H.-J. Schmid. *An Introduction to Cognitive Linguistics* [M]. Beijing: Foreign Language Teaching and Research Press, 2008: 49, 118.

Van Dijk, Teun A. *Text and Context Revisited* [C]. In: Proceedings of the First Seoul International Conference on Discourse and Cognitive Linguistics: Perspectives for the 21st Century, Seoul, Korea, 2001a: 582.

Van Dijk, Teun A. *Discourse, Ideology and Context* [C]. Folia Linguistica XXXV, 2001b: 11-40.

Van Dijk, Teun A. *Discourse and Context: A Sociocognitive Approach* [M]. Cambridge: Cambridge University Press, 2008: 28-106.

Ventola, E. *Generic and register qualities of texts and their realization* [C], in P. H. Fries & M. Gregory (eds.), 1995: 3-28.

Venuti, L. *The Translator's Invisibility. A History of Translation* [M]. London, New York: Routledge, 1995.

Vinay, J-P. & J. Darbelnet *Stylistique compare du francais et de langlais: methode de traduction* [M]. Paris: Didier, 1958/1972.

Weissbort, D. & A. Eysteinsson (ed).*Trasnslation—theory and practice: a historical reader* [C], Oxford: Oxford university press, 2006: 188-194.

Wilss, *The Science of Translation: Problems and Methods* [M]. Shanghai Foreign Language Education Press, 1982/2001:134.

Youssef, A. F. *Cognitive processes in written translation* [D]. Unpublished doctoral thesis, University of Houston, 1986.

Zandvoort, R. W. *A Handbook of English Grammar* [M]. Groningen: Wolters, 1961.

Zhao Fa: *The Nature of Imagist Poetry*, Chongqing: Chongqing Publishing House, 1997:19.

艾芜：《艾芜小说选》（英汉对照），外语教学与研究出版社 1999 年版。

巴尔胡达罗夫 (Barkhudarov)：《语言与翻译》，蔡毅译，中国对外翻译出版社 1985 年版。

蔡毅、段京华：《苏联翻译理论》，湖北教育出版社 2000 年版。

曹雪芹、高鹗：《红楼梦》，人民文学出版社 1982 年版。

陈福康：《中国译学理论史稿（修订本）》，上海外语教育出版社 2000 年版。

陈海涛、尹富林：《语篇信息结构认知对英汉翻译的影响》，《外语研究》，2007 年第 6 期。

陈康：《论信达雅与哲学著作翻译》，见罗新璋编：《翻译论集》，商务印书馆 1984 年版。

陈敏哲、白解红：《单域整合网络的意义建构机制探微——以网络新词 blogebrity 和 celeblog 的意义建构为例》，《外语教学》2014 年第 3 期。

陈音稳、陈海英、尹德谟：《从英汉双语范畴化差异的角度论证"双元结构"理论》，《西北农林科技大学学报(社会科学版)》2009 年第 2 期。

陈望道：《修辞学发凡》，上海教育出版社 1979 年版。

陈道明：《隐喻与翻译——认知语言学对翻译理论研究的启示》，《外语与外语教学》2002 年第 9 期。

狄更斯 (Dickens). *David Copperfield*，张谷若译，《大卫·考坡菲》，上海译文出版社 1979 年版。

丁声树：《现代汉语语法讲话》，商务印书馆 1979 年版。

董桂荣、冯奇：《从概念整合的角度看翻译创造的合理性》，上海翻译，2005 年版。

方红：《浅析英汉翻译中词汇的范畴转移》，《齐齐哈尔大学学报(哲学社会科学版)》2005 年第 6 期。

费道罗夫 (Fedorov) 著:《翻译理论概要》,李流译,中华书局 1955 年版。

冯广艺:《变异修辞学》,湖北教育出版社 2004 年版。

傅雷:《高老头》重译本序,见罗新璋编:《翻译论集》商务印书馆 1984 年版。

高芳、徐盛桓:《名动转用和语用推理》,《外国语》2000a 年第 2 期。

高芳、徐盛桓:《名动转用语用推理的认知策略》,《外语与外语教学》2000b 年第 4 期。

高芳:《名动转用与含意》,《外语教学》2002 年第 2 期。

高航:《动词化机制的认知语法考察》,《解放军外国语学院学报》2008 年第 5 期。

龚光明:《翻译思维学》,上海科学社会出版社 2004 年版。

桂诗春:《冗余现象与英语教学》,《外国语》1980 年第 1 期。

韩子满:《翻译等值论探幽》,《解放军外国语学院学报》1999 年第 2 期。

何星 (He). *A Study of Denominal Verbs in English and Chinese: From the Perspective of Cognitive Linguistics*,上海外国语大学博士学位论文,2006 年。

胡裕树:《现代汉语(修订本)》,上海教育出版社 1995 年版。

胡壮麟:《语境研究的多元化》,《外语教学与研究》2002 年第 3 期。

贾平凹:《贾平凹小说选(英汉对照)》,外语教学与研究出版社 1999 年版。

姜秋霞:《文学翻译中的审美过程:格式塔意象再造》,商务印书馆 2002 年版。

蒋勇:《特别概念结构的借代功能》,《外国语》2003 年第 6 期。

金隄译 (Jin).《尤利西斯》,人民文学出版社,1994 年版。

金隄 (Jin):《等效翻译探索(增订版)》,中国对外翻译出版公司 1998 年。

竟成：《现代汉语里的名词动用》，《语言教学与研究》1985 年第 1 期。

居祖纯：《汉英语篇翻译》，清华大学出版社 1998 年版。

居祖纯：《高级汉英语篇翻译》，清华大学出版社 2000 年版。

居祖纯：《新编汉英语篇翻译强化训练》，清华大学出版社 2002 年版。

居祖纯：《汉英翻译强化训练》，上海辞书出版社 2004 年版。

李长栓：《非文学翻译理论与实践》，中国对外翻译出版公司 2004 年版。

李成：《"江南 style"系列的内在语义关系与概念整合》，《现代语文》2013
　　年第 3 期。

李德超：《TAPs 翻译过程研究二十年：回顾与展望》，《中国翻译》2005
　　年第 1 期。

李福印：《认知语言学概论》，北京大学出版社 2008 年版。

李和庆、张树玲：《原型与翻译》，《中国科技翻译》2003 年第 2 期。

李敏修：《介词的动词化现象》，《中学生英语读写》2002 年第 9 期。

李忻洳：《从概念整合视角探析翻译过程》，《外语研究》2014 年第 5 期。

李占喜：《关联与顺应：翻译过程研究》，科学出版社 2007 年版。

梁晓波、孙亚：《致使概念的认知观》，《外国语》2002 年第 4 期。

廖七一：《论翻译中的冗余信息》，《外国语》1996 年第 6 期。

廖七一：《当代西方翻译理论》，译林出版社 2006 年版。

林秉璋、刘世平：《英语词汇学引论（第三版）》，武汉大学出版社 2005
　　年版。

林克难：《汉英翻译多"蛇足"》，《上海科技翻译》2000 年第 1 期。

林语堂：《论翻译》，载罗新璋编《翻译论集》，商务印书馆 1984 年版。

凌伟卿：《21 世纪大学英语教程—翻译》，上海大学出版社 2009 年版。

刘国辉：《名词与动词的认知问题以及转换效用》，《外语教学》2004 年
　　第 5 期。

刘炜：《等效翻译理论研究述评》，《重庆文理学院学报》2008 年第 4 期。

刘华文、李海清：《汉英翻译中运动事件的再词汇化过程》，《外语教学
　　与研究》2009 年第 5 期。

刘华文、李红霞:《汉英翻译中再范畴化的认知特征》,《外语研究》2005
　　年第 4 期。

刘会珍:《翻译中的语境意义》,《湖北经济学院学报》2008 年第 5 期。

刘宓庆:《当代翻译理论》,中国对外翻译出版公司 1999 年版。

刘宓庆:《中西翻译思想比较研究》,中国对外翻译出版公司 2005 年版。

刘绍棠:《刘绍棠小说选(英汉对照)》,外语教学与研究出版社 1999a
　　年版。

刘士聪:《汉英·英汉美文翻译与鉴赏》,译林出版社 2002 年版。

刘宇红:《认知语言学:理论与应用》,中国社会科学出版社 2006 年版。

刘震云:《刘震云小说选(英汉对照)》,外语教学与研究出版社 1999b
　　年版。

刘正光:《名词动用过程中的隐喻思维》,《外语教学与研究》2000 年第
　　5 期。

陆谷孙:《英汉大词典》,上海译文出版社 1993 年版。

陆国强:《现代英语词汇学》,上海外语教育出版社 1983 年版。

陆俭明:《现代汉语语法研究教程(第三版)》,北京大学出版社 2005 年
　　版。

罗新璋:《我国自成体系的翻译理论》,见罗新璋编《翻译论集》,商务
　　印书馆 1984 年版。

吕叔湘:《吕叔湘文集》,商务印书馆 1990 年版。

马海燕、温中兰:《〈红楼梦〉英译本中文化词语处理的比较》,《宁波大
　　学学报》2005 年第 4 期。

马海燕:《论古汉语诗词翻译的"阈限"性——从主题与主题倾向看译
　　者主体艺术性的发挥》,《外语与外语教学》2009 年第 7 期。

马永良、张尚莲:《对话主义与意象翻译中的他性解读》,《上海翻译》
　　2010 年第 4 期。

毛荣贵:《翻译美学》,上海交通大学出版社 2005 年版。

毛荣贵、沈沁、焦亚萍：《新美国短文精品选译：轻松走出忧郁》，中国对外翻译出版公司 2005 年版。

孟霞：《概念整合理论评介》，《西安外国语学院学报》2004 年第 4 期。

苗菊、王少爽：《从概念整合理论视角试析翻译准则》，《中国外语》 2014 年第 1 期。

缪俊：《从概念整合理论看比喻的句法形式》，《修辞学习》2007 年第 1 期。

莫言：《天堂蒜薹之歌》，作家出版社 2012 年版。

帕默尔 (Palmer)：《语言学概论》，李荣等译，商务印书馆 1983 年版。

潘文国：《汉英语对比纲要》，北京语言文化大学出版社 1997 年版。

彭新竹：《从%概念整合理论&管窥学科整合趋势》，《外语学刊》2013 年第 5 期。

钱冠连：《语言冗余信息的容忍度》，《现代外语》1986 年第 3 期。

钱钟书：《钱钟书集：七缀集》，生活·读书·新知三联书店 2002 年版。

邱文生：《认知视野下的翻译研究》，厦门大学出版社 2010 年版。

沈家煊：《"糅合"和"截搭"》，《世界汉语教学》2006a年第4期。

沈家煊：《"王冕死了父亲"的生成方式——兼说汉语"糅合"造句》，《中国语文》2006b 年第 4 期。

沈苏儒：《论信达雅—严复翻译理论研究》，商务印书馆 1998 年版。

石毓智、白解红：《汉英形容词概念化的差别及其句法后果》，《四川外语学院学报》2006 年第 6 期。

束定芳：《认知语义学》，上海外语教育出版社 2008 年版。

司显柱：《英汉名转动词比较研究》，《外国语》1996 年第 3 期。

司显柱：《功能语言学与翻译研究——翻译质量评估模式建构》，北京大学出版社 2007 年版。

宋苏玲：《合成空间理论对语篇连贯解读的解释意义》，《外语与外语教学》2000 年第 5 期。

苏晓军：《复活节翅膀》的认知符号学分析，《外语学刊》2007 年第 1 期。

隋晓冰：《现代英语词汇学概论》，哈尔滨工程大学出版社 2005 年版。

孙亚：《心理空间理论与翻译》，《上海科技翻译》2001 年第 4 期。

孙亚：《语用与认知概论》，北京大学出版社 2008 年版。

孙艺风：《文学翻译过程》，见谢天振编《翻译的理论构建与文化透视》，
    上海外语教育出版社 2003 年版。

孙迎春：《汉英双向翻译学语林》，山东大学出版社 2001 年版。

谭业升：《转喻的图式及其例示的语言差异—以英汉名词动用为例》，《外
    国语文》2011 年第 3 期。

谭载喜：《翻译学》，湖北教育出版社 2000 年版。

谭载喜：《西方翻译简史（增订版）》，商务印书馆 2006 年版。

王斌：《关联理论对翻译解释的局限性》，《中国翻译》2000 年第 4 期。

王斌：《映射及其认知运作》，《外语研究》2001a 年第 3 期。

王斌：《交织与隐喻的比较研究》，《外语学刊》2001b 年第 1 期。

王斌：《概念整合与翻译》，《中国翻译》2001c 年第 3 期。

王斌：《隐喻系统的整合翻译》，《中国翻译》2002 年第 2 期。

王斌：《翻译与概念整合》，东华大学出版社 2004 年版。

王初明：《从补缺假说看外语听说读写》，《外语学刊》2006 年第 1 期。

王德春、陈晨：《现代修辞学》，上海外语教育出版社 2001 年版。

王冬梅：《现代汉语动名互转的认知研究》，中国社会科学院研究生院
    2001 年。

王克友：《翻译过程与译文的演生——翻译的认识、语言、交际和意义
    观》，中国社会科学出版社 2008 年版。

王健坤、孙启耀：《概念整合理论对语篇连贯的解释力》，《外语学刊》
    2008 年第 1 期。

王金波、王燕：《从信息论的角度看汉英翻译的冗余现象》，《中国科技
    翻译》2002 年第 4 期。

王晶虹:《基于概念整合理论对大学英语阅读教学的研究》,《华中师范大学学报》2014 年第 2 期。

王立弟:《翻译中的知识图式》,《中国翻译》2001 年第 2 期。

汪立荣:《概念整合理论对移就的阐释》,《现代外语》2005 年第 3 期。

王蒙:《王蒙小说选》,外语教学与研究出版社 1999 年版。

王弄笙:《汉英翻译中的 Chinglish》,《中国翻译》2002 年第 2 期。

王全智:《可能世界、心理空间与语篇的意义建构》,《外语教学》2005 年第 4 期。

汪榕培、李冬:《实用英语词汇学》,辽宁人民出版社 1988 年版。

汪少华、郑守疆:《从合成空间理论看隐喻的意义建构》,《解放军外国语学院学报》2000 年第 6 期。

汪少华:《合成空间理论对隐喻的阐释力》,《外国语》2001 年第 3 期。

王薇:《名词动用的认知修辞研究》,上海外国语大学 2008 年。

王薇:《国内外名词动用研究》,《山东外语教学》2007 年第 6 期。

王薇、杨宁宁:《现代英汉语名词动用对比与异同探因》,《北京第二外国语学院学报》2010 年第 8 期。

王文斌:《概念合成理论研究与应用的回顾与思考》,《外语研究》2004 年第 1 期。

王晓丽:《语篇转化中的心理空间网络构建》,《外语学刊》2008 年第 4 期。

王心洁、马仲文:《翻译过程的空间理论描述》,《语言学研究》2006 年第 6 期。

王旭红:《马克·吐温短篇小说精选（英汉对照）》,大连理工大学出版社 2005 年版。

王雪明:《认知范畴对英文翻译的启示》,《太原大学学报》2007 年第 1 期。

王寅:《认知语言学》,上海外语教育出版社 2007 年版。

王占馥:《语法修辞新论》,百花洲文艺出版社 2006 年版。

王正元：《概念整合理论的发展与理论前沿》，《四川外语学院学报》2006年第6期。

王正元：《浮现意义对语言不完备性的自救》，《外语学刊》2008年第2期。

王正元：《概念整合理论及其应用研究》，高等教育出版社2009年版。

文军：《冗余信息与翻译中的省略》，《中国翻译》1990年第3期。

吴慧坚：《主题与主题倾向规约下的关联性语境融合—林语堂《记承天寺夜游》译文评析》，《社会科学战线》2010年第5期。

吴莉：《心理空间理论关照下的语篇分析认知图式解读》，《外语学刊》2006年第3期。

习近平：《在博鳌亚洲论坛2010年会开幕式上的演讲》，*Beijing Review* [G]，April 22.

萧乾、文洁若译 (Xiao & Wen)：《尤利西斯》，译林出版社2010年版。

熊学亮：《认知语用学概论》，上海外语教育出版社1999年版。

徐盛桓：《论英语名——动词的转化》，《山东外语教学》1981年第1期。

严复：《天演论》译例言，见罗新璋编《翻译论集》，商务印书馆1984年版。

杨彬：《心智的门铃——英语新词的认知阐释》，山东大学出版社2008年版。

杨贵章：《从主题与主题倾向关联理论看古汉诗视觉意象之英译——以"床"之语义变迁及其英译为例》，《文史博览(理论)》2010年第5期。

尹富林：《论概念整合模式下翻译的主体间性》，《外语与外语教学》2007年第11期。

尹洪山、胡刚：《汉英翻译的迁移性冗余》，《中国科技翻译》2006年第2期。

尹世超：《汉语语法修辞论集》，中国社会科学出版社2002年版。

曾利沙：《对"Altogether Autumn"两种译文的比较评析——兼论多种译本"批评"的方法论》，《中国翻译》2000 年第 5 期。

曾利沙：《小议翻译操作中的"多度视域"——兼对第十二届"韩素音青年翻译奖"英译汉参考译文的几点商榷意见》，《中国翻译》2001 年第 2 期。

曾利沙：《论"操作视域"与"参数因子"——兼论翻译学理论范畴——"文本特征论"的研究》，《现代外语》2002 年第 2 期。

曾利沙：《论文本的缺省性、增生性与阐释性——兼论描写翻译学理论研究方法论》，《外语学刊》2004 年第 5 期。

曾利沙：《对〈2002 年中国的国防〉（白皮书）英译文评析——兼论对外宣传翻译"经济简明"原则》，《广东外语外贸大学学报》2005 年第 2 期。

曾利沙：《主题关联性社会文化语境与择义的理据性》，《中国翻译》2005 年第4期。

曾利沙：《论翻译的艺术创造性与客观制约性—主题关联性社会文化语境下的译者主体性个案研究》，《广东外语外贸大学学报》2006 年第 2 期。

曾利沙：《主题与主题倾向关联下的概念语义生成机制——也谈语篇翻译意识与TEM8语段翻译教学》，《外语教学》2007a年第3期。

曾利沙：《论语篇翻译的概念语境化意义生成的认知机制》，《英语研究》2007b 年第 3 期。

曾利沙：《从对外宣传翻译原则范畴化看语用翻译系统理论建构》，《外语与外语教学》2007c 年第 7 期。

曾利沙：《从翻译理论建构看应用翻译理论范畴化拓展——翻译学理论系统整合性研究之四(以旅游文本翻译为例) 》，《上海翻译》2008 年第 3 期。

曾利沙：《论古汉语诗词英译批评本体论意义阐释框架——社会文化语境关联下的主题与主题倾向性融合》，《外语教学》2010年第2期。

曾利沙：《体验-建构融通式笔译教学法理念与方法论——兼论语境参数与体验-建构的互动性》,《广东外语外贸大学学报》2011年第4期。

曾利沙：《翻译学理论多维视角探索》,上海外语教育出版社2012年版。

张传彪：《论名词动词化与"语言经济原则"》,《中国科技翻译》2006年第3期。

张定兴：《略谈英语数词动词化及其翻译》,《中国翻译》1995年第5期。

张定兴：《略论动词化的新趋向及其翻译》,《上海科技翻译》1998年第4期。

张定兴：《再谈英语商标词的动词化及其翻译》,《上海科技翻译》1999年第3期。

张光明：《认知隐喻翻译研究》,国防工业出版社2010年版。

张辉：《熟语及其理解的认知语义学研究》,军事谊文出版社2003年版。

张辉、杨波：《心理空间和概念整合：理论发展及其应用》,《解放军外国语学院学报》2008年第1期。

张基佩：《外宣英译的原文要适当删减》,《上海科技翻译》2001年第3期。

张军平：《英汉语法标记手段对比与翻译中原作内部意义的再现》,《外语学刊》2009年第6期。

张宁：《旅游资料翻译中的文化思考》,《中国翻译》2000年第5期。

张新红、李明：《商务英语翻译（英译汉）》,高等教育出版社2003年版。

章宜华：《意义驱动翻译初探——基于认知语言学的综合翻译法》,《学术研究》2006a年第1期。

章宜华：《认知语义结构与意义驱动释义模式的构建——兼谈外汉双语词典的释义性质与释义结构》,《现代外语》2006b年第4期。

章宜华：《语义•认知•释义》,上海外语教育出版社2009年版。

张媛：《英语人体器官名词动用的语法转喻阐释》,《山东外语教学》2010年第3期。

张忠梅:《二语词汇习得的认知观》,《西南农业大学学报》2008 年第 1
        期。

赵爱萍:《名词动用的语用认知解读》,《外语艺术教育研究》2010 年第
        2 期。

赵刚:《汉语中的冗余信息及其翻译》,《国外外语教学》2004 年第 4 期。

周道凤、刘国辉:《语法整合对句式翻译认知过程的阐释——以英语致
        使移动句式的汉译分析为例》,《外语教学与研究》2007 年第 5 期。

周领顺:《英汉名-动转类词对比研究》,《外语教学与研究》2000 年第
        5 期。

周领顺:《试论企业外宣文字中壮辞的英译原则》,《上海科技翻》2003
        年第 3 期。

周志培:《汉英对比与翻译中的转换》,华东理工大学出版社 2003 年版。

http://baike.baidu.com/view/4598367.htm

http://www.en8848.com.cn/yingyu/74/t-9674.html

http://www.indianmoney.com/news_n_updates_details.php?page_id=3&subc
        at=52&news_id=16686

http://tool.xdf.cn/ch/

后 记

    本书是在我的博士论文基础上修订而成。2008 年 9 月，我来到广东外语外贸大学进行访学，师从曾利沙教授，开始了我的学术之旅。曾先生乐观积极的生活态度、严谨求实的学术思想，宽广深厚的理论根基，执着无畏的探索精神启迪了我，同时也激发了我进一步求知的欲望，我随之报考了他 2009 年的博士生并如愿考取，有幸成为他的门生，从此，在美丽的广外开始了我的求知之旅，白云山曾见证过我为选题受阻、思路不通时"消得人憔悴"，也见证过我与师友们在爬山过程中思想碰撞、灵感忽现时的"乐得人高歌"。三年的时间一晃而过，我也顺利毕业，又经过三年的修订，本书终于要付梓出版，内心洋溢着满满的感动和感激之情。

    衷心感谢导师曾利沙教授，这些年我在学术上的点滴进步，都凝聚了他辛勤的汗水，从我博士论文的选题到答辩，从本书稿的修订到成形，导师都给予指导和期望。在本书即将付梓出版之际，导师又不辞辛劳为之作序，我真切地感受到他对自己的学生就像对待园子里的幼苗一样，乐得辛苦栽培、适时浇灌、及时扶正，期待幼苗有朝一日长成参天大树。正因如此，学子虽然不才，却也不敢太懈怠，也在努力向上成长。读书期间的点点滴滴凝成了我最美好的记忆，学习和生活自然是辛苦的，导师对我们要求也很严格，每周五晚上对我们进行导读，常常是讨论到半夜还没有收场，遇到我们有进步或有新的想法，他就很兴奋，喜悦之情溢于言表，但有时候看着我们木讷的样子，他也会很恼火，对我们发一通脾气，最后搞得不欢而散。不过，多数时候导师对我们还是充满理解，他经常告诫我们要吃好饭、养好胃、锻炼好身体，并分享他如何合理利用每天早中晚几个时间段的经验，以便让我们能最大化汲取知识养分、产出新观点，逢年过节，他和师母还会露一手，做几个拿手好菜，让我们去品尝一番，当然在饭桌上他仍然不忘为我们"讲课"。正因为有了导师的言传身教，我在广外的几年过得非常充实，虽苦亦乐，而且这种乐观积极的态度和正确务实的方法会一直伴随我，使我受益终身。

感谢刘士聪教授、王宏印教授、王东风教授、余东教授、张保红教授、莫爱萍教授、杜金榜教授等。我多次聆听他们的讲座，从中获益良多。尤其是王东风教授的博士生沙龙，为我们提供了一个校级之间的交流和学习平台，从中我得到很多启发。余东教授对我的论文提出过不同的看法和修改意见。杜金榜教授在导读课上对认知语言学理论的深入探讨使我在撰写论文时对概念整合理论有深入了解，与他多次的交流和探讨使我下定决心要从新的视角研究翻译。莫爱萍教授对我的论文也很关注，经常询问进展情况。刘士聪教授和王宏印教授是我读研时的恩师，多年来一直对我充满关爱和鼓励，遇到困难我会聆听一下他们的高见。

感谢仲伟合教授、王友贵教授、霍永寿教授、刘建达教授、马建军教授等，他们的课精彩纷呈，高屋建瓴，富于启发，使我受益匪浅。

感谢我的同门师兄妹陈光亚、颜方明、杨贵章、杨洁、严亮、罗娜、邓薇、王俊超、陈霞和学友李跃凯、田其林、马军军、蔡激浪、何嫣、徐睿等，我们相互勉励，以苦为乐，共度过一段美好时光。

感谢我挚爱的双亲，他们总是在背后默默支持和鼓励我一路向前，分享着我的快乐和忧愁，在我最需要的时候，他们总是能挺身而出，为我遮挡一片风雨。在我读博的攻坚阶段，孩子缺人照顾时，老母亲毅然拖着年迈体衰之躯担起重任，为我解忧。想想这么多年无法回报他们的恩情，还要一直从他们身上索取，愧疚之情便油然而生。

感谢我的爱人李应伟先生，没有他的理解、支持、体谅和帮助，我是不可能在广外专心读书的。他既要工作又要照顾孩子，这对于一个大男人来说其中滋味可想而知，尤其每天早上要用一双大手为一个小姑娘梳头扎小辫儿，三年如一日照顾孩子的衣食住行，真的难为他了。感谢我的女儿李佳洋小朋友，从她读幼儿园中班起我就开始读书，不能常陪伴她左右，她虽然对母爱非常渴望，但是还是很支持妈妈，每次离家时孩子那依依不舍的神情都令我心碎，这也转变成了我学习的动力。可喜的是孩子健康成长，经过这些磨砺之后她也变得更加坚强和乐观。

特别感谢中国社会科学出版社的编辑老师，他们为本书的出版付出了大量的心血，在编辑过程中提出了很多中肯的意见和建议，他们的敬业精神令我敬佩。